D1741912

Australian Expats:

Stories from Abroad

Bryan Havenhand and Anne MacGregor
Editors

Global Exchange
Newcastle, Australia

Australian Expats: stories from abroad

First published 2003

Published by
Global Exchange Pty Ltd (ABN 66 006 887 556)
PO Box 852
Newcastle NSW 2300
Australia
Tel: (02) 4929 4688
Fax: (02) 4929 4727
Email: info@globalexchange.com.au
Web: www.globalexchange.com.au

Cover design by Salt Creative, Melbourne.
Front cover photo from Getty Images.
Page design and layout by Anna Kaemmerling, Global Exchange, Newcastle.
Printed in Australia by McPherson's Printing Group, Maryborough.

National Library of Australia
Cataloguing-in-Publication data:

Australian Expats: stories from abroad

ISBN 1 876438 05 3

1. Australians - Foreign countries. I. Havenhand, Bryan, K., 1951-.
II. MacGregor, Anne, 1966 -.

325.294

Disclaimer

The author, publisher and their agents believe all information supplied in this guide to be correct at the time of printing. However, the parties are not in a position to provide a guarantee to this effect and accept no liability in the event of information proving incorrect. Opportunities, regulations, organisations and addresses change over time. This guide does not take the place of professional advice from travel agents, employment agencies, doctors and relevant others. The listing of organisations in this publication does not imply recommendation.

GLOBAL EXCHANGE

Global Exchange is a publisher specialising in titles along the theme of 'working and learning across borders' with particular reference to opportunities available to Australians and New Zealanders. Current titles with this theme include:

International Careers for Australians

Working Overseas: a working holiday guide

Teaching Overseas for Australians and New Zealanders

Japan: a working holiday guide

Volunteer Work Overseas for Australians and New Zealanders

Working in London & the UK

Going Overseas on a Budget: An A-Z

Netting a Job in Australia and New Zealand

Inspiring Adventures Overseas: special interest travel

Work Around Australia

For details of these and forthcoming publications check our website at www.globalexchange.com.au.

CONTENTS

FROM THE EDITORS

In January 2003, when we met at a pleasant outdoor cafe in Sydney for the first time, both of us brought the same idea to the table: a book containing a collection of stories written by overseas Australians. Anne was in Australia for the Christmas holidays and was shortly due to fly back to Brussels. Bryan was down from Newcastle where his publishing business is based. We reached consensus on the basic shape of the Southern Cross Group (SCG)/Global Exchange Book Project during that meeting and decided to endeavour to have the collection in bookshops in Australia in time for Christmas 2003.

After much to-ing and fro-ing, in June 2003, an e-bulletin finally went out across the globe to the 4000 expat Australians on the SCG's email address list, announcing the Project and asking people to 'tell their story' and spread the word. The SCG's website (www.southern-cross-group.org) carried further information and details for aspiring authors, and SCG volunteer committee members went forth brandishing bundles of flyers with instructions to nab any expat Aussies who crossed their paths. The submission deadline was 31 July 2003.

Stories began arriving just a few days after the Project was announced, first as a trickle, then gradually becoming a flood. Some mornings our computers struggled to download the vast numbers of new email messages arriving along with their carefully composed attachments. Any temporary crises of confidence we might have had that we wouldn't receive enough stories to fill the book were quickly dispelled. The response was overwhelming. It seemed that our idea had struck a chord with Australian men and women of all ages living in many countries.

The book would evolve into a global effort, with one editor in Brussels and one in Newcastle, and 166 contributors submitting almost 180 stories from over 40 countries. Throw a tight schedule into the equation due to launch dates set months ahead, and we were counting our blessings for the existence of email, a wondrous invention!

Much to the chagrin of the editors we have been limited in the number of stories we could include in this book. If we had been able to print everything we received, we would have ended up with a volume rivalling *War and Peace*, in excess of 1200 pages. Some difficult and often agonising decisions on what was 'in' and what was 'out' had to be made during a series of transcontinental phone calls conducted at inhospitable hours for one or both editors. Just reading through all the stories once was a big job in itself.

In choosing the stories for inclusion in this volume we have first and foremost looked for what many would simply describe as a 'good read'. But we have also sought to present a true cross-section of Australian expat life. At the end of the day, there were lots of 'good reads' that didn't make it in. Unsurprisingly, a large proportion of stories came from the US (43) and the UK (24), but we had always planned on a broader representation than just these two countries, or rather, two cities, New York and London. We were also looking for a broad cross section of age, occupation, experience, activities, perspectives and a mix of styles. About one third of stories came from men and a sizeable number came from accompanying spouses and partners. A strong sense of place also helped selection.

A list of all those who submitted stories for the Project is included at the end of the book. All contributors put a great deal of thought and hard work into putting their personal journey into words. Many had never attempted this before. We understand that those whose stories are not included in this book will be disappointed. To those people, we extend our warmest thanks for your participation and contribution. Without you, the final product would not be as diverse a collection as it has turned out to be. As we promised at the outset, authors whose stories are not included in this printed work will be given the opportunity to have their story published on the SCG's website.

Bryan has more than his fair share of relatives and friends living overseas. One cousin hasn't lived in Australian for about thirty years. It was during Bryan's time working for a youth-orientated travel company that he became aware of the numbers of Australians wishing to work overseas. While with this company he established—after a long process— the Australian-USA work exchange program which continues to this day. He also wrote his first guide to working overseas in 1988, the fifth edition of which, will appear late in 2003. More details of this and similar publications can be found on Global Exchange's website at www.globalexchange.com.au.

Though a fuller account of her life as an expat and co-founder of the Southern Cross Group appears elsewhere in this book, Anne has taken the Australian expat issue on as a crusade, albeit, like all others involved in SCG, as a volunteer, fitting in her SCG life around her paid job. The entire SCG volunteer committee, which now numbers over forty individuals worldwide, pulled together to make this book a success, but particular honorary mention must go to Rita Holt in Canberra, who along with Anne, Bryan and Debbie Robson (of Global Exchange), read through every single story we received. A great vote of appreciation must also go to Lorraine Buckland in London for her untiring sterling efforts as SCG's coordinator in the UK, the country where some 300,000 expat Australians live.

A central purpose of this book is to raise awareness, at home, of the extent and nature of the Australian diaspora—some 860,000 Australians living in other parts of the world. This book has allowed just a smattering of the members of this now extensive expatriate community to tell their accounts of life overseas. All contributors provided their stories for the Project at no charge. Royalties will go to the SCG to help it continue its work in representing and supporting Australians far from home.

We are much appreciative of Nikki Gemmell for her support and her willingness to contribute a foreword that so aptly summarises the highs and lows of expat life.

We hope you enjoy reading these stories as much as we did.

Bryan Havenhand and Anne MacGregor

Editors

September 2003

FOREWORD

Auden said 'to be free is often to be lonely,' and yes, there's the loneliness of the outsider in this collection of stories by Australian expatriates; adventurers who've sought a different kind of freedom in all corners of the globe. But to be free is also to be enriched, humbled, exhilarated, enchanted, challenged—as these contributors so eloquently and passionately point out.

There are 33 stories from 22 countries in this book. The writers are markedly different in age and ethnic background, where they've settled and why; but a fervent enthusiasm for the unknown unites many of them, a fearless desire to travel forth into a fresh environment, expectation blazing under their skin.

Why were these contributors lured so strongly by the siren song of Elsewhere? For some, the reasons are not so far removed from the sentiments expressed by Miles Franklin in *My Brilliant Career* in the late nineteenth century. Robert Miller writes, in frustration, of 'the prison of isolation' he was escaping from by moving overseas—and he wasn't talking about the back of beyond, it was Sydney. A tight little world where everyone went to the same school and university; got a job in the CBD and never moved beyond a radius of twenty kilometres. Rebecca Thistleton says her country town in southern NSW had become 'like a well worn pair of slippers;' she was eighteen, and bored, when she boarded a plane for Paris. I left for London when I was thirty for a similar reason: to take a detour from the highway of the probable and the predictable. A road that wasn't clearly sign posted, and I wasn't too sure how long I'd be travelling—or when I'd come home.

Few of the contributors have found the expatriate's journey a smooth ride, but most recognise the gifts that come with being severed from your comfort zone. Rupture is good, sometimes necessary. Some talk of the freedoms of anonymity, of being a different person to the one they are back home: looser, more relaxed, less in control—and more tolerant when things go wrong. Some talk of the greater understanding they have of Australia when it's viewed from a distance, in a world context. For many, the whole tone of their living has been toughened, grubbied: but gloriously so. They revel in it, and it makes them appreciate, so much more, what they have in Australia.

Trains where you can always get a seat. Sparse city pavements. Efficiency. Good showers. The cleanliness of our streets. Ready smiles. I miss all of those things, but much more so, I miss the unique physicality of our land: the hurting light, the vaulting blue skies, the silence that hums in the central Australian desert. The flint-sharp smell of a Southerly Buster on the breeze. The sound of whip birds. And so much more. A bold stream of light stealing through a gap in a curtain in the early morning. Shadows. Napisan and Chocolate Monte biscuits. The honesty of Aussie girlfriends. Family, of course, achingly. Australia floods my heart. And yet, and yet ...

So, to the vexed question of return. How to respond to the mantra from parents, grandparents, siblings and friends—'when are you coming home?' It's the number one dilemma for a lot of expatriates, which is sharpened by brief visits back where they're confronted by the shock of the aging in older relatives. By nephews and nieces they've never met and friends who've disappeared into a different, domestic world. The insistent query about homecoming, down the phone line and in emails, is extremely difficult for a lot of us to answer.

Unlike many of those Australians who left their country in anger and frustration in the fifties and sixties—the Greers, the Hughes et al—the current generation doesn't seem to have that burning desire to put Australia behind them once and for all. We travel to enrich our lives, but a lot of us now aim to bring that experience home at some point, to enrich our nation. The question is when.

A friend in his mid-thirties, who's lived in London for fifteen years, said recently that wherever he spends his fortieth birthday will be where he spends the rest of his life. He still hasn't worked out where exactly it will be—but considers this resolution a good start. At thirty six I have no idea where I'll be at forty, and hate to think my journeying will stop by then. But I feel guilty even writing this. For the restlessness that's been tugging at my skirt since my early twenties is still with me, and haunts me now: the greed of it. It's a restlessness that's forever luring me on, willing me to find fresh landscapes. Fresh fuel for my fiction.

But I'm a mother now and it's changed everything. My two little boys were born in London, and my Melburnian husband and myself would like them to grow up as Australian men. To have a childhood like we did—where a backyard is a given and not a luxury. Where sunshine and fresh food grow children tall. Where they know what a rash shirt is, and a boogie board. Where they learn to walk through long grass with caution, and swim that beautiful Australian Crawl. Where the culture is enthusiastic and positive and friendly and open.

I feel selfish denying my children a constant presence in their lives of cousins and grandparents. My husband and I cling to a London life for our careers, and a loose sense of adventuring we still desire. Despite all the advances in communication and travel that the world has seen over the past couple of decades, Australia still feels, to us, like it's at the edge of the world rather than the centre. We love the energy of Europe and living within it lightly, like nomads—but a lightness of living is not sitting so easily with a household of children. When will I settle into a proper, grown-up life? As contributor Gabrielle Brabander says: 'it's about wanting to leave, but at the same time not being able to go.' When will the decision to return home feel right?

Home. Such a loaded word. Especially when a relentless gypsy within me has pulled from place to place for so long, obscuring my sense of where home actually is. Certainly not in Wollongong, the town where I spent my childhood. Perhaps my husband and I are slipping towards some expatriate, no-mans-land: outsiders not only in the country we have chosen to live in, but our own country as well. We wonder if we will ever settle contentedly into Australia again, and fear we won't. Perhaps we've entered, without even realising it, that strange state of exile where a memory of home is all that is left.

All I know is that I want to be buried on Australian soil, I will never stop wanting that. But I'm grateful, as are so many of the contributors in this book, for the challenging, exhilarating, frustrating expatriate experience, for the texture it's given my life—a richness I would not have had by floating, restlessly, in the comfort zone of 'home.'

Nikki Gemmell is an Australian novelist based in London.

AUSTRALIA REMAINS PART OF US

Ask an Australian at home how many Australians live overseas, and you'll usually get answers ranging from under 100,000 to about 500,000. Very few people know that the Australian Department of Foreign Affairs and Trade estimates that there are about 860,000 Australians living overseas.

I am one of the estimated five hundred Australians living in Belgium. We are a tiny and dispersed fraction of our country's total diaspora, resident in a nation of 10.26 million inhabitants. Belgium is a miniscule country, with a surface area of just 32,545 square kilometres. Australia, by contrast, has 20 million inhabitants, in a surface area about 237 times as large.

Not many Australians realise that less than a century ago, there were thousands of Australians in Belgium for a protracted period, during the First World War. It seems to be a feature of Belgium's tinyness that it is often overlooked. Even Australia's official war historian Charles Edwin Woodrow Bean, who was present on the Western Front as well as at Gallipoli and left us the extraordinary twelve-volume *Official History of Australia in the War of 1914-1918,* didn't mention Belgium in the title of any of his books, although his four volumes on Australian operations in France do relate what took place there: Australians fought and died in huge numbers in Belgian Flanders. My father is the proud owner of a complete set of Bean's *History,* acquired, I believe, before I was born. As a child growing up in Canberra, I was in awe of these impressive missives which had pride of place on the family bookshelf. It is only in my adulthood, as a result of living in Belgium and visiting sites in Belgium and France on the Western Front, that I have begun to understand the importance of that war for Australia as a nation.

The Australian Imperial Force (AIF) was on active service in France and Belgium from March 1916 until the end of the war. On the Menin

Gate alone, at Ypres (called 'Ieper' in Flemish), in the modern Belgian province of West Flanders, are inscribed the names of 6176 Australians who did not return home. Since 1928, except for a break during the German occupation of Ypres in the Second World War, every night at 8 pm, whatever the weather, the Last Post is played at the Menin Gate. In total 59,330 Australians died in the First World War, and most AIF men who reached the Western Front between 1916 and 1918 would have passed through Ypres, although probably all most of them saw was a pile of rubble. Australian servicemen are buried in 163 cemeteries in Belgium, including 1368 in Tyne Cot Cemetery, in Passchendaele, the largest Commonwealth war cemetery in the world.

Napoleon met his Waterloo in Belgium, and there's a quirky Australian connection there too: legend has it that the great C E W Bean was extremely impressed as a child when his father took him to visit the historic Waterloo battlefield, which is just a few kilometres south of Brussels. The Australian War Memorial website tells us that 'His experience at Waterloo was a foretaste of the labours that would occupy most of his adult life: the establishment of the Australian War Memorial and the writing of the official history of Australia during the First World War'. So the man who probably did more to establish the Anzac legend than any other individual in our history had an important connection with Belgium from a young age.

Perhaps Bean didn't devote a volume of his *History* specifically to Belgium because the border between France and Belgium was inconsequential for his purposes at that time. What mattered was the Front, and the AIF's area of operations was from Nieuport in Belgium to east of St Quentin, in France. In mid 1917, this section of the Front would have been a distance of about 250 kilometres. While the war was about territory, and therefore about national boundaries, the territorial gains along the Front were amazingly small over several years despite the enormous human cost.

Today, you can move between Belgium and France and other continental EU countries almost without noticing it. There are no border controls on the road and if you're looking the other way or dozing off in the car you'll miss the signs announcing you've arrived in another country. With Euros in your pocket, you don't need to stop to change money anymore.

This modern phenomenon of a 'borderless Europe' is the positive legacy of two world wars in which Australians fought and died. Following the Second World War, the European Coal and Steel Community was created on the initiative of the French Foreign Minister Robert Schuman, who declared on 9 May 1950 that 'the coming together of the nations of Europe requires the elimination of the age-old opposition of France and Germany' and proposed as a first step that Franco-German production of coal and steel be placed under a common High Authority. A few years later, the European Economic Community—today's EU—was created by the same original six nations: Germany, France, Italy, Belgium, the Netherlands, and Luxemburg. The idea behind the concept was to economically integrate these nations to such an extent that they could never go to war against each other again.

Brussels, a city of a million people dating back to 977 AD, is the heart of the European Union, and its central role in a united Europe is the reason I live there now. It is the seat of many of the European institutions and NATO. I first came to Brussels in the northern summer of 1992 on a university excursion with my European Law class from Hamburg where I was doing a Masters while on a German government post-graduate scholarship. As part of the trip, we talked to students who were doing traineeships (*stages*) in the European Commission (EC), and I resolved on the spot that this was the logical and vitally essential next step for an aspiring Australian lawyer who wanted to practice EC law. So in October 1993, I arrived in Brussels for a five-month unpaid traineeship in the anti-dumping section of the Commission's Directorate-General for international trade.

To this day I'm convinced they only took me because I badgered them to death. In Brussels circles, the lobbying efforts required to land a *stage* position in the Commission are legendry. Today, a decade later, my paid job and my voluntary work with the Southern Cross Group often involve lobbying, and I smile when I remember that I first learned how to lobby in the summer of 1993 when my traineeship position in Brussels was by no means assured. In Hamburg, my professor and some of his former students enlightened me as to what would be required, and put in a good word for me with various contacts. Taking the Australian approach, and simply applying and relying on the merits of a written application, is no way to land a European Commission *stage*. First I had to get onto the short list, also known as being in the 'Blue Book', and then I had to get someone in the Commission to pick me out of the Blue Book and give me a position. With Blue Book status achieved, difficult enough for a non-EU national, I was devastated to receive a rejection letter in late September. More desperate and persuasive phone calls from Hamburg to various Commission officials ensued.

To my amazement, finally a Scotsman in the Commission took pity on me and I was on my way. The fact that the position was unpaid and I had no savings meant that my long-suffering father had to go to his credit union in Canberra and take out a loan to support me during the training, which I later had to repay. In December 1993, half-way through the traineeship, and with no job prospects lined up in Europe, I turned down a lecturing position at the University of Adelaide Law School, because by then I knew that I wouldn't be ready to go home for quite some time.

After the Commission *stage*, I sent applications to just about every law firm in Brussels. The result was a job running the small Brussels outpost of a German law firm that was based in Freiburg in the Black Forest. It seems there is a niche market in Brussels for native English-speaking lawyers who have good German. Clueless and naive, I took on what was initially a one-year glorified trainee position, relying heavily on the only other person in the Brussels office, my secretary, to explain to me what I was supposed to be doing. My boss was rarely in Brussels. But the job, though scary and overwhelming at first, was a challenge and an incredibly thorough grounding in the Brussels Euro-scene, and I met many people during that period who remain good friends to this day.

The position in the Freiburg law firm became permanent, but after two years, I decided it was time to move to a larger law firm to gain experience in bigger European law cases. So in early 1996 I went to work in the Brussels office of a much larger German law firm which was later swallowed up by one of the huge London 'magic circle' law firms. Those years were extremely busy and professionally rewarding, exciting, and challenging, involving a great deal of travel all over the world. But they were also, over time, exhausting. It took me several years to realise that I had to find a work-life balance, and that there are few, if any, rewards in sacrificing one's entire self to an employer.

For some time, I had had in the back of my mind a niggling desire to take the New York bar exam and to live in America. I decided to give it a shot in late 1999, when I was finally fed up with my job in Brussels to the extent that I was motivated to actually take steps to change my situation. I sent off email CVs to some of the trade law practices of law firms in Washington DC, and landed a job with a US firm. The firm applied for a US visa for me which took nine months to come through, but in the meantime, I worked out my four-month notice period in Brussels, then crossed the Atlantic to study for the New York bar exam in the summer of 2000.

If I had known how horrible taking the New York bar exam was going to be, I would never have entertained the dream of doing it for so many years. I spent a very unpleasant two months during the summer of 2000 in DC attending preparatory bar exam video lectures and living in a tiny student dormitory room on the campus of George Washington University. I felt ancient at 34, next to all the US law school graduates, mainly in their mid-twenties, and very isolated as a result. It was hard to knuckle down and study and I was petrified that my brain simply wasn't capable of remembering everything I had to remember when all my exams at ANU law school in Canberra had always been open book.

Two minutes after arriving in the US, I missed my life and friends in Brussels profoundly, despite the fact that walking away from my old job in Brussels was a huge relief to me and absolutely the right decision. I tried with difficulty to focus on studying for the bar exam, held over two days in Albany, NY in the last week of July. Although I think I put in a fair effort despite feelings of displacement, circumstances ultimately conspired against me. On the night between the first and second days of the exam, I fractured a wisdom tooth and couldn't complete the test, instead having to rush off to a dentist to have the offending tooth extracted in emergency surgery in downtown Albany.

Two days later I flew back to Australia, via Brussels, feeling squashed and unhappy, for a pre-planned two-month holiday with my father while I waited for my US visa, knowing that I would have to re-take the exam the following February, and apprehensive that I was going to have to explain to my new employer that I would need time off to do so. But the long holiday caravanning around Australia with my father was the tonic I needed. Ultimately, I returned to DC to start my job in October 2000 and successfully passed the bar in February 2001.

America was not what I expected. Perhaps that's an unfair statement, because I had never properly thought about what I did expect before I went. The job opportunity was there and it seemed too good to pass up. I arrived in time for the Bush/Gore presidential election, and I was in DC—like the Australian Prime Minister John Howard—on September 11, 2001 when the Pentagon was hit by an aeroplane. It was a curious—even atypical time—to experience the US. Before I went, friends told me that being Australian, I'd have no trouble fitting in. But I had more culture shock in the US than I'd ever had in Germany or Belgium. Sometimes, although I was conversing with Americans in English, I really didn't have a clue what they were talking about. I made some friends, but it was difficult. Suddenly I was spending all my holidays back in Brussels.

By this time, a great deal of my spare time was being devoted to the Southern Cross Group. While in Brussels during the 1990s, I'd been a member of the Belgium committee for Australian Business in Europe (ABIE), essentially a networking organisation for Australians and those doing business with Australia, originally founded in London. Myself and another ABIE Belgium committee member felt that ABIE should be lobbying for change on various issues which negatively impacted Australians overseas. While there was support among our ABIE Belgium colleagues, ABIE UK felt that this was outside ABIE's mandate. Eventually, we decided to form our own advocacy organisation for overseas Australians.

The Southern Cross Group (SCG) was 'born' at a meeting of Australians in Brussels, attended by about 35 individuals, in late January 2000. Several people came forward as our initial volunteer committee members. Later that year we established a website (www.southern-cross-group.org) and in an instant we were global.

Little did we realise at the time that the organisation would flourish and grow to the extent that it has. That fact in itself is proof that there is an enormous need for an international non-governmental organisation which has the special interests of overseas Australians at heart.

One particular issue quickly emerged during the SCG's formation as pressing for many hundreds of thousands of expat Australians everywhere, and soon we were coordinating a global and concerted effort to convince the Australian government to repeal Section 17 of the *Australian Citizenship Act 1948*. The provision (which was finally repealed with effect from 4 April 2002) operated to automatically strip Australian citizens (whether born in Australia or naturalised) of their Australian citizenship when they took a second citizenship in adulthood. Essentially it impacted only on Australians overseas—people who had lived in another country long enough to qualify to become citizens of their host country. Many Australians took another citizenship without realising they would lose their Australian citizenship. Finding out that they were no longer Australian some time later when they went to renew their Australian passport was often a devastating and upsetting experience. Others held-off taking a new citizenship because they knew about Section 17 and couldn't bear to think they'd lose their Australian citizenship. Although Australia allowed dual citizenship for about five million citizens, primarily migrants and their children, expats were being discriminated against.

Even before the Southern Cross Group was founded in January 2000, we had contributed a short letter to the Australian Citizenship Council (ACC) in early 1999 when it began to review the *Citizenship Act*. We called for the repeal of Section 17, and the ACC also recommended repeal to the Government in February 2000. Then we waited until May 2001 for the Government to respond to the ACC's recommendations, but when it did, it still wasn't sure whether Section 17 should be repealed or not. Finally, after over 800 individual submissions were received in just one month in mid 2001, in response to a further discussion paper, the Government announced it would repeal Section 17 in August 2001.

That's the short version: behind the scenes, we were madly writing letters to high profile expatriate Australians, and contacting as many other expat Australians as we could, often through existing expat organisations around the world and various websites, urging everyone to write to Canberra. Some nights I lay awake in bed and wondered who else we could possibly contact and what else we could possibly do to make the repeal of Section 17 a reality. Very few stones were left unturned.

Over the entire period several thousand letters, faxes and emails were received by politicians in Canberra from expats. This was unprecedented. It's very hard to get something changed when you aren't where the action is, and indeed, when many of the people negatively impacted no longer have a vote in Australia. But our voices were eventually too numerous to be ignored.

Most of the Section 17 campaign took place while I was in DC. After September 11, 2001, I decided that I really wanted to move back to Brussels, and interviewed successfully for jobs there in late 2001. I was back in Canberra waiting for my Belgian work permit to come through in February 2002 when the Bill to repeal Section 17 was introduced into the House of Representatives. My father and I were in the peanut gallery at Parliament House, with broad grins on our faces. He had been at the SCG's founding meeting in Brussels, and continues to be an active volunteer for the Group, as well as a huge support for his daughter.

Some people might have thought that the SCG was just about Section 17 and dual citizenship, and that we would collapse in a heap once it was repealed. In fact, it was the catalyst of something far more important—the Australian diaspora movement—which I believe will prove in the longer term to be vital for Australia as it goes forward in a globalised world. We started using the term 'Australian diaspora' several years ago, and now it regularly appears in the media and elsewhere. It denotes the some 860,000 Australians who live overseas, and probably also includes others who are not Australians but who have close family or historical links to the country. We can say that the Australian diaspora today is at least one million people. That's a figure equal to about five percent of Australia's resident population.

We in the diaspora all have one thing in common—Australia. We didn't stop feeling Australian just because we moved overseas. If anything, many expats tell the SCG that they feel more Australian outside Australia than when they are at home. A whole army of unofficial ambassadors roams the world on Australia's behalf and is Australia's home-grown global network. This should allow Australia to be somewhere that can be tapped in to from anywhere.

But many expats are bitterly disappointed how Australians at home, and Australian governments, treat them—perhaps subconsciously—as traitors for having left. At the very least, it's usually 'out of sight, out of mind'. The tall poppy syndrome may play a role, which we will never be able to properly measure. Expats are also punished—inadvertently perhaps—by the failure of Australian governments to properly consider the impact of laws and policies—or in some cases, the lack thereof—on

Australians living abroad. Some of this may simply be because our voices have never been heard in any organised fashion before. If something's broken and you don't phone the repairman, he's not going to appear magically of his own accord.

Many other countries have policies and structures in place to include their overseas nationals in the life of their countries, and to harness the huge resource that their diasporas represent. Australia lags sadly behind on this front.

It is my fervent hope—shared by the other volunteers whom I work alongside at the Southern Cross Group—that there'll be a time, perhaps a decade or two from now, when it's simply part of our culture, a given for all Australians at home, that Australia is the sum of its entire people. Although a significant proportion of Australians do not reside within its territorial boundaries, that should not result in their exclusion from the life of the country and is just a natural corollary of globalisation. The Southern Cross Group will continue to chip away, in small ways and on a number of fronts, to eventually achieve this paradigm shift.

When Australians go overseas today, like their Digger countrymen before them, every single one of them embarks on their own adventure. In this book, we've only got space to share a handful of personal journeys. But all adventures lead to growth and change, strengthening our adaptability, perseverance and determination as a nation. We're a thousand times more pampered than those First World War heroes— no trench foot or Bully beef today. And I bet the Anzacs never had 'Filet Kangourou' jump out at them from a Belgian restaurant menu.

But one thing hasn't changed since the Great War. It doesn't matter when or whether the adventure ultimately leads back to Australia's shores, because wherever we are, Australia remains part of us and we remain part of it.

Anne MacGregor is co-editor of this book and a co-founder of the Southern Cross Group. She lives in Brussels.

THE OLD WOMAN AND THE FLY

The blows of the sledge hammer in our bathroom sends plaster crumbling into our kitchen below. It's day five of the plumbing repairs to our house in Mozambique's second largest city, Beira. We've recently moved here for two years as volunteers to work at the Catholic University of Mozambique. What starts as a blocked pipe in our bathroom turns, inadvertently, into a complete home renovation. We expected poor drainage in Mozambique. What we didn't anticipate was the flow-on effect of a different kind; a multitude of tradespeople arriving daily at lunch time, carrying ladders, buckets and spanners. Like the song, 'The old woman who swallowed the fly', the plumber soon comes to fix the pipe, the builder comes next to render the wall, the painter soon follows to paint it white, then the electrician arrives to rewire the whole-damned mess-of-disconnected-wires back together again. Exasperated, and with limited Portuguese to speak with our *canalizador* (plumber), we let off more steam than the pipe's release valve.

We are experienced travellers and prepare ourselves thoroughly in anticipation for our two year placement. We pore over guide books, purchase the latest high-tech gear, from shoes to pocket knives, pickle our clothes in mosquito repellent and inadvertently 'trip' out on malarial prophylaxis. We watch TV documentaries on the HIV/AIDs virus and brief ourselves on the UN poverty objectives. But even this cannot prepare us for some of what we will face.

Mozambique's population of approximately 17 million is made up of 16 main ethnic groups or tribes. Portuguese is the official language but most of the population prefer to use their local Bantu language. The country is still emerging from a sustained period of civil war which ravaged the country for 17 years between 1983 and 1990. The ruling Frelimo Government renounced its Marxist ideology in the early 1990s and after the formal peace accord was signed in October 1992, there has been significant movement towards capitalist ideologies. In fact, with its seven to nine per cent growth rates and multi-party democratic elections, Mozambique—rightly or wrongly—is now the darling of the IMF and the World Bank. Foreign aid has been flooding into the country and significant development has occurred, lifting it off the bottom of the UN human development indexes. And yet the shadow of poverty and hardship is never far away: 80 per cent of the population is unemployed, one-third is infected with the HIV virus, and per capita GDP is around US$145.

Our home city of Beira is built on a swamp. It is also sunk right in the middle of poverty that plagues much of the central and northern region. Beira itself is still largely in ruins, and dilapidated multistorey buildings house hundreds of families and children who live, as does 70 per cent of the population, with no electricity or running water. Piles of rubbish lie at intervals along the streets and large puddles of water lie stagnant, breeding the ubiquitous malaria-carrying mosquito.

Like many volunteers, we are keen to absorb ourselves into the lifestyle and live like 'locals', whatever we think that means. To this end, prior to embarking on our adventure, we have no intention of employing an *empregada* (maid), or night guard, who are normally associated (we mistakenly think) only with wealthy locals and expats. However, on our arrival, we learn that both the maid and guard will prove essential, at the very least to lessen the numerous enquirers ringing the bell to ask about work opportunities. Within a week of our arrival, *empregada* Dona Maria becomes part of our household.

Dona Maria is a diminutive 52-year-old mother and grandmother with two missing front teeth and a Felix the Cat-like smirk. She is the sole breadwinner for a household of thirteen. Dona Maria quickly adapts to her new surrounds, washing, ironing, waxing the floor and making herself invaluable. But before long, we discover grey frizzy hairs in our plastic comb, loosened lids on moisturiser bottles, and fresh red Elizabeth Arden nail polish smears on the crockery. Slipping her foot into a well-worn Birkenstock, she is quick to remark that Senhora's shoe size conveniently matches her own. She is as far from the image of the housemaid from the film *Gosford Park* as Mozambique is from Australia. We smother our giggles at her childish exploits and debate how we should 'reprimand' her with our limited Portuguese. All is forgotten when, in the second week of her employment with us, she is summoned from our house one afternoon to the local hospital where her daughter has been admitted. Dona Maria is too late. The doctor tells her that her daughter has died from TB. As is so often the case in local hospitals, HIV/AIDs is not cited as the responsible illness, despite it being the cause of a large proportion of the total hospital deaths.

Food becomes an important focus of passing our spare time. With ample supplies of fresh seafood, we are excited at the prospect of tasting an array of gourmet recipes, marinated monk fish in coconut milk, *goropa* fish curry and rice, and a local version of the French bouillabaisse. However, with little culture of competition, the restaurants offer the same dishes as each other; it's a bit like choosing between a peanut butter and vegemite sandwich at every eatery in town.

Despite the lack of variety offered, the local *bolos* (cakes) are one of the sweeter legacies of the Portuguese. Custard tarts, rice cakes and custard-filled donuts emerge daily from electric ovens and consuming them becomes our daily ritual.

Food becomes an unexpected means of currency. One day we receive an official notice telling us there's a parcel waiting for us at the post office. We line up excitedly, ready to hand over our receipt in exchange for the mystery packet. We can see several packages sticking out of the grey metal filing cupboard. For fifteen minutes we endure a woman pulling out one package at a time, peering at it to match up our name (so foreign to her), stuffing it back in, only to pull the same ones out again. Our hopes rise and fall with her every move, especially when we spot the all-too-familiar Aussie airmail stickers. We can even make out the name Lester, an expat friend, on one of the parcels. When we subtly point out to our myopic mail sorter that we most definitely have a parcel, she slams the door shut and hands our single packet to one of four women, all of them sitting at a table reading newspapers.

The large and buxom handler is dressed in an official blue shirt and tie, the compulsory public servant uniform of *Alfandega* (Customs). With a lazy gesture of her hands, and a gleeful note in her voice, she demands money in exchange for relinquishing the package. We do not hand over money in response to her illegal plea. She reaches over, picks up a large pair of metal tailor's scissors and dexterously hacks open our packet, a birthday box of goodies as it turns out. Out spills a packet of Cheezles. We are as eager to get our teeth around our much-missed Aussie snack as we are to leave the building. But as she slowly and deliberately puts her hand in to pick out the packet, it is clear someone has to give in. We grab the packet of Cheezles, toss them onto her desk, whip up our box and turn on our heels cursing furiously under our breaths.

Later that night, we visit a bar with Lester and recount to him our tale. He is delighted to hear that he has a parcel awaiting his pick up. We order a drink to celebrate and ponder how he can claim his property without his official collection docket. Then, an incredible coincidence occurs. It is our first time in the bar, and we are shocked to see our friend from the post office customs sitting at the next table. (We don't recognise her at first without specs and tie). She seems embarrassed by our encounter but gives us a cheesy grin. We tell her about Lester and his parcel. She undertakes to hand it to him personally the next day. She keeps her promise.

Not so promising is our form of transport, the humble bicycle. Eager to try to fit in with our bike-riding counterparts and not wanting to be seen to be flaunting 'white wealth', we avoid buying state-of-the-art mountain bikes, instead opting for the popular imported Indian bicycles. With regal names such as 'Hunter' and 'Hamilton' the bikes promise a luxurious riding adventure. With their white mud guards, silver metal rod hand brakes, and rear vision mirrors the bikes are a fashionable accessory. We plan to ride everywhere and rival Lance Armstrong in speed, as Beira is flat and swampy. The bikes' construction, however, doesn't match their aesthetics. The bumps and potholes render them mirrorless, brakeless, and missing various bolts and screws.

Riding them is like cycling on an exercise bike with the resistance set at the hardest gradient. They have only one gear so we dread having to stop at one of the two sets of traffic lights. Our sweat trickles into the potholes below with the effort of having to get going again. Nevertheless, we persevere, spending much time with the local roadside bike repair man who bangs the bikes' wheels, caresses their tubes and makes a show of keeping them on the road.

Another useful form of transport is the *chapas* (mini bus), which defies all safety regulations, and is a claustrophobic's nightmare.

Crammed in four to a narrow row, you can be confronted by the most basic of smells and sights: from unwashed bodies and body odour, to babies whose heads, in many cases, are covered in lesions (also a legacy of HIV) as well as alcohol-imbibed men. Yet this is the place where friendships are formed, where children sit on your lap, and where you share, for a brief moment, the same vistas as they flash past your face at a jerkily breakneck speed, until you screech to a stop to avoid a goat, or to pick up another passenger.

Yet do we really see the same vistas as the locals? What appear to us to be piles of rotting rubbish, are for others, convenient dumps and sources of plastic bags, empty bottles and food. The overpowering stench of sewage bubbling up through the drains is merely an expected part of a failed utility to many. (It is said that the Portuguese, furious at being asked to leave the country, destroyed much of the infrastructure as they left. Ships were run aground and cement was poured down the drains.) The dilapidated colonial buildings juxtaposed against the discoloured sixties concrete apartments seem an outrage to us, and a means of living for the locals. Behind these dirty concrete facades some occupants live in luxury in these apartments, yet, it is claimed by some, no-one is keen to form a body corporate or ensure that the public areas are maintained—a legacy of living under communism, where property was forcibly shared.

The living conditions exacerbate health problems, and with a hospital system (and knowledge) inadequate to respond to these issues, diseases such as cholera and malaria are rife. It is not only AIDS, but malaria too, which is responsible for a huge proportion of deaths among the Mozambican population. Malaria is to a Mozambican what the common cold is to an Australian. The difference is that 30 per cent of all hospital deaths and 60 per cent of hospitalisation are due to malaria.

Naturally, we didn't want to contract malaria. We brought enough prophylaxis to set up a pharmacy, more mozzie coils than the neighbourhood mosque has incense, and sufficient tropical strength repellent to ward off the mosquitoes. Yet, one mother of all mozzies bites one of us several times. We notice the bites, but don't ponder on the possible consequences. That is, until the next week, when flu-like symptoms, chills and a migraine-like headache set in. We trudge into the nearest health clinic which resembles a half-painted concrete toilet block rather than a medical facility. Out the back in the 'lab', bloodied syringes sit soaking in a rectangular bucket, and a few staff peer into microscopes below peeling posters which promote vaccinations and hygiene practices. Several people wait outside on benches, holding their heads in pain. What strikes us is that, unlike most hospitals, there's not a whiff of cheap antiseptic. We inspect the small pin-like finger probe and decide that it's hygienically wrapped and safe to use. The test is over quickly and efficiently, testimony to the number of times the staff perform it each day. A drop of blood is smeared onto a small glass slide. Thirty minutes later we ask hopefully, 'Negativo?' 'No,' says the orderly, as the doctor has already left. 'Positivo.' Before turning back to his colleagues (outside on a smoko) he delivers a matter-of-fact verdict: 'Quatro, quarto, dois?': the number of chloroquine pills required to treat this type of malaria. We hurriedly write an email seeking further advice from our Australian insurance company, whose medical arm replies within hours. Their medical staff confirm that this remedy is not effective, the mosquitoes are chloroquine-resistant. They recommend another, more appropriate medication, and a week later, the patient emerges from her malarial mist.

Which brings us back to remedies of another kind—the electrician who arrives at our house to reconnect the wires. He drills a hole in the wall to gain access to the power outlet, which has been inadvertently plastered over. He hits a pipe. The pipe springs a leak. It's the old woman and the fly all over again. Responding to our tale, the locals smile knowingly and say, 'It's Mozambique. You have to expect it here.'

Kate Armstrong and Christopher Nelson are yet to reach the mid-point of their two-year posting to Mozambique through Australian Volunteers International. As much as they were tired of hearing the clichéd advice, 'expect the unexpected', they reveal that the age-old adage is relevant for all travellers and expatriates, especially those who think they've seen and done it all.

LEAVING AND BELONGING

I grew up on the beautiful coastline of Sydney's beaches. The beauty of my homeland inspires me. I draw strength from my childhood memories of the oceans and cliffs, and the freedom of the wind sailing beneath the hot sun.

My friend Karen and I were taking part in a sailing race in the Caribbean before flying on to London. We were workmates at Westpac Training. It was 1993 and there were widespread retrenchments following a decision to reduce overheads and bring the subsidiaries back under the roof of Westpac Banking Corporation. Whole departments were dismantled. Most of Karen's department was gone. At the time, many corporations were restructuring as a consequence of the indulgent 80s. As Karen and I were in our 20s, we chose to volunteer for retrenchment, seeing this as an opportunity to go on a global walkabout. Neither of us expected to become expatriates.

'Can't we stopover in the US? I have always wanted to see Disneyland,' Karen urged. I tried to talk her out of it. After Disneyland, we flew to Antigua Race Week. Karen and I were fortunate enough to sail with a crew that made history: we became the first Australians to ever win line honours.

Karen flew on to London. America was not on my list of 'must see' except for New York., I arrived in New York City late at night. A cab took me around the same block ten times before arriving at a seedy hotel on 42nd Street. That night blared gospel singing and gunfire. I stared at the three heavy bolts on the door and waited for light.

Light came with the pure energy of a million lives whirling around me in a moving tapestry. I moved to a hostel uptown and joined the rush. My days blended with the sights, smells and noises of New York's many cultures as I walked the neighbourhoods: from the chic of Soho to the Village, Chinatown, Little Italy, Lower East Side and on. New York has many faces and raw heartbeats of humanity. Coming from our vast and isolated island in the Pacific Ocean to the extremes of New York was like waking up inside a movie set. There was a quality of the fantastic and unreal: from scene to scene, I was captivated.

If the city streets were a passionate whirlwind, Central Park was a slow dance: an emerald island of tranquillity with misty lampposts along a lazy lane, cheeky acrobatic squirrels chat to steal my lunch. A 20 foot Sesame Street Big Bird blades past on roller skates, makes me laugh. I slept cocooned, the skyline surrounded, enfolding my dreams. If I could weave this timeless energy, I could awaken my dreams to magic.

The early morning sunlight was playing hopscotch in the garden of the hostel. Soft warmth danced on my skin, distracting me momentarily from my thoughts. I knew I would have to leave New York; my childhood friend from Australia would pick me up from Heathrow airport in a few days. Yet, it was undeniable that I felt a compelling invitation to life in this city. It was hard to believe that I had barely arrived.

A young man threw shadows on my reflection. I looked up to a smile. He was telling me that his volunteer for the day had not shown. He worked for God's Love We Deliver, a non-profit organisation that ran out of the basement of the hostel. He asked if I would like to help him deliver hot meals to people homebound with AIDS. Here was my chance to give back to the city that was giving me so much. When I fervently answered yes ten years ago, I had no idea what I was truly volunteering for. The young man, Andy, became my husband.

Shortly after we met, Andy was visiting his Mum in Florida and asked if I would mind his kitten at his Upper West Side of Manhattan studio apartment. Wood floors. Arches. I would be delighted. When the door closed behind him, I turned up the stereo, listened to funky jazz, and danced around the spacious apartment. I looked to the ceiling claiming, 'I want an apartment just like this one!' I didn't think I would soon live in the apartment I danced in, but I did. I stayed in the city I fell in love with.

Andy and I created a garden on a concrete slab joining two apartment buildings. When we would have parties, we would all squeeze like contortionists through the bars on our window to get outside. There we had it: our spot of nature on the second floor: flower boxes, two chairs, a table, and a barbie. On steamy summer nights, we slept in our tent in the garden staring through the mesh skylight. I was remembering what stars looked like in an Australian night sky. What I realised that summer was that I did not have to compromise my love of Australia in order to love another place.

I waded into the yellow sea of cabs as I once waded into the effervescent waves of home. Newness: intellectual dinner parties, politics over free trade coffee. Excitement: *Law & Order* filming in our apartment, a Stradivarius violin stolen from work, investigation and intrigue. Dive: skydiving from a plane at 2000 feet, seeing Andy disappear into the sky before me. Play: first snow, first snowman, summer at the Hamptons. A different world: a winter midnight alone at Niagara Falls, a Key West sunset with a buoyant crowd, horse riding through Hawaiian rainforests, Scottish lochs, European flavours. Australia is a rugged land and sea, but the beauty of this earth is exhilarating, no matter what geographical perspective.

From an Upper West Side perspective, when a catastrophe strikes, it is time to stock up on sushi. Therapists for neurotics and pets abound, as do Great Danes and pocket pooches wearing raincoats or sun collars. People become waves of obstacles around ignored traffic lights. On sidewalks, faces blur and separate—each unique, coloured by their culture, animated by another, lined by life experience—pass and converge.

From the many faces of this city, I chose to look upon grass roots creativity. With an air of the impromptu, visual, performance and literary arts flow and fill the neighbourhood streets, claiming this city as the international meeting place for artists. Australia's geographical isolation creates a curiosity to learn and participate in the world. To New York the world comes.

How does one connect in a culturally complicated place? As an Australian living overseas, the question of belonging is a reoccurring theme. Challenges squeeze in under your apartment door. Freedom? Mobility? The cost of belonging, pleasure or pain?

It is a circus out there, and bureaucracy is holding the training whip while you are leaping through the hoops of immigration, jumping the hurdles of health care and the cost of education. I share with most Australians a healthy scepticism about authority, however, these ordeals trained me to quell my rebellious nature and focus on personal goals. While waiting out the challenge, one becomes admirably resourceful, an investigator in search of loopholes. One of the biggest fears in the US is to become ill. Those without health insurance delay visiting a doctor in the hope an illness will go away by itself. Because no other hospital would take an alien without health insurance, I ended up in Harlem Hospital for a week under emergency care. During that time, I did not see one other fair-skinned person among the doctors, nurses, or patients. Socio-economic segregation? Ward after ward filled with testimonials: for the older, poor health not attended to earlier; for the younger, gun shot or knife wounds.

During the long waiting period for my permanent residency status, my mind roamed the shores and headlands of my childhood, my adolescence, my becoming a woman. I still miss drinking a cup of tea with my Mum and sharing my life with her. I miss sunset walks on an endless beach with my Dad, sharing our philosophies, watching the brushstrokes of mauve blend with crimson, indigo. Laughing, digging toes in wet sand, hunting for pipis. My heart aches because it is pulled and stretched across seas, across lands, to encompass births, deaths, marriages, first homes, losing a job, gaining a job, minor concerns, major setbacks. When the phone receiver is replaced, I smile in a distant land. Do they know or believe how much I care? I hardly express it in the rush of life. The younger ones don't know me nor I them.

Being a global citizen means developing a web of support that spans the planet. Each time a loved one flies, we weave one more silver thread. Loving community is spun until we understand home as the smiles of our extended family. When I open emails from loved ones, I hear the words read to me in their voices, their unique body gestures. The touch? There are times I would gladly give what I have accomplished abroad to sink into a long warm Aussie cuddle.

After working with the Australian Mission to the UN, I decided to attend to college in the US. It took me a year and a half to be accepted into the public education system. Although I had studied Engineering Drawing at Sydney Technical College, no prior education was acknowledged. I sat for the High School Equivalency Diploma and started with zero credit towards my undergraduate degree. I was assigned to a two-year community college with other foreigners the city did not know what to do with. As it turns out, the multicultural environment at the

Borough of Manhattan Community College further exposed me to worlds of colour, culture, art and ideas. Seventeen different languages were spoken in one class of 35 students with English as their second language. My patience and appreciation grew for these intelligent students, acquiring new concepts in a language not their own, as I struggled to learn French as a second language. I excelled in my studies from desire, but my advantage was the high quality of my Australian education. Since receiving permanent residency, the US has been very generous in scholarships and grants, allowing me to continue to do what I love: to learn.

I was studying for a French final when a friend called, asking me not to leave for school. It was September 11, 2001 and a plane had just crashed into a tower of the World Trade Center. Confusion. Then the second tower was hit. My college was only a few city blocks from the World Trade Center. I rang the security office at my college to ask if there would be classes as usual. A panicked woman shouted into the mouthpiece, 'We are being evacuated NOW!'. The mounthpiece clunked against the table. The students were evacuated in time, but we lost one school building, damaged in the blast. As the tower crumbled, the earth stood still and watched. The incessant hustle and bustle of New York was silent, in shock. The wailing sirens below and the whirring helicopters above jolted everything and everyone.

I called my parents early. It was night in Australia, and Dad groggily answered the phone. 'Dad, something has happened in New York, but I want to let you know I am alright. This might sound strange but you will understand in the morning. Go back to sleep now.' 'OK,' Dad said, still in the haze of sleep. Ten thousand miles away my island of birth felt safe and abundant. My grandmother was turning ninety that day. It was when the phone lines died, that I found myself again on an isolated island wanting to reach into the world.

I, like most New Yorkers, felt frustrated I couldn't do more, to somehow effect a change. On day one, the Red Cross turned us away; too much blood. In the days following September 11, many volunteered with the Red Cross. I worked the midnight shift on the Chefs with Spirit boat moored off 'ground zero'. Spirit Cruise Lines, the Red Cross and chefs from all over the city came together to create a temporary shelter for the rescue workers. Twenty-four hours a day hot meals were provided, a person to speak to, and a place to sleep for a couple of hours before returning to the site. Due to the proximity to ground zero, security was high. As volunteers, we were told that if we left the boat and kept walking, we would be shot.

During a quiet time in my shift, I went to the top deck of the boat for fresh air. This gave me a moment to really see and feel. It was eerie. Rays of floodlight lay in pools swimming in surreal darkness, illuminating buildings torn open like tin cans. To me, the surrounding buildings cocooned the site in compassion and protection. They stood like tall loyal guardians, bearing witness to every action of the men below. For myself and many other people from around the world, the role of bearing witness became a form of honouring the passing.

Two hours after the last tower fell, I wrote a poem to capture the emergency and urgency of the day. Upon reading this poem in my Modern Poetry class, the professor requested that I write a booklet of poetry for an honours project. The theme of 'Loss Poems' was clearly established from my first poem and by the intensity of feeling that was expressed by both the professors and students when we returned to college after the tragedy. There had been talk of the city not reopening the college; it was closed until October and used in the rescue operations. We could only enter the building through the back door, and security was strict. The front entrance was still locked in the frozen zone.

I wrote on the experience of walking to school, recoiling from the thick acrid air as the subway doors opened. Many of us put on masks as we climbed the subway stairs into a grey world of twisted metal. We walked past paper faces of lost rescue workers lining deserted storefronts. Frozen smiles fluttering in the wind, catching against our shoes, swept away, littered like confetti down empty streets. Loss of loved ones, career, faith in mankind; the future questioned. September 11 and its repercussions catapulted many of us into a new phase in our lives. I would leave the city I fell in love with.

One day in class, my philosophy professor made a random comment that two of his students applied to Mount Holyoke and Wellesley Colleges under the non-traditional student program. After class, I found out that the deadline for college applications was closed. However, my college representative said, 'Why not call them and ask if they will extend the deadline for you.' I rang two colleges and to my surprise, they did extend the deadline on condition that I had a full application completed and on their desk in three days. I had no sleep but I managed to fax the two applications in on time.

Much to my great joy, I was accepted at Yale University. In submitting my late applications and at other times, I have experienced the advantage of being Australian. Our directness and honesty creates an openness, which cause others to relax. Our easy humour is unencumbered by formality, which gives us an unassuming charm that people warm to. We have strength and perseverance when necessary and we are satisfied to achieve our goals with hard work. We have an effect on others we are not aware of. I have Karen to thank for being at Yale. She talked me into seeing Disneyland: 'go on, let's try something scary, exciting, fun with unexpected twists and turns'. We both unexpectedly lived and married overseas. When overseas Aussie friends and I talk, we do not ask each other if we will ever return to Australia. We ask, 'WHEN are you going home mate?'. Karen left London and returned to Australia with her husband, David.

I will be going home for *Chrissy*.

We Aussies who are on a global walkabout are weaving stories worth telling. I am typing my story on a laptop covered with Vegemite paw marks and a platypus sticker. I am listening to Hunters and Collectors. How could anyone question my connection with home? Australia raised me wild and free. Today it is my identity and strength. The land taught me rugged individualism and idealism. Aboriginal dreamtime cradled me in ancient wisdom, instilling a deep connection and respect for this earth. Wherever I roam, Australia and I can never be separate. I celebrate my homeland with the world. I enjoy others celebrating their homeland with me.

Antasia Azure is a student at Yale University undertaking a major in Comparative Literature. She is interested in journalism and hopes to write a book on identity and belonging from the point of view of a global citizen.

NGILOZI, THIS VEGEMITE IS TERRIBLE!

It's late afternoon and a thunderstorm rolls in over rural Swaziland, threatening the outdoor wedding proceedings. In the middle of the group is the bride, almost completely covered with a huge blanket and wearing a huge headdress of bright feathers. Around her wrists and ankles seedpod bracelets rattle. Surrounding her are women in brightly-coloured cloth, carrying her possessions on their heads. Leading the procession is a young warrior wearing jackal and leopard skins. They dance and sing around the cattle kraal.

A wedding guest is urged forward and the rituals are explained to her in whispers. The dancers are announcing to their ancestors and the gathering that this woman is now to be married and thus will join the groom's family.

I am the wedding guest—an Australian volunteer in Swaziland with my husband, Adrian. I am privileged to meet this family, share in their food and dancing, and have their wedding ceremony explained to me. I'm on the adventure of a lifetime.

Through Australian Volunteers International, I am now working with the Family Life Association of Swaziland (FLAS) as a youth officer, and Adrian is an instructor at the Manzini Industrial Training Centre (MITC). Having never worked directly with youth, we knew our new roles would be challenging, but we had no idea just how much we would enjoy them.

Coming from rural Australia, we miss the wide-open spaces and the connection with the land. But in our own ways we are finding something akin to an affinity with the land here. Swaziland is geographically a stunning country. When we first flew in, we came down across low hills saturated by the deep green of an early wet season and the vibrant purple of a million Jacaranda trees in full bloom. We couldn't wait to be part of it. For Adrian, connection with the land deepens each day in a very literal sense as he feels the rich red soil in his hands, alongside the future farmers of Swaziland. For me, the bonds come 'through the lens'—capturing images of Swazis in their landscape.

Volunteering means facing the unknown and using skills you didn't know you had—that's the challenge, that's what makes it interesting. You have to be able to laugh at yourself when others do. Once you stop taking yourself so seriously it's a lot of fun. It's also about time for reflection about who you are and your place in the world, both as an individual and as an Australian.

Africa for me is about extremes—all the experiences are more intense. Sunsets over flat-topped Acacia trees in the African lowveld affect me not just visually, but emotionally. Equally intense and moving are the widows who must wear deep black mourning gowns and scarves for three years. Or the despair in the sunken dark eyes of the woman in rags as she begs for bread for the baby on her back. The good times here are among the best I have ever experienced; the bad times the worst.

Unemployment in Swaziland is incredibly high and the majority of people are forced to take very low paying jobs. High living costs force people to live in squalor—66% of Swazis live below the poverty line. The HIV/AIDS pandemic is causing devastation throughout the country. During the past two years, hardly a week has passed at work without a memo about the death of a staff member, or a staff member's relative. I am constantly surrounded by death.

Being here is a rollercoaster ride—attempting to reconcile your own rationale for living among so much suffering while knowing that at any time you can go home with the freedom that having an Australian passport affords. It's about wanting to leave, but at the same time not being able to go. It's seeing and hearing things you never wanted to, but growing as a person because you have to.

One of the most significant issues facing Swaziland (and many southern African countries) is the HIV/AIDS pandemic, and youth is the most vulnerable group. Looking at our young friends, we realise that, statistically, only about half of them will live past 30. The HIV/AIDS pandemic has left behind thousands of orphans and a society unable to cope with large extended family groups that lack a working-age breadwinner. Lack of access to education means that many young people with no family support are forced into crime and prostitution to survive.

FLAS, where I work, operates youth and adult clinics, and runs peer education programs on sexual and reproductive health issues. They also run two youth centres. I spend my days producing radio programs, running activities at the youth centres and organising awareness campaigns for young people. Most of the youth I deal with are in school and aged between 10 and 20. On my first day at FLAS I was affectionately given the Siswati name *Ngilozi* (Angel). Swazis are very honest and direct—'Ngilozi, this vegemite is terrible!'.

Often the voices of youth go unheard, but our radio program gives them a voice and I feel proud to be a part of that. Sitting in the studio each week and recording them talk about their hopes, fears and dreams—being allowed an insight into their lives—is a privilege. You cannot help being caught up in their enthusiasm and hope for the future. Recently we interviewed an aspiring young rap group. Their music describes the devastating effect of HIV/AIDS on their friends, but there are also songs of hope—messages of young people who have nothing but making good.

My background is admin/finance, so undertaking youth activities has been an enormous personal challenge. At FLAS we deal with some really serious issues, but working with the youth here also means having a lot of fun. Where else would I get the opportunity to stop the traffic in the CBD of a capital city and march with hundreds of youth handing out condoms and making lots of noise about youth issues?

However, I cannot describe my despair when a colleague told me that at a recent workshop where young participants were asked to draw a picture of what Manzini City will look like in 10 years, they all drew tombstones and empty offices. Nor can I express the heartache of looking into the eyes of a young person who knows they are dying from AIDS-related illnesses. Or when a young girl recently raped comes to FLAS and asks you to arrange a HIV test for her. You feel powerless and inadequate.

Yet for generations, Swaziland's proud traditions and culture have embodied a strong sense of self-determination and optimism for the future. We live next door to a home for street boys. These kids have been sponsored to attend an HIV/AIDS conference in Spain to perform the traditional Swazi Sabhaca dance. For weeks now we've had drumming, singing and dancing day and night as they practice. They are so excited about going on an aeroplane and are constantly asking us questions about what it will be like. Seeing their huge smiles and the excitement in their eyes is magical.

Swaziland can be a difficult country to understand. The culture is very traditional, complex and often secretive. If you ask a question you get an answer, but you have to ask the right questions. In many ways I am still a mystery to many of my co-workers (as they are to me), but they enjoy teaching me Siswati and telling me stories—I at least contribute humour to their work day! Many of them share very personal stories, which is testimony to their openness.

As an Australian woman, dealing with gender inequality and attitudes in Swaziland is difficult. For Swazi women and girls, it hinders every aspect of their lives—economic, emotional, social, legal, and otherwise. It is particularly difficult for young women who find they are unable to negotiate safe sex within relationships. They have no autonomy or independence, and are without decision making powers. As a result many unwanted pregnancies occur, with the responsibility for the child falling to the woman.

More than 40 per cent of women aged 20-24 seeking anti-natal care are HIV positive. Most of these women suffer alone, without the means to access proper medical care for themselves or their babies. As an Australian used to having medical rights and support structures, this is something I struggle to come to terms with.

A general lack of opportunities for Swazi youth is a problem. Education in Swaziland is not free and many youth find themselves unable to attend even primary school due to financial constraints. Without education it is difficult for youth to complete any form of employment training.

Adrian teaches agriculture at the Manzini Industrial Training Centre. The centre takes trainees with little education aged between 18 and 25. The emphasis is on practical instruction to empower young people with the skills and encouragement they need to enter vocational trades. For Adrian, agriculture in a tropical climate is a long way from the broadscale cropping and livestock industry of southern NSW. He says that seeing the pride his trainees take in producing and selling vegetables makes this the most rewarding work he has ever done. It's also taught him a lot about himself. With no teaching experience, re-starting the agriculture program, writing and designing a syllabus (and doing it all under the pressure of making a profit at the end) has been a huge challenge.

The key to Adrian's success has been treating his trainees with respect. He's a farmer, so instead of sitting in the classroom, he mostly works one-on-one among the plots, helping them individually. It is more a friendship than a student-teacher relationship.

Each day is an unexpected adventure. Adrian spent weeks in the rural areas trying to find a rotary hoe to hire. When he did find someone with the right equipment, the negotiations were less than straightforward. The 50-year-old farmer had learned Waltzing Matilda at school some 45 years ago. He remembered the song but didn't know what some of the words meant. Before he would agree to hire his machine Adrian had to sit with him all afternoon and explain about jumbucks, billabongs, swagmen and tuckerbags.

As outsiders we are often seen as having all the answers, which is very unsettling. Volunteering means leaving your pre-conceptions and expectations at home, especially ingrained and sometimes irrelevant Australian ideas about working and doing things. It's also a process of re-assessing your accomplishments. My new Siswati words—*kubeketela nekuphokophela* (patience and determination)—have been helpful in this regard.

Recently I was talking with a young friend who has a very traumatic past. We were looking at photographs of her; comparing ones when I'd first met her in 2002 with some I'd just taken. I couldn't believe how beautiful and happy she looked in the recent images.

When I commented on the change she said, 'You know why I look so different, Gabstar? It's because you've helped me change my life by being my friend—you taught me how to smile and how to be happy.' That one sentence made the previous 18 months worthwhile. It felt far better than anything else I've ever achieved, here or at home, and will remain the highlight of my time in Swaziland.

Adrian and I have found that we have a lot to offer. Not in a monetary or material sense, and not necessarily through skills transfer or by performing well in our jobs, but through friendship and respect for others. Many of our friends have traumatic pasts and uncertain futures—they are vulnerable and have never been able to trust anyone, nor have they ever experienced respect or love. Holding someone's hand while they wait for the results of their HIV test doesn't require special skills, it's about supporting friends and breaking down barriers and prejudices.

We've also found that we have a lot to learn about ourselves—about courage and strength and determination. About facing challenges and not only learning to work through them, but also finding a way to enjoy them. About living life *now* regardless of the past or the future. Most importantly we've learned the joys of opening our minds and our hearts to new experiences, both good and bad.

Living in Swaziland has challenged my beliefs and ideas about Australia. Being an Australian here brings mixed feelings and raises more questions than it answers. Who are we? Where are we going as a country? What's important, what's not? What kind of roles can and should Australians play both at home and abroad to make the world a better place?

People ask what Australia is like. Initially it was very easy to answer, but after almost two years it is much more difficult. Our Swazi mates are now very 'tuned in' to Australian headlines. Fortunately most of these are about sporting triumphs and for me, sport is always a comfortable topic. However, when asked about people in detention centres or the 'Stolen Generation' I am lost for explanation. *Rabbit Proof Fence* recently screened here. My friends asked why children were taken from their families—they couldn't understand a culture that would do that. How do you explain such insanity and such injustices? And how do you do it as a 'proud' Australian?

Under the shadow of the huge Aussie flag we proudly pinned up the day we arrived in Swaziland, I look at the photos we have pasted on our 'home wall'. Family and friends stare back at us, a reminder of our 'other' life. On the shelf are jars of vegemite, an empty Cherry Ripe wrapper is stuck to the fridge, and there's a bottle of Australian red wine we are saving for Christmas Day. Our memories of Australia are at times surreal, and we wonder how easy it will be to return home. Next to our Aussie icons are brightly decorated African pots, masks, baskets, and photographs of our friends and travels here. It's like having a split personality.

Sometimes we still feel like outsiders, but through our new friendships we are slowly unravelling a small part of the mysteries of Swazi culture. When we feel down we turn to the humour and warmth of our Swazi friends. They are so easy to be around, and remind us why we made the decision to come. Individuals and families generously include us as part of their lives. They show us love, compassion and tolerance. This reinforces the wonderful opportunity we have as Australian Volunteers. We love Swaziland and cherish our days here.

As an Australian abroad, I feel I have enormous opportunities, but with that also comes responsibilities—not just within my communities here and at home, but globally. Traditionally Australians have always 'helped our mates', but maybe it's time to re-define who our mates are.

We need to look beyond our own beliefs, to break down barriers caused by ignorance and fear. Being a volunteer has shown us how much we have to learn—both from within and from the outside, and for us it has shown what can be achieved.

Volunteering in Swaziland means living and working with wonderful individuals who continue to inspire us with their determination and resilience under often extremely difficult and disturbing conditions of inequality and suffering. Their warmth, good humour and curiosity makes each day here very special. It also offers the opportunity to grow as an *Australian*. To value what we have, to realise there is still a lot that needs to be done to truly make Australia the 'lucky country' for everyone, and to encourage peace, tolerance and understanding, both at home and abroad.

Gabrielle Brabander, came from Deniliquin in regional NSW and has been working in Swaziland since October 2001. She is a youth officer with the Family Life Association of Swaziland. Her husband Adrian works as a vocational agriculture trainer with the Manzini Industrial Training Centre.

HEARTS LIE BLEEDING

Three masked guerrillas materialised out of the pitch-black Mexican night. Their eyes glinted in the light of a handheld torch in the cavernous hall where we were meeting them, in a Zapatista rebel stronghold guarding the entrance to the Lacandon jungle. We had driven all day over bone-rattling roads with only a photocopy of a pen-sketched map a fellow journalist had filched from the army. Much of Chiapas state, riven by conflict between the government and Zapatistas holed up in their jungle bastions, was so remote that countless villages did not appear on any map; its few sealed roads existed only because the army built them for access to flashpoints across the region. We made the journey, in a clapped-out car with shot suspension, because several days earlier 45 Indian refugees, 35 of them women and children, had been killed by paramilitary gunmen who came crashing through the undergrowth firing automatic weapons. Most of the victims—Zapatista sympathisers, died with a bullet in the back of the head.

The attack on the hamlet of Acteal, 70 km northwest of the old colonial capital San Cristobal de las Casas, was Mexico's worst single act of violence since New Year's Day 1994, when Zapatista rebels claiming Indian rights staged an armed rebellion against the state. Rumour had it that the massacre, whose death roll included four pregnant women, had been designed to draw the rebels into a clash with the army; Zapatista foot-soldiers would rally at one of five meeting places like this to carry out any organised response. Mistrust, meanwhile, rolled across Chiapas' mountains like the morning mist. Burning houses lit up the valleys at night; refugee shantytowns burgeoned as villages polarised into pro and anti-rebel camps; and vigilante gangs with names like Peace and Justice were reportedly on the move across the state. As journalists, we huddled with the rebels in their freezing outpost that night trying to find out how they would respond to the mayhem.

I hadn't been sent to cover Mexico's most fraught political conflict deep in the Chiapas heartland because I was Australian, but rather, because it was Christmas. Most of my colleagues who were heading home to celebrate had already gone, so we were a minimal staff left running the bureau in Mexico City. That Tuesday I had been assigned the early shift, opening the office at 7 am. As I left my flat in the capital's leafy Condesa district, on the radio of the green VW Beetle taxi I caught that morning to work, I heard confused reports of first 11, then 19 dead in some sort of assault in Chiapas. As I logged into my computer the death toll continued to rise. By the time my bureau chief called I had already filed my first urgent report; when he started seeking someone to send, it seemed logical that I should volunteer.

It was 23 December 1997. I threw a tape recorder, batteries, notebooks and my laptop and mobile phone into a pack with some clothes and headed for the airport. Families laden with Christmas luggage were crowding the check-in desks and all the direct flights were full; I eventually found a standby to state capital Tuxtla Gutierrez with a stop in Oaxaca, where the trainee pilot overshot the runway the first time we tried to land. We got into Tuxtla by late afternoon, and I made my way to San Cristobal in a communal taxi filled with silent, long-faced Mexicans. I checked into one of the few hotels with phone connections in the rooms and agreed on a rough plan of action with my bureau chief.

The next morning I headed to San Cristobal's main hospital. I suppose any middle class person, not just an Australian, would feel the same shock the first time they entered a remote hospital in the developing world. It was utterly bare—in this time of emergency—of equipment, medicines, staff. It could have been any concrete-floored government building with the addition of metal beds. I had been dreading the sight of Indian women and children, their bodies mangled by machetes and AK47 rifle-fire, so I was secretly relieved to learn the worst cases had been taken to Tuxtla. But what I saw was painful enough.

In one room a tiny woman in bright Indian dress and long black braids stood beside the bed of a four-year-old girl so small she looked no more than two. Semi-conscious, the child's leg had been shattered by bullets. Someone had handed the woman a plastic cup; the coffee inside it was rippling with her uncontrollable trembling. In a faint voice she told me in

Spanish—I didn't speak the Tzotzil Indian language—that she was the girl's aunt and only remaining relative, and that her mother and brother had died in the massacre. 'I am all alone,' she kept repeating with the anguish of someone who has spent most of her life in a community of extended families. It felt wrong to pull out a tape recorder. Instead I put my arm around her shoulder, both of us fighting back tears. In the same hospital I recognized a cameraman who had also flown down from Mexico City; later we stood in the yard with our arms around each other and wept with the pity of it all until we could pull ourselves together enough to work.

That afternoon we drove up the winding mountain roads to Acteal trying to piece together, like everyone else, what had happened. The roads were thick with checkpoints; the radio said 5000 army reinforcements were rumbling in from Campeche and Yucatan states. So many questions remained unanswered. Who had armed the gunmen with military-issue assault rifles? How could this have happened within earshot of an army patrol? Why had officials not responded to warnings the church said it had sent even as the five-hour bloodbath unfurled? Fingers pointed at local members of Mexico's ruling party, seven decades in power, and their alliance with the *caciques* or powerful landowners who considered the Zapatistas a threat; at the army; even at the liberation theology of the San Cristobal bishops whose inspirational preaching, opponents said, exposed the Indians to greater risk.

Those who died, it turned out, were unarmed civilians already displaced by violence in their own municipalities onto land to which others had prior claim. Witnesses said 25 men in blue uniforms drove up in trucks and opened fire. The army had cordoned off the hamlet, but we gained access later in the day. Not much was left—a plastic shoe in the mud, discarded bedding, bloodied clothes. We slid our fingers through the bullet holes in the timbers of Acteal's church where many had died seeking sanctuary. It took days for the last of the terrified wounded—31 in all—to emerge from hiding.

Fear set Indians on the move all over Chiapas; their makeshift camps increased the pressure on its deforested hills with their thin yield of corn and coffee beans. In some places the tension was palpable. Polho, the nearest village to Acteal, had already declared itself an autonomous community in opposition to the state, stringing up a banner across the road and checking the ID of anyone seeking access to its few wooden huts. It was fast becoming an extended refugee camp as sympathisers, survivors and their families streamed in from miles around. Smoke billowed from outdoor fires where silver-toothed women baked tortillas for legions of children; younger women in traditional dress rummaged through hillocks of Red Cross clothes. It was also the place where officials would bring back the dead, after a double set of autopsies in Tuxtla.

We spent most of Christmas Eve in Polho—a village whose only luxury was Coca-Cola—waiting for the coffins to arrive. The mountain road below it was heaving with personnel carriers. Waiting in the roadway to use Polho's only phone, I suddenly felt a tickling in my hair—three giggling Indian girls were stroking it and comparing their jet black tresses with my light brown. We had no common language but I was probably the first foreign woman, and no doubt the first Australian, they had ever seen.

Though few in Chiapas knew it, international indignation was raining down on Mexico; Bill Clinton and Kofi Annan interrupted their Christmas breaks to condemn the 'odious crime'. Opposition politicians travelled 750 km from Mexico City to support the families. Meanwhile, Acteal's daughters and sisters who had been at school in San Cristobal that fateful day made their way to Polho in government-supplied buses nursing armfuls of white lilies for the dead. Night fell and still the bodies did not come.

Finally, towards midnight, four trucks with cheap plywood caskets stacked under a tarpaulin parked on the narrow road, right beside the busload of mourners. The diminutive coffins of children, blood staining the cheap white satin, were unloaded first. Men carried them down the gravel path, past mourners holding a candlelight vigil, to Polho's basketball court, the only horizontal space in such steep terrain. But it was too dark to identify the bodies. Instead three Catholic priests, surrounded by barefoot children and women in embroidered *huipils,* performed a service in Tzotzil and Spanish amid a sea of coffins. 'I have never before assisted at a Christmas mass with 45 people dead,' Father Oscar Salinas told me, visibly moved. The next day the bodies would be taken to Acteal for identification, and burial.

That scene too was unforgettable. The sickly sweet stench of death turned acrid in the midday sun. More reporters, local and foreign, had arrived in Acteal; one discreetly passed around a pungent jar of Vicks gel for smearing under our noses. The hillsides filled with keening as women knelt over lifeless children. Families brought clothing and objects for the journey to the afterlife. But the bodies were too swollen, and too disfigured by the rough stitches of the autopsy physicians, to be dressed in their best clothes. So they stuffed the little backpacks into the coffins and resealed them, and the names were checked off by state prosecutors who had set up their typewriters under a canopy of banana leaves. The priests held another service, mixing Catholic and indigenous rites, and the bodies were lowered into a common grave.

There was political fallout as the state governor, and then Mexico's interior minister, both stepped down. I made the trip back to Tuxtla several times to interview Governor Ruiz Ferro, and broke news of his impending resignation. I also had to find a taxi prepared to run the gauntlet of burning logs that blocked the sinuous road back to San Cristobal after dark. Meanwhile dreadlocked students in rainbow-hued jumpers, many from Italy and Spain, poured into the rebel zones in solidarity. The government would soon try to turf some of them out for 'meddling in Mexico's domestic affairs'.

I only began to realise how my own views were evolving when I ran into those student idealists, and wondered why I found some of them so naive. Perhaps after 17 days without a break I was just too close to the story, could no longer see the big picture. Human rights after all are not negotiable. But the closer I got to the broader conflict in Chiapas, the more complex its origins appeared.

The problems that ravage this most underdeveloped corner of a developing nation, and which culminated in the Acteal massacre, are political but not only political. They have historical roots most clearly seen in how much fertile land is owned by the rich *caciques*, and how little of it by the Indians. There are environmental pressures too, as the Lacandon jungle is logged and overworked. Chiapas is rich in oil, gas and reportedly uranium, which make it strategically sensitive. It is also a border state, and conservatives fear its Mayan Indians have more in common with people in Belize and Guatemala than with Mexicans in the capital. Constitutional concerns made the emergence of autonomous communities a dilemma for the government, which also feared the consequences if restive states like impoverished Guerrero, with a guerrilla movement born of its own brand of desperation, followed suit.

Complicating matters was rivalry between the Protestant and Catholic faiths, and worries about weapons flowing over the border after the end of Guatemala's civil war. The Zapatista movement, led by the pipe-smoking Subcommandante Marcos, came into being for a reason, and there is no doubt that Chiapas' indigenous people suffer more from the ills of underdevelopment than almost any other group in Mexico. But it seemed to me that the conflict between the Zapatistas and the government was the culmination rather than the cause of Chiapas' woes.

I am not sure I can say I brought special 'Australian' skills to my reporting of Chiapas, since I was working for an international news organisation full of reporters who cover situations of conflict. But being Australian, I think, helped bring me into that community, with whom I shared a sense of caring about big issues and a curiosity about the world. I also brought a sort of resourcefulness, and a willingness to take calculated risks, the spirit of which is familiar to Australians. Beyond that came the advantages of a liberal education that gave me a framework for my dealings abroad.

But more than what I brought to Mexico is what Mexico brought me, and how it impacted on my Australian worldview.

No place has challenged me more, nor forced me to reexamine my values and beliefs as much as Mexico, as much as Chiapas itself. The closer you get to a conflict that seems so black and white from afar, the more the pixels start separating and the less clear-cut it seems. Growing up in Australia, with so little contact with Central or South America, left me unprepared for the real Latin America. But I found my own romantic views of the region quickly subverted the nearer I got to it.

Most reporters go into conflict zones with the desire to produce honest, truthful work. But war, even a low intensity war, sets all sorts of traps, while injustice can tug at objectivity in all sorts of ways. You have to keep checking yourself against a backdrop of values like impartiality and fairness, guard against the distortions of anger, and remind yourself you are not judge and jury but only an observer, and one who never has the whole picture. You have to be wary of easy labels, and aware that everyone you meet, sometimes even other reporters, has a vested interest.

What disarmed me in Mexico was realising that coming from a rich country puts you automatically on the wrong side, no matter what you believe or how you live, because of how you are perceived by others. Inequality, like corruption, is difficult to fight single-handedly, though surely changing it must begin in small, individual acts. Was it because I was Australian, and unwilling to relinquish certain principles, that I sometimes felt discouraged, despite rejecting the fatalism around me? It took me a long time to accept that exploitation is part of what it means to live in what could be called a still-colonial society. Exploitation, I came to realise, is not only how the rich, or how foreigners, treat the poor in developing countries; it can work in all directions in all sorts of small, ambush-like ways. Strike an emergency—illness, say—and watch a cab driver double his fare. Request a service, and pay more to rectify shoddy work. It was a system, and it was also a survival strategy. I had to learn not to take it personally.

Women have a rough ride in the developing world and my situation in comparison was extremely privileged. Even so, I was not inured to an atmosphere of gender inequality. Though 'No Women' signs at cantinas these days are rare, the fact that more than 250 young women can be murdered over 10 years in a city on the US border without the crimes being solved sends a discouraging signal to women nationwide. I came to understand that the freedoms enjoyed by women, which as an Australian I took for granted, and which had made it possible for me to be in Mexico under such circumstances at all, were more closely linked to prosperity, education and culture than I had ever surmised. They no longer seemed so inalienable, and suddenly became much more precious.

It is also true that Australians can feel isolated in countries like Mexico in ways that expatriates from more populous nations do not. Compatriot colleagues are rare—I met just two other Australian reporters in nearly three years in Mexico. Meanwhile the 'tyranny of distance' never leaves us—Australia is simply too far away for a weekend break. Most of us accept a degree of isolation as an inevitable part of being an Australian abroad. What I hadn't expected was that the experiences you have can also isolate you from people back home.

Although what I was writing from Chiapas was being published in newspapers from London to Los Angeles, the cultural distance one needs to bridge can make it difficult to communicate with family and friends. Just getting a phone line to Melbourne from Chiapas at Christmas felt like a triumph, without trying to explain what I was doing in the Lacandon jungle. Yet becoming an expatriate has also opened my eyes about the world in ways not available to me had I stayed home. I am well aware that this way of life has a price—missing defining experiences, both public and private, at home. But I characterise myself as an Australian member of an internationally minded community, who just happens to live her Australianness abroad.

Caroline Brothers was born in Hobart, brought up in Melbourne and obtained a doctorate in history from the University of London. She is the author of *War and Photography: A cultural history* (Routledge, 1997). She joined Reuters in 1990, has worked as a foreign correspondent in various countries in Europe and Latin America and is currently based in Paris. The opinions expressed in this account are her own.

HOMELANDS: REAL AND IMAGINED

The other night I dreamt that I was back in Indonesia. I was on my grandmother's verandah in one of her rickety old rattan chairs, observing an orange-red sunset. I was leafing through her old photo albums, into which she had also placed old postcards I'd sent her as a child. My favourite was a close up of a rather proud-looking kookaburra. This was also one of granny's favourites. A frustrated ornithologist, she and I would try to mimic the kookaburra's call and often end up in a giggling fit. I always believed her version to be more authentic than mine. She could, after all, perform a kookaburra mating call, a song heard at dawn and, the most beautiful, a song of early evening. My repertoire was limited to one call, and even then it sounded more like a dying pigeon than a kookaburra.

The prickly heat of the daytime had passed, and the tall fruit trees in granny's front garden had cast long shadows over the driveway. There was a distinct chill in the air. The jasmine flower which smelt its most fragrant at night, was like an elegant jazz singer in one of those intimate after-dark jazz clubs. She was setting up her microphone and humming her scales in preparation for the evening performance. The late afternoon sounds of the mountain village were my faint elevator music: the tofu seller calling out; the distant horns of buses, motor bikes and other two-wheeled modes of public transport; children singing as they passed our front gate. In the garden before me, granny was tending to her dozens of orchid plants which peeped out of small clay pots, and collectively hung off three parallel rows of bamboo lattice. She was mumbling to herself, as usual, and glanced over at me when she asked herself a question, as if to check whether I agreed.

When I awoke, I lay in bed, looking at the sun of a London winter morning. It was making soft dappled effects through the curtains. I asked myself from where this dream memory must have stemmed. I couldn't determine whether this was one of the last times I remember seeing granny before she died, or was it a memory described to me by my mum from her childhood? Was it my own youthful recollection, something akin perhaps, to Marcel Proust's 'taste of a little piece of madeleine which on Sunday mornings ... my aunt Leonie used to give me, dipping it first in her own cup of tea ... '? A recollection triggered, in my case too, by a smell or a taste. I had, I recalled, made granny's recipe for banana fritters just the day before.

I remembered Salman Rushdie's inversion of the famous opening line of L P Hartley's novel *The Go-Between*: 'The past is a foreign country, they do things differently there'. For Rushdie, it was the present, not the past, that was foreign, and the past was home, albeit a lost home in a lost city. In his case, the past was his memory of Bombay as he wrote and researched *Midnight's Children*. It was a place he had not visited for almost half his life.

Was it the same for me, I wondered, as an Australian in London, having lived overseas for much of my working life? Was the past strange and foreign for me, or was it the present which I found more strange? I decided, as the sun grew brighter through the bedroom curtains, that for me, neither the past nor the present was foreign. Something is strange and foreign if it is peculiar and unfamiliar. Moving homes with regularity and to different countries, was not strange. The act of travelling itself had become something regular, as predictable as a tropical downpour during the monsoon season. And the regularity of travel had, I supposed, rendered living overseas the rule rather than the exception. Home therefore, was ever-changing. A comforting fact, which served to reassure me in my travels, was the frequency with which I met friendly fellow Australians. It was like discovering new species of green growth pushing up in the garden after rain. I was always surprised how quickly flowers and trees grew in the tropics. Plants, like new friendships, seemed to blossom quickly in an expatriate hothouse.

My Mum had more in common with Mr Rushdie, I decided. She was like the Indian emigrants about whom Rushdie wrote, who on occasion look back at India through guilt-tinted spectacles, where the present sometimes feels more foreign. In my mother's case, I felt sure she must have wondered whether the move from Indonesia to Australia in the 1950s was wrong. She was not exactly a Muslim who had started eating pork, but she had crossed over (geographically), and had become partly of the West. She was a celebrated bridge-builder, straddling two worlds successfully. At times, however, she had fallen down the proverbial divide between the two cultures, left wondering with which she identified more, and whether in the end, someone in her bi-cultural position should be forced to choose anyway.

Working in Indonesia in the early 1990s I am sure I was at first looked upon as an oddity. Although being able to physically blend into the local landscape, I spoke Indonesian with an Aussie twang; I walked twice as fast as my bewildered workmates; and I confounded my colleagues with my quest for a good salad sandwich, politely declining any offers to try the local specialty. By the end of the 90s I was crazy about local cuisine, local art forms and literature. I sat at the feet of local and foreign journalists, eager to get a handle on the political intrigues which would emblazon the newspapers every week. I even adopted the local style of crossing the street, the key to which was to traverse in a manner oblivious to all beeping horns and shouting, calmly waving one hand in the knowledge that a magic force field surrounded your body.

In the days leading up to the fall of President Soeharto in May 1998, university students expressed their discontent with the regime through demonstrations. Everyone knew this action reflected a wider unhappiness among the general population. Students would peacefully march the main thoroughfares of Jakarta, enormous flapping banners hoisted high, megaphones blaring, and participants sporting matching t-shirts. They set out to cause maximum disruption. And they succeeded. Jakarta's already heavy traffic became nightmarish. Movement around the CBD often became gridlocked. My office building was located smack in the centre of the demo hub. It was next door to Atmajaya University, regarded by many as the hotbed of student activism. The building faced Jalan Jendral Sudirman, one of the city's main business areas, and was to unknowingly play host to one of the most shocking student shootings in Indonesia's recent history. It would precipitate three days of the worst rioting ever seen in the capital.

Having missed an opportunity to evacuate the building at lunch time, I then was under strict orders not to leave the building. I slowly came to realise I was kidding myself that the completion of urgent documents was more important than the personal safety of all in my office. From front row seats, I saw a barrage of tear gas grenades being hurled by the army towards a mass of students slowly inching its way forward. The crowd of innocent demonstrators was forced to disperse in a frantic scramble, the scene reducing into an uneven battle of firearms against the unarmed. All I saw and heard was a constant barrage of gun shots, clouds of wafting smoke, young voices shrieking, and frenzied movement of human figures seeking bodily protection from the line of fire.

Later that night I found myself downstairs in the open-air car park, now a makeshift emergency ward, trying to ferry my staff home, pleading with willing moped drivers to make the short trip south. Milling around me were hundreds of university students, some hobbling towards the nearby hospital, some wrapping the arms of their injured friends around their own necks. They were trembling and tearful. All were in shock.

Some students lay by the wayside. These bodies lay very still. By an accident of birth, I had attended Monash and Melbourne universities. But I could have been you, I muttered, trying to address a river of anguished soft-skinned faces, their sweating, dusty bodies pressing past me in the melee. During my attempts to help the wounded, my thoughts clicked momentarily to my unfinished legal documents, intended for a government infrastructure project. It crossed my mind that over the coming days all this paperwork might be rendered completely irrelevant if a change in power were to occur. I picked up a satchel accidentally dropped by a passing teenager. I passed it to its rightful owner, and yet was struck by a sense of complete uselessness. Someone's university cap caught my attention on the ground, trodden on and filthy. I wanted to be sick.

Mum had always tried to explain that a certain double perspective would make my life a challenge. Whether I was geographically located in Indonesia or Australia, I would sometimes feel at odds, because I was at one and the same time an insider and an outsider in society. I had always liked to call it my in-built bi-culturalism. And I was finding it an advantage rather than a liability in the Indonesian work context. But as an emigrant, my Mum was haunted by a sense of loss, an urge to reclaim, to look back. She often quoted Rushdie. If we look back, she would say, we should do so knowing that our physical distance from our 'India' means that we will not be capable of reclaiming the thing that we have lost. We will create fictions, not actual cities or villages, but invisible ones—imaginary homelands. Mum thought about Indonesia a lot. I always believed her memories were not always historically accurate. But like all memories, they were personal to her and impossible to label right or wrong. Now being away from both Asia and Australia, I asked myself whether I too was haunted by a sense of loss or whether it would kick in at a later age.

On second thoughts, perhaps I am already haunted by a certain sense of loss. I rolled over in bed and inspected the stripes on my pillow cover. The day my father died one stinking hot summers day in 1989, my mother asked me to fetch his car from where he had parked it. Earlier that day, he had suffered a fatal heart attack. On the front seat of the car, I found a few bills to be posted, the files he was working on, his daily TO DO list, with some items ticked and crossed out in his unmistakably small handwriting. I remembered thinking the down strokes of his fountain pen were unusually strong and wide. I drove the car home slowly down Toorak Road, as if I was somehow driving a part of him home too. I imagined him there in the front passenger's seat. Maybe a part of him was there. After all these years, I still think back to that moment and I still ask myself how I managed to drive home so numbly, without so much as a wet eye. Andre Aciman once wrote about just such a moment as being not so much looking at the beauty of the past, as the beauty of remembering, realising that just because we love to look back doesn't mean we love the things we look back on. I couldn't be there at the moment of father's death, but I could still drive him home in my head.

Mum reminded me of what Goenawan Mohamad called 'the type of person ... who still has the unsettledness of one who has not yet set down anchor: someone who does not love his place of origin enough to stay there, but yet cannot tie his heart to his new place'. Goenawan was describing people who had moved from towns or villages to Jakarta where they found work, but which they could not really grow to love. He may not have had my mother in mind as he wrote this description. (She was an ageing woman of nearly seventy, who had moved to a foreign land and seemed now to be falling out of love with her second home.) But his words fitted her current mindset. She had just emailed me to explain that she wanted to return to Indonesia. She wanted to die and be buried there. Perhaps I felt Mum was somehow floating between worlds and that she believed (wrongly in my opinion), that an old 'India' lay waiting, open-armed, a place secure and unchanged, yet ultimately a place imagined more than real. I felt she was more emotionally in limbo than she realised, or cared to admit. Mum's old photo albums quickly came to mind—sepia-toned pictures of attractive, laughing, partying young Jakartans. How could she reclaim this thing that was lost?—a fairytale Indonesia of the 1950s, where her life was full of hope, and her bands of school friends surrounded her like a human comfort zone. Surely this was an imaginary homeland which could not be recaptured on her return?

If I look back and romanticise my memories of the Far East and beyond, am I too trying to recreate an 'India' in my mind? Or am I like all humans, as Bruce Chatwin suggested in his travel writings, who are intrinsically nomadic at heart and united with all others, trying to learn from our journeys, particularly when we stop for a period of cave-dwelling? I rolled over in bed again and faced the curtains. I cringed when I thought of one of the questions I was asked during a job interview for a position in a Jakarta firm. 'I want to rediscover my roots' was my reply. In my case, I have travelled to places to experience where I've come from. And in the end I did find those roots. The move to Asia made me settle within myself. The family links rekindled, the new friends made, the cultural experiences gained. So much seemed fresh, intense and exciting, yet it was all bathed in a reassuring familiarity.

Travelling, as Mark Mordue suggests, teaches us how to find home and how to respect it. Living for many years away from the country of my youth, made me cherish my childhood in ways I could never have realised. It helped me accept what things have made me the human I am. When I smell a certain brand of sunscreen I am back on the Kooyong tennis courts playing in Melbourne's summer heat. I can even remember my dark blue tennis skirt and matching striped top, and the butterflies in my stomach as I psyched myself up for the impending round robin. Then, as now, I was worried about my weak backhand failing at a crucial point in the match. The culinary skills of my aunties also guarantee the continuation of those 'madeleine' moments. When I smell granny's Dutch vegetable soup I don't just think of its taste. I think of her old white china with the gold rim, the family portraits in her dining room with the unfriendly facial expressions, and the two still life paintings painted by a very distant cousin. Such buoys of multi-sensory nostalgia are like navigation marks, keeping memories afloat.

In the biting cold of London's winter, I seemed to be reminiscing more and more about the sultry heat of the tropics, of my life in Asia, and my even earlier life in Australia. I pulled the quilt from my body and stretched my arms above my head. The sun had grown brighter and it was time I opened the curtains. I imagined for a moment, the early morning sun shooting its rays into my old Jakarta bedroom and hitting the foot of my bed. Somewhere in this image I heard a rooster crow. A rooster not belonging in the metropolis which is Jakarta, but in granny's home in the mountains of East Java. I could almost smell a Melbourne summer morning—the fumes of my father's lawn mower. Rushdie got it right when he explained that human beings do not perceive things whole. He said we are capable only of fractured perceptions.

Not long after receiving my Mum's email, I heard an old farmer being interviewed on BBC radio. He was asked why he had decided to return to a little village in Lancashire, the place of his childhood years: 'Let's face it,' he said, 'your village is your village. It doesn't mean anything to someone who didn't ever live there. It was where you grew up. It's in your mind'. I marvelled at this impressive timing and made a beeline for my laptop. As I did, I thought again of my granny and the smile she gave me as she tended to her orchids. Suddenly I felt a real yearning. I needed to revisit the verandah, the sunset, and the late afternoon sounds of her mountain village. And I smiled when I thought about that rather proud looking old kookaburra on the postcard.

Yanti Brown grew up in Melbourne and is a graduate of both Monash and Melbourne universities. She has practised law in Australia, Indonesia and the UK. Yamti experienced the early 90s economic boom in South East Asia and later, the turmoil following the fall of President Suharto She lives in London with her husband James.

GREEN FROGS AND BODHRÁNS

In December 1989 I left the convent after twenty-three years. It was a sudden and unexpected decision, not one I had ever anticipated making. I suddenly found myself, at 42 years of age, looking for a job and a place to live. I had been working in education for years as a secondary school teacher and principal, so I headed toward people I knew in education. Got the job and tried to settle. Materially, life was soon as smooth as ice but emotionally just as cold.

I had grown up in Cairns in the 1950s—in an idyll of freedom and adventure. We were the classic Catholic family—seven children, living across the road from the church, the school and the convent. I went to that school from kindergarten to Year 12. And returned some years later to be a teacher and the principal. I felt so rooted there that I envisaged being buried in the school yard.

Memories of the 1950s are plotted and pieced with sport, music, picnics. As well as competitive sport we had family games on the front lawn and out at the beach. Beautiful beaches. We scraped oysters off the rocks where the marina now stands in Port Douglas; we spent annual holidays in the cool greenery of Kuranda, before the hippies discovered it in the 1960s. We loved to hang by our legs from the poinciana trees in front of our home; we loved catching crabs at the nearby esplanade. We ran about bare-footed and fearless. The key was always in the front door and coins were always in the green jug in the kitchen for a matinee and an icy pole. Sunday nights were often around the piano. A family bond, a network of cousins and friends and parents who gave us security and belonging and also a taste for adventure and independence.

I entered the convent when I was a very idealistic nineteen years. At the time my brother told me I wanted 'to escape being a housewife,' and I was indignant; but on more mature reflection, he probably had an insight. When I was young, all the women I knew were either housewives or nuns. Not that I regret those twenty-three years. Whatever was driving me to enter it felt like an imperative that I, despite much repugnance, just had to follow.

They were certainly twenty-three years of grappling with life and identity and meaning and challenge. I believed utterly in the meaning of religious life, and thought it just had to be updated from its monastic origins to be more relevant and meaningful in today's world. The Vatican Council of the early 1960s had expressed that ideal: that a return to the origins could renew and revivify the life. We filled our holidays listening to gurus, re-visioning, re-imagining religious life—reading, debating, clarifying and distilling. For years I was fired by the ideal of integrating my work and my prayer/reflection, trying to find the ways that made the monastic roots meaningful now in a busy active life. I hit a cul-de-sac. From early in 1988 I experienced a huge grief from loss of purpose. Grief for the old monastic ways that really puzzled me. All around me I was hearing loss of purpose and experiencing loss of purpose. I made a sudden, peaceful, clear decision that I had to leave. The imperative that drove me in, now drove me out. My understanding of vocation was utterly dead; the meaning was gone, so I had to go.

That's when I found myself working in Catholic education in Brisbane. Socially, I felt like a displaced person, trying to make friends with people whose lives were already full. It was a strange period, the first time in my life that I was feeling rootless and non-belonging. Certainly it was a time when I was reshaping my sense of personal identity; I took initiatives like joining groups and made several friends, but that did not assuage my low-key sense of not belonging.

During the 1970s I had begun researching my ancestral roots. On both Mum and Dad's side, every ancestor that was not Australian-born had come from Ireland in the nineteenth century, starting with the first arrival in Sydney in 1841. I was sixth generation Australian and had nine Irish-born Australian ancestors. I became interested in the names and Irish places of origin. I had Byrnes from Wicklow, Lonergan from Kilkenny, O'Mahony from Cork, Doherty from Donegal, Gallen from Donegal, Henry from Derry, Savage from Down, Kelly from Tyrone, and Dunne from Dublin. And if I included all the maiden names I would add another four. I delighted in claiming the ancestors—they flowed through me like a peace river.

Within a year of departure from the convent, I had bought a unit and had a holiday in the US and Mexico. While walking along Bourbon Street in New Orleans I spotted an Irish music pub and experienced a mixture of repulsion and attraction: 'same old thing' versus 'they're having a great time in there.' I stayed for hours. During the next year, when I realised that I would not have to spend my annual holiday sitting at the kitchen table completing a Masters thesis, I hurriedly booked a trip to London and Ireland. From Dublin I hired a car and drove around to most of the towns the ancestors had come from. I felt euphoric. The sense that this is where my people came from saturated me. Genetic memory just reached across the generations and said: 'This is my place.'

The following year I felt very unsettled in Brisbane. One Friday night while shopping in Brisbane city, I walked into an Irish souvenir shop and, like an *eejit*, felt overwhelmed with everything Irish. I had to sort out this Irish thing. Several evenings I sat on my balcony with a view of Brisbane and decided that I would really like to move to Dublin to live, but that I did not have the finances to do it and that if it were to happen, then the money would have to 'arrive.' And it did.

An exercise in down-sizing was occurring in my office. One Friday afternoon in late 1992 we were all assembled for the announcement of the decisions about the restructuring. Anyone (not just the over 55 year-olds) could ask for a package. After the meeting I flew up the stairs in a tingle of excitement, realising the possibility that the money would arrive. The kindness of people in that office I will never forget. That evening I had a dream in which a Brisbane friend, who had just returned from a holiday in Ireland, was standing under the Spanish Arch in Galway and saying very earnestly to me 'Denise, come!'. It seemed irrefutably right for me to go.

Within a year of that holiday in Ireland, I had resigned my job, rented my unit, sold my car and arrived in Dublin with four suitcases in February 1993. I was 46 years of age. I was warned there were no jobs for teachers or for anyone. Despite that, I started the lengthy process of getting my academic qualifications recognized and preparing for an oral test in the Irish language. Like thousands of other Irish, I now have only a *cupla local* (few words) but I knew enough nine years ago to pass the test.

Ten years later I have a great job in education, a share in a mortgage, great friends, a fantastic social life and a deep sense of belonging.

When you begin living in another culture, it is similar to a one-to-one relationship in that you start by noticing similarities and differences, and after a time you just sink into the arms of the other, warts and all. But the experience of difference does help you to appreciate your own identity. I have a certain perspective on the Irish Australian comparison, but I also have a sense that identity with both is very compatible. Let's use a little magnifying glass to consider some areas of comparison.

In the two secondary schools where I taught I found much similarity with Australian schools in student behaviour and staff discussions. It was like putting on old socks—walking into such a familiar environment. It is at the system level that most differences occur. There is immense confidence in the education system here, but the economy has not, until recent years, provided a big investment, so that school resources and supports are lacking. For the past seven years I have worked in research and report-writing, formulating policy recommendations for the Minister for Education and Science. Our work is in the area of infrastructure for education. For example, I am currently writing a report that addresses the criteria and procedures for the establishment of new second level schools. My very Australian problem-solving ability serves me well.

Australians are great problem solvers. This is a key element of the sunny Australian disposition—the belief that there is always something that can be done to sort out a problem. The Irish approach to problems is much less direct. The tendency to draw back from making the hard decisions that really sort out a problem is called 'an Irish solution to an Irish problem'—no solution at all. 'She'll be right, mate' is really more Irish than Australian. This is evident even in the law-making of the *Dáil* (parliament). The blood alcohol level for drivers was reduced from 1.00 to 0.08 in the mid 1990s amidst an outcry, so the law is seldom imposed (with no random testing) and the high rate of death on the roads continues.

The Irish enthrallment with the spoken and written word is legendary and real. The pun is part of the air you breathe. With the favourite Irish phrase, 'Having said that ... ' a person can espouse an opinion that is the total opposite of the one they had just expressed.

Their minds do not demand resolution of the opposites. It is a quality that recognises the complexity and the creativity of life! The sharpness of the ear is also clear in the Irish gift for music. Indeed, all ear skills are well ahead of the visual skills, although I do like the preferred style of well-dressed Irish women—understated, minimal and natural.

Compared to the Irish, Australians have a cohesive, missionary-like way of addressing issues and doing something, even if all they can do is say 'sorry.' This very serious streak in Australians is seldom known. The strong work ethic of young Australians now working in all kinds of employment in Ireland is noticed and appreciated.

The Irish intellect values knowledge and creativity much more than analysis. The articulate and knowledgeable person can engage in non-sequesters without challenge. Willingness to chat, to engage in inconsequential talk, to establish connection and to socialise is a big part of the national personality. In Ireland it is not uncommon to arrange to meet friends for a drink or to pop unannounced into a neighbour at 10 pm. 'Neighbour' is a rich word in Ireland. Centuries of urban and rural poverty have ensured mutual dependence on neighbours, and modern Dublin suburbia still carries the expectation that neighbours are significant friends. That is part of what makes living here so pleasant.

In Irish social situations there is an ease of relationships between males and females, between males and males and between the generations. It is easy for people to have significant friends of either gender. Also, the gay—macho continuum is much less polarised. It is common and acceptable for a high-testosterone man to be talking about poetry or language or music.

In spite of their sociability, the Irish are more introverted than Australians. They keep more of their inner world to themselves. This quality gives rise to a host of others: meeting the direct question with an oblique answer; 'Whatever you say, say nothing!'; the capacity to be *cute*—which in Ireland means 'cunning or clever in a clandestine way'; the mentality of getting around the law or the bureaucratic requirement—so much so that one wonders what statistics can ever be believed. Maybe it is because they have a strong inner world that they are people with affinity for a spiritual life. Despite the economic boom of 1998 to 2002, the greater materialism and political correctness, it is still a marvellous country for knowing that it is people that matter.

I have a wonderfully ordinary contentment with the rich challenges of ordinary living—relationships, opportunity for reflection, the sources of meaning. I have a three-generation family network whose warts-and-all acceptance has enabled me to integrate well into Irish life. Their love of feisty conversation is second only to their love of singing. I have a boss who wears his Kerry cuteness on his sleeve; he is the sunniest 'Mr. Fix-it' in Ireland and his ability to relate with every single person in his universe is nothing short of charismatic. A good friend, who is a committed *gaelgeoir* (Irish speaker), can be found in O'Donoghue's pub every Monday night because it is the best night for a *seisiún* (traditional music). He is a navigator between the traditional and the modern in a culture that has moved from *piseog* (superstition) to cosmopolitan in one generation.

Being Irish and being Australian fit together well, like scoops of ice cream in a cone. Maybe all I have been doing is digging for a deeper scoop. Something to do with both ancestral roots and stage of life; something to do with both genes and nurturing. It takes more than deciding who to support in an Australia and Ireland football match to integrate the two affinities. I realise I am working on it when I have dreams of North Queensland green frogs playing the *bodhrán* (one-sided drum covered with goat skin and played with a stick).

I suspect that firm deep roots enable us to feel at home anywhere at all in the world. At all, at all. And that's the real challenge. Joseph Campbell said: 'Where we had thought to travel outward, we will come to the centre of ourselves.'

Denise Burns is a sixth generation Australian born into a family with deep Irish roots. She lived in Cairns and Brisbane before moving to Dublin in 1993. She works in a commission consisting of all the partners active in Irish education and is involved in formulating policy recommendations for the Minister for Education and Science.

To teach to learn

Almost a year ago, with tears sliding down my cheeks, I hugged my family and friends goodbye. There was no turning back. The bags were packed, papers signed and I was to leave behind the place I call home. Even though I knew I would see my family at Christmas, the thought of leaving home for the first time and venturing to a foreign land all by myself scared me tremendously. As I walked away reluctantly, my vision becoming more and more blurred by the flood of tears, I met the brave faces of other JETs (participants in the Japanese Exchange Teaching program). With one last look at my loved ones and with heavy steps, the flow of passengers forced me through the departure gate.

Now sitting in my Board of Education office in a small town of 7000, reminiscing on that moment and recalling my experiences over the last year, is a JET who is renewing her contract and planning to stay in Japan indefinitely! Here I have come to teach, yet have been taught much more in return. For I have come clueless, a fresh face out of university and now a year older and hopefully wiser, I know exactly where I want to go next. And that is to stay. To teach. To learn.

The JET program has placed me in Takebe, a town unheard of unless you live in Okayama. True, Tokyo, Osaka and Kobe sound more exciting. I remember agonising over the application form a year ago. All the places, apart from the few I had heard of, meant nothing to me. I left it up to fate for I did not want to exclude myself from opportunities unknown to me. I did the right thing. Takebe is well known for beautiful cherry blossoms in spring and relaxing hot springs in winter. Located in the middle of the sunny prefecture, Okayama, it is the ideal country town in which to work and live. The town consists mainly of the elderly and children. Most people my age have left Takebe for bigger things and those remaining are very few or hail from neighbouring towns. The beautiful Asahi River runs through Takebe and I encounter this magnificent view on my way to school everyday. I work at one junior high school (which is my base school), three elementary schools and have a free day preparing lessons at the Takebe Board of Education.

My job is to assist Japanese Teachers of English (JTEs) to teach English and encourage students to harbour the desire to study English. Hence, the job title of an Assistant Language Teacher (ALT) has been bestowed upon JETs. It warms my heart to see that whenever there is a Team Teaching (TT) lesson (where I teach with the JTE), the students anticipate it with excitement. Normally, when students have English lessons without the ALT, they must study grammatical points and textbook material that are sleeping catalysts. During my lessons, the JTE and I try to incorporate grammatical points into games. Most of the time, I plan the lessons and attempt to make them as much fun as possible. When I see their happy faces and comments of '*ureshi*' (fun) or '*omoshiroi*' (interesting), I know I have come to Japan to do what is expected of me. It is even more rewarding when I know I am not only teaching my students English but general knowledge as well. It is quite interesting to note how many students do not have a good grasp of general knowledge such as countries and capital cities. I hope, in addition to teaching English, to pass on what has been taught to me about the world community.

Born in Taiwan and immigrating to Australia when I was nine, I have been blessed with the knowledge of two cultures. Having arrived in Japan and being bombarded by questions about my identity, there were times when I doubted who I really was. Some people would accept I was Australian (especially those who became my good friends and derived conclusions beyond my appearance) but some would insist I was Chinese. I have realised the truth is neither one nor the other. My roots are Chinese and I accumulated my first knowledge in Taiwan. However, I spent the rest of my childhood and teenage years in Australia and it was during those troubled years that I had begun to realise the Chinese girl was more Australian than she had thought. The arguments with my parents, the frustration and confusion were the result of a girl stuck in the midst of two cultures. At home, we spoke Chinese and abided by Chinese customs. Naturally, the Australian culture that I brought home would threaten the fundamental values and beliefs that my parents have always held strong.

So, now this Chinese Australian girl is in Japan, teaching English as required and teaching culture by accident. She teaches about Chinese New Year and other traditions as well as occasionally teaching Chinese. She is also delighted to talk about Australia, Ian Thorpe and koalas. She would often surprise her students and colleagues with her love of *wasabi* (green mustard) and knowledge of *Kanji* (a form of Japanese writing that was adopted from China). She loves bringing Vegemite to class. She is from not just one lucky country but two. Being Chinese has meant that the cultural shock of living in Japan was minimised; being Australian meant that she could share the knowledge of what it is like to live in a multicultural society, and to have friends from many cultures who have helped shape her into who she is today.

Even though my main purpose is to teach English to children in my town, my presence also affects the community and faraway places that I visit. I remember when I first arrived in this small town, I could feel myself as the little pebble setting off ripples across the pond. I can safely say that many people in my town doubted my Australian nationality and ability to speak English until they saw me talking with my American neighbour. After all, I looked too Japanese to be a foreigner. As the old saying goes, if I received a penny (or dollar) every time someone said I looked Japanese, I would have made a nice saving by now. On numerous occasions, I would be out in Okayama city or be travelling somewhere in Japan with other JETs and people would assume I was the Japanese friend of the group. At shops and restaurants, I would be approached first to ask if we needed service. The irony of it is, as many Asian looking JETs can tell you, quite often we speak less Japanese than the other JETs! It can be quite embarrassing when I shake my head and stutter in my limited Japanese, with the shopkeeper or waiter looking confused. It is after some explanation that they begin to comprehend that I am not Japanese and that I am as foreign as any of my friends! Initially the misunderstanding can be annoying but it is often satisfying to see their faces change into one of realisation and understanding. Having seen the large number of Asian looking JETs at conferences, I know we have added, invisible responsibilities. For every misunderstanding, there is a lesson learned. I am glad that my presence here is contributing to the knowledge of both the young and the old, the near and the far.

Life in Japan never ceases to amaze me, for I have learned a new definition of teaching. For example, just being a teacher has earned me more respect than I really deserve. Many people in my town are surprised that I do not have a teaching license and have only graduated from university. The Japanese have a high regard for teachers and the title that is now synonymous with my name, *sensei*, is also reserved for doctors. This revelation has made me realise the difference in Australian and Japanese culture. Comparatively, teachers have less responsibility back home. Japanese teachers not only teach but also oversee club activities after school. They wait until all the students have gone home, bidding them goodbye before going back to the staff room to attack the pile of work that is constantly building on their desks. All the teachers know every student and their family background. Students are often the topic of conversations in the staff room. Recently, a boy has been a victim of domestic violence and a girl's father passed away due to a car accident. Many meetings were held in the staff room, with grave and concerned faces. Next week, there will be parent meetings where home-room teachers visit the students' houses. Apparently, this is so that the teachers can see the students' studying and living conditions. From my experience growing up in Australia, students were taught to be independent and responsible for themselves. The job description of a Japanese teacher is an essay in itself, for everyday I seem to discover a new task that they do.

'*Sai sho gu, Jianken poi*', this is the chant that I find myself saying as often as I say 'hello'. Even though I have no idea what it means, I have learned that these few words play a big part in the everyday lives of the Japanese (and of the foreigners who are woven into the fabric of their daily lives). These words are popular in battling boredom. Children often *Jianken* (the name of this game) or Scissors, Paper, Rock as we have come to know it in Western culture, for fun. Most importantly, however, it often acts as the decider of an argument. When I first saw it played out in the staff room among a group of teachers, I could not believe my eyes! So, this is how conflicts are resolved, I thought to myself in disbelief. As a race that is well known for conflict avoidance, this method of resolution is quick and as one JET puts it, 'You can't argue a *Jianken*'.

Jianken is more than just a game, it represents Japanese culture and Japanese beliefs. It is an effective method as it is not only quick but also unanimously accepted. When I studied about Japanese organisations being efficient and effective, little did I realise it could be partly due to their decision making system and something as simple as *Jianken*. This sense of conflict avoidance and quick resolution is instilled in the Japanese, from an early age. This school yard game transcends many settings, whether it be in the classroom, at home or when they are out and about. It decides who will sweep the floor to who will have the last serving. The children grow up into adults, bringing this efficient and effective decider into adulthood. The outcome is accepted, the loser concedes loss while the winners marvel at their own *Jianken* techniques. I now have also taken on this method of decision making, with Japanese people and fellow foreign friends. And if I lose, well, as one ten year old put it, '*Shoga nai* ... ' (What can you do?).

Many JETs want to be placed in cities where knowledge and opportunities are more evident. I came with the naïve belief that a city girl would have a lot to teach this small town of 7000. That may be true in some aspects but to this day, I am still surprised how much more Takebe has taught me in return. Having lived in the city all my life, it took me a while to get used to country life. An incident in my first month in Takebe is also one of my favourite stories to tell. I had hung out my futon and some sheets one day and went out to the city. When I came back later that evening, I found my futon and sheets folded neatly and placed on my bike. The first reaction I recall having was fear: my stomach churning accompanied by a large temperate drop to my body. I yelled for my neighbour, an American JET, to come over. He entered my house and checked all the rooms, coming out with the okay signal. I went to my Board of Education the next day and told them the story. They reassured me that it was probably some nice old granny near my house. I thought about it later and found myself thinking how stupid I was. Why would someone rob my house and fold my laundry? There were numerous occasions where I would also forget to lock my house when I was out or asleep. Previously needing to always guard my own safety to almost a state of paranoia, living in Takebe is a nice change. People tell me I should still be careful, which I acknowledge gratefully. But knowing that if I forget to lock up, my house will still be in the state I left it in when I return, is great reassurance.

This small community where everyone knows each other and looks out for one another is a refreshing change from the city life I previously led. What I consider as kindness and people going out of their way would be viewed as nothing out of the ordinary for the Takebe residents. I have learned that small communities rely on their people to promote harmony and stability, whether it is my supervisor volunteering as a fireman, the mothers looking after the elderly at the local nursing home or the nice old granny who startled her local JET by extending a helping hand. The sense of being part of the community, being looked after, is something that I have learned to deeply value. Therefore, I am always glad when given the chance to do volunteer work in my town, Takebe.

It is natural to learn through your friends, people with whom you share laughter and tears. However, the opportunity to be a JET has given me a circle of friends who I would never have had the privilege of meeting back home. They come from all walks of life, the JETs, the non-JETs, the Americans, the Canadians, the Irish, the English, the New Zealanders, the Chinese, the Japanese, the young, the old, the veterans, the new faces. The list goes on. We learn about each other's culture. Jewish music is soothing, Halloween costumes are a headache, Japanese calligraphy is not for the impetuous, and Australians and New Zealanders do not sound the same! As much as being a JET is a learning experience for me, it is also a lesson about stereotypes and assumptions for my friends. We learn to be strong. Whether it is conquering the great Mt Fuji and emerging from the fog alive, touching the velvety white snow for the first time and attempting to ski down great heights alive, or just getting lost and attempting to communicate in a foreign tongue. We tried, we survived.

We learn about our differences. The different accents, the different slang, the different terms. Through arguments of capsicums and green peppers, we accept that English is a universal language with many variations. And so we learn to appreciate what makes us the same, what makes us different. (I have been told my American accent is atrocious!) Living in Japan has enabled me to gain insight into places that I have never been to through the people I have been fortunate enough to befriend. Once again, I have been blessed to learn, not only about Japanese culture but about other cultures that I have yearned to experience. I have been taken out of my fish bowl and put into the sea, forced to examine breeds other than my own. Indeed, I have been very lucky to be given the opportunity to live in a foreign land as a minority, to learn about others and for them to learn about me.

'I knew it', was my mother's reply when I took up the courage to tell her my plans for the future. Many people back home were expecting me to return after a year, but not three years later or more! Coming to Japan has taught me more about myself. I was forced to examine who I was, as Chinese and an Australian. This country has reminded me of the old: my innocent childhood days and how I enjoyed learning through games. Most importantly, Japan has enabled me to experience the new— the language, the culture, the way of work, the way of life. I had a vague idea of what I wanted to do prior to coming to Japan. Being on the JET program has opened my eyes to new experiences and new opportunities. The ambiguous goals had suddenly become clear. I cannot go home now. There is still much more to learn, to experience. I have a dream. And it is to stay in Japan, to study the Japanese language and take internationalisation to many places. It is to use my knowledge of English, Chinese and Japanese in international work and promote understanding between cultures. *Ganbarimasu*! (Trying my best!)

Chia Chien Cherry Chang was born in Taiwan in 1979, emigrating to Australia when she was nine years old. She is currently working with the JET program in Japan. Her interest in the country stemmed from her Japanese-speaking grandparents, her parents and a trip to beautiful Hokkaido in the Japanese summer of 2000.

I JUST WANT TO LIVE HERE

Bir daha (one more), the 3000 strong crowd chanted. I gazed out from my vantage point on the upper balcony toward the Bosphorus. Tarkan broke out into a huge grin and launched into the third encore of his new song, 'Dudu'. The evening was cool for a summer evening. I was pleased that I had opted for my short black denim jacket over a slightly more chic bright orange sleeveless top. The beat of the song had the audience swinging and swaying along, the rhythm drawing arms up into the air in typical Turkish fashion, the words already imprinted in minds and repeated after only the second rendition.

Tarkan is probably the most popular pop idol in Turkey and, from my limited knowledge of the world pop scene, is known in other countries throughout Europe and perhaps even Australia (Holly Valance being one of his greatest fans!). I smiled to myself thinking, how did I get from romanticising about living in Istanbul to being one of so many at the launch of a major pop singer's new album? What did I do to be rewarded with nights gazing at the Bosphorus, lights twinkling like fairy castles from the mosques dotted in the villages along the shore? I had a dream.

I first set foot in Turkey as a tourist in 1997. Four or five weeks of travelling; soaking up the sun, the sea, the food and Turkish people's incredible warmth and hospitality. I remember leaving the country by ferry, from Kusadasi to Samos, a neighbouring Greek island in the Aegean Sea. As the ferry bounced through the choppy sea, a real sense of sadness enveloped me, an unexpected feeling given the limited time I had spent in the country. The magic of the mosques, the allure of the Istanbul skyline, the beauty of the tufa landscape of Cappadocia, and the complex and fascinating history had forged a bond between this ancient land and me.

Upon returning to England I found myself in a small bookshop rummaging through the foreign language section, searching in vain for

Turkish resources. Many larger shops later, I found the text and tape of *Teach Yourself Turkish*. Clutching it in my hand, I walked home wondering where this was leading. I was a typical product of the early 1980s Victorian public school system with little grasp of any language other than Australian-English. I tentatively opened the book and learned that there were over 100 million speakers of languages closely related to Turkic languages. At the very least, I thought to myself, some self-study would help me when I travelled back to Turkey and on through some of the countries of the former USSR!

I visited Turkey twice during 1998, the bond growing stronger each time. At the end of the year, my sister Kay joined me in London. She had originally travelled with me for those four weeks in September 1997 and while she loved her time in Turkey, Kay did not feel the connection that I did. I talked with her about how I wanted to spend more time in Turkey, with vague and sometimes random thoughts gathering strength and focus as they were verbalised. Kay has always been my biggest fan and has encouraged me to pursue my happiness. I, however, felt that my profession, that of a dietitian, was a language-based job that was not transferable in the short term, given my limited Turkish. I was also keen to change the focus of my work. I wanted to be more food-oriented rather than nutrient-oriented.

A plan was formulating and gathering definition. In January 2000, I started a six-month intensive course in food and wine. During the term break, I returned to Istanbul and met two women who would give me the light and the encouragement I needed to inch toward my growing desire to live in Turkey. Burcu and Ebru run a cafe called Cookbook; at that time a themed cafe, highlighting different cuisines from around the world each week. Cookbooks from Turkey and around the world were also for sale in the cafe. There were changes on the food scene that suggested Turkish people were really embracing other world cuisines. Cafes and restaurants were opening up with variations on local dishes as well as international choices. While this style of eating establishment had been open for some time, the clientele tended to be people at the top end of the socio-economic scale. It seemed to me that there was some movement to offer something for middle-income earners. While I love almost all Turkish cuisine (although I must personally draw the line at intestines served in any way, or chicken breast pudding), I was also excited to find European-style cafes serving Italian coffee appearing more regularly along the streets and boulevards. My personal comfort level increased, I felt that there might be space for me in this city, that I could find a niche. Despite the exotic appeal and glamour of foreign countries and cities, I had travelled enough to know that some touches of familiarity are important and sometimes lifesaving.

I wrote to the Australian Embassy in Ankara, the Turkish capital, expressing my wishes to live in Turkey and perhaps open some kind of food establishment. A letter arrived from the Australian Trade Commission in Istanbul. A woman named Ingrid who had written the letter offered very little information but said that should I require more assistance I should make further contact. I did this on my next trip. I met her in her office and briefly explained what I wanted to do. Could she give me any direction? Whom should I contact? I wanted to know how I could move my dream closer to a reality. She seemed the obvious person, she appeared to be a Australian of Turkish origin, her accent was almost as thick as mine. The woman barely listened to me, but launched instead into a diatribe about foolish young Australian women who meet carpet sellers in the bazaars, get swept off their feet and throw their lives and money away without thinking about it. I sat there stunned. I could not recall mentioning any carpet sellers, any bazaars, or in fact any relations with Turkish men. She went on to talk about how being a woman trying to get house renovations completed by crooked and lazy Turkish tradesman was beyond ridiculous and if you could not speak the language, an impossibility. Her outburst offended me and I left her office with my confidence shaken. She almost succeeded in making me feel stupid and foolish for thinking I could do such a thing as a 'single, white, foreign woman'. Almost.

The most recent collapse of the Turkish economy towards the end of 2000 was felt in full force in early 2001. Kay and I planned a ten-day trip to Istanbul then to Antalya and Kas on the south coast in April. We found the roads of Istanbul deserted, petrol prices having risen by 60% in the past few weeks, shops, cafes and restaurants closing. People were anxious about their future; some seeing their cash savings diminish virtually overnight. The crisis seemed more acute in the capital, and I could feel my own gloomy thoughts about opening up a business where people were suddenly cautious about spending money, settling like a stone in my gut.

I returned to London, depressed. My dream would remain just that. The light at the end of my tunnel seemed to be extinguishing. There seemed to be only a faint hope of cementing my attachment with Turkey through Kay's and my decision to purchase a flat in the small village of Kas. During our most recent trip, we had stayed with a friend Dorothy and her partner Tevfik. They lived on the top floor of an apartment building in the centre of the village. The view from their balcony took in the mountains, the Mediterranean Sea and a small Greek island across the way. Kay sat transfixed for hours, gazing at everything and nothing. Tevfik told us the flat next door was up for sale. Two months later, we owned it. This became my lifeline over the next ten months as I worked often 70 hours a week as manager of a nutrition and dietetic service, lecturer and chef in London.

Life went on. Kay and I decided we would sell our house in London in May 2002. This could give me the financial freedom to approach a life in Turkey in a different way. In April of that year, I left all except my part-time lecturing post at King's College University and went back to Istanbul. I rented an apartment for two weeks through the magazine *Cornucopia* and decided to work hard at finding a way in. I enquired about a course in Turkish language and culture at the prestigious Bosphorus University. Somehow, I had misinterpreted the information on the internet and had missed the application closing date for the summer course. Nevertheless, I visited the administrator of the course on campus and she hinted that there might be an opening. I was hopeful. As I was thinking of settling in Istanbul, she thought I might be interested in renting a flat in a village along the Bosphorus, not far from the university. A teacher at the university was just finishing some refurbishments and was planning to rent it from the commencement of the course in mid-June. I visited the flat and met my potential landlady, the light flickering just a little brighter at the end of the passage.

I left Istanbul and spent a few weeks in Kas, pondering over the monumental changes I was making in my life, yet again. The flirtation of the past years was becoming a serious relationship. I left Australia only days after I turned 30, now days before turning 35 I looked set to move to Istanbul. All I had worked for was coming together, and for the first time I was scared. I tallied up my acquaintances and friends in Turkey; Dorothy and Tevfik in Kas, and in Istanbul, Ebru, Burcu and Emine, the administrator of *Cornucopia*. I was leaving behind an established life in London with many more friends and more importantly, my sister.

Suddenly my abhorrence for London turned to faint dislike, my previous salary looked very attractive compared to the meagre income I would now receive. The London underground seemed an amusing adventure rather than the disgusting event that it was, and Londoner's coldness, hostility and aggression seemed just the quirky characteristics of a city's people. Yet my heart was not there, it was on the shores of the Bosphorus, in the alleyways of Galata, in the fresh produce markets and grand bazaars, among the throngs of people moving down Independence Street on a Saturday night.

I emailed the owner of the flat in Istanbul and agreed to rent it, not for the duration of the eight-week course, but for the year. Until Kay and I sold and settled on the house in London, I would need to cover the mortgage there as well as rent in Turkey. I felt faintly sick at the thought, not one to embrace uncertain personal financial situations. I swallowed the bile and took comfort in the fact that if things got bad I could return to the UK for a short-term contractual job as a dietitian, the national shortage of health professionals coming at an opportune time.

I arrived in Istanbul with as many bags as I could manage and Turkish Airlines would allow on Thursday, 13 June 2002. It was my fourteenth entry into Turkey in less than five years. To my disappointment my new landlady, who occupied the two floors above me, had not quite prepared the flat. I spent the first few days purchasing various things, an ironing board, clothes drying rack, kitchen and bathroom items. I was not concerned about price as I would deduct it from my rent, and I was not quite prepared to step into the negotiating ring for these items with my limited Turkish. For larger items that I would purchase myself such as a small stereo, I enlisted the help of Ebru. We spent an exhausting afternoon sound testing the various possibilities and bargained for the best possible price. Come Monday morning I was as settled as I could be and set off for my first class of a gruelling eight weeks of Turkish language.

My landlady departed for England days after my arrival so when I detected a small gas leak in the kitchen I rifled through the cards and numbers in case of emergency and rang the service. With my three days of formal Turkish instruction, I communicated the following. 'I am Sharon Croxford. Arnavutkoy. Boyali Kosk Sokak 48, Flat 1. There is a gas problem'. Thankfully, this was enough. The serviceman was able to come to the flat the next afternoon.

I woke the next morning to horrendous, twisting gut pain, knowing that the fish from the previous day was not as clean as my sensitive gut required. I spent the next five hours between bed and the toilet while waiting for the gas serviceman. As the leak received attention I realised that the swishing, hissing noise I had intermittently heard was not gas, but the main water pipe in the foyer. I flopped down on the stairs, the pain from food poisoning making me feel faint while the thought of a burst water pipe bringing tears to my eyes. Again, I tested my limited Turkish. 'Excuse me. There is a water problem. Friend?' The next morning someone arrived to fix the water pipe that by then had burst and flooded the foyer and was running down the street.

I trudged through the following weeks, quickly realising that if I was to keep up with the language course I would need to study every night and all day Sunday. Problems with the flat kept me otherwise occupied. A water leak in the main bedroom resulted in the carpet going mouldy as well as the wooden base under the bed and many of my wicker baskets that keep my possessions in order. Sporadic cutting of the neighbourhood water supply coupled with a faulty emergency water pump had me showering in the girl's dormitory on-campus. Finally an attack of something like fleas from the lounge carpet left me feeling exhausted and defeated as well itchy and scratchy.

In the first weeks I also had some sad news from home. My grandmother died suddenly one afternoon. She went to buy her paper from her local shop, a daily exercise she had practiced for most of the past years of her life. She suffered a minor stroke and later a major stroke. She died that evening. Grandma was in her late eighties and had lived an adventurous and independent life. She went in the best way possible, with little pain and indignity. I grieved for her, walking the streets of this foreign city, feeling detached but still able to bring forth all the happy and quirky memories of our times together. I did not return for the funeral but sent a story for the minister to read during the service. Kay and I would both return later in the year for a family memorial and scattering of the ashes.

My undoing came a few weeks later. I went to an internet cafe to check on life outside Turkey. I clicked on what I thought would be a humorous note from a friend. Instead, I learnt for the first time that my friend's husband, Ian, had been killed in car accident a few weeks earlier. Some confusion in the UK had left me out of the initial communication and Susan assumed that I knew. I logged off and went into the street. The tears rolled down my cheeks. I blindly walked toward home, the gulps of hysteria building up. I sat on a small fence to collect myself. Unable to call Susan, I called Kay. I swallowed the solid mass in my throat and told her the news, asking her to ring a mutual friend and find out what happened.

Life went on behind a haze of confusion. Uncertainty about my decision to move to Istanbul looming before me, threatening my resolve. I felt incredibly sad and alone. People surrounded me everyday, but these people were virtual strangers and seemed to intensify my isolation. I felt I was at breaking point. There had been too much change, too quickly and my determination to do it alone, my inherent difficulty in asking people for help left me stranded. Why had I moved, yet again, to another foreign city, where I knew virtually nobody and did not speak the language?

During my next term teaching at the university in London, I took a long weekend and went to the Slow Food Salone del Gusto in Turin, Italy. I was booked into several tasting workshops, including the only Turkish session. Turkish cheeses and wines. An interesting combination given that cheese is usually eaten for breakfast in Turkey and wine was only gathering momentum as a drink of choice, competing with the strong ouzo-like liquor, Raki, and beer. After the workshop, I introduced myself to the panel. Frank, from Slow Food—Bodrum, Sibel from Doluca Wines and Yadi, a friend of Sibel's. Despite the few moments that we spent talking, meeting them strengthened the feeling that there was a real place for me in Istanbul, that people really did have similar interests to me. It also added to my confusion!

Following a six-week visit to Australia, when a incredible clarity in my head and heart told me that Istanbul, Turkey was now my home, I re-entered Turkey in February 2003 with a green residence visa in my passport. Istanbul can seem like a crazy mess of a city, but it is one of the most beautiful cities in the world. It has its challenges, but none greater than any I have faced in other places. A friend, Alper, recently said something like this to me, 'Other cities just have other problems'. He is right. What some of those other cities do not have are a friendly, brave and resilient people who never give up hope. Sounds a little like my other home.

People ask me 'Why have you come to Turkey?'. I seem a bit of a freak to them; no job, no husband or boyfriend that tempted me to move, no family. My answer of 'I feel a connection with Turkey, something in my gut, in my heart. I just wanted to live here so here I am', leaves them a little bewildered, wanting more. The answer is much bigger than that but so difficult to put into words that unless you experience a similar journey and similar emotions you may also find it bewildering.

Sharon Croxford left Australia in 1997, spending five years in England, plotting, planning and dreaming of a life in Turkey. In 2002, after much hard work she found she was able to find a life in Istanbul, supported financially through periods of lecturing at King's College University, London each year. Her ultimate goal is to open a School of Food and Cooking in Istanbul, where she hopes to share the wonders of Turkish and other world cuisines with those who want to learn.

Two Hours Ahead

I am always two hours ahead in this country. To an Australian brought up on the eastern seaboard like me, the South Island of New Zealand's close proximity to the South Pole is evident in more than the cool winds and icy seas. I can feel the difference in my relation to the sun when the summer days stretch well into the evenings, and winter nights begin in the afternoon. Mountains and hills reflect sounds, so that it seems to me that I am always indoors.

Seasons are distinct and crisp. My eyes, used to the smoke-mauve greens and muted beige-golds of the Australian landscape find the intense primavera green of New Zealand spring and summer growth almost painful. So young! So fresh! Such an innocent colour; in keeping with the bluebells and daffodils that tilt prettily in the Scottish gardens. Six months later the winter-dark manukas and pine forests range soberly over the hills. Grass is the colour of hay, with new verdant growth like swansdown pushing up from underneath. New Zealanders stare when I remark how lush it is—for them the autumn conditions are worryingly dry.

As a little girl in Adelaide, I believed that New Zealand was another state of Australia. I'd never even known New Zealand was more than one island. In fact, until I was 19 my experience of the country had been limited to Ruth Park's marvellous novels, and one disastrous viewing of Jane Campion's film *The Piano* with my boyfriend. I was deeply affected by the dark gravity and repressed emotion inherent in the cinematography, scenery and Michael Nyman's intense score; and I spent most of the movie sobbing on my boyfriend's annoyed and unsympathetic shoulder. My inability to explain my distress was one more weight on our overburdened relationship; and we broke up soon afterwards. My grandmother died, my parents separated, my job was a bore. In June 1994, three charming Kiwi men were billeted with my household for a week.

They told me about a ski trip our church's Young People's group was taking to New Zealand in October. Later I found one of them was to be married in Dunedin the weekend before the trip began. 'Why don't you move to New Zealand?', another well-travelled friend suggested when I told her of my interest in the ski trip and my lassitude towards Melbourne. Two months later I arrived in New Zealand for the first time.

Dunedin enchanted me. The staunchly Scottish university town is located on the east coast of the South Island. I instantly loved its green hills rumpled like a blanket on a bed, its old-fashioned gardens, its avant-garde cafes and Victorian architecture. I returned for visit after visit and finally moved over at the end of 1997. The next year I went to work for a well-known and well-loved dairy company.

You will be singled out if you are an Australian in New Zealand! While working on telephones for Mainland's customer service department, sales reps around the country told me I had quite a 'suhxy' voice, that I had in fact been voted the company's 'suhxiest' voice—did I look like Elle MacPherson? Was I 'divuhstated' that the Wallabies had lost again? Feeble retaliatory taunts of 'you're a buhg puhg' fell flat—many people simply didn't realise that I was mocking them. One never thinks of language barriers in two English-speaking countries, but how many Aussies know how to translate the remark, 'Oh, box of fluffies, thanks' in response to asking a friend how they are? I took umbrage when I was called a 'hard case', I was concerned when a friend was described as a dag—I never thought of myself as jailbird material, nor of my friend as particularly lacking in style. I was relieved to learn that I was simply something of a larrikin, and my friend a humorous joker. On the other hand, I caused offence by calling a workmate a 'dork', and didn't know why, until a year or two later, when someone took me aside and explained its private and anatomical significance for gentleman whales. Whoops! Which brings me to that remote-but-well-known Australian region, 'Whoop-Whoop'—known in New Zealand as the 'Wop-Wops'—I ask you.

Sport is like war for most New Zealanders; and teams are their armies and heroes. Australia is the archetypal enemy. The Olympic season was a trying time for me—many Kiwis seemed to hold me personally responsible whenever New Zealand failed to win any medals. It just wasn't fair that Australia took so many medals—after all, New Zealand has only the population of one of Australia's cities, didn't I know? Was it worth my pointing out that Australia has only the population of one of the cities in the UK? The economy seems to rise and fall on the success of the All Blacks. I'd been quite a fan of the All Blacks since 1995 but received so much ragging whenever the Wallabies lost a rugby game that I switched sides—right on time for the growing number of Wallabies' cup wins. This certainly aggravated my detractors. On the other hand, I received only respect for supporting the regional Otago Highlanders—'Southern Men' are known and esteemed around the country.

I spent 2001 and 2002 working as a trainer for the company; travelling around New Zealand to train sales reps and contractors on the use of pocket PCs for sales, inventory and account work. It was a wonderful way to see the country and learn about the locals. Away for weeks at a time, I'd spend a whole day or two with many people of different backgrounds and cultures; travelling around their town or their region. My memories of those days are precious and occasionally surreal.

Imagine me in Kawakawa, a tiny rural town in the heart of Northland. At 4 am I am stacking 20 litre crates of milk on the damp footpath outside a local store, trying to think of an appropriate reply to the shopkeeper's frank remark, 'Cripes, the milkie told me he'd have a bird in the truck with him today, but I was expecting a horrible blonde, not a lovely brunette!' At 9 am I am negotiating recalcitrant software with Alex, a burly Kiwi bloke who is politely concealing his growing irritation with the 'townie' technology that won't print an invoice. It's easy to impress a Kiwi male if you have even a slight knack for mechanics. When all else has failed I whip out the screwdriver I pinched from the Wellington depot, take the printer apart and tighten every connection, then reassemble it with flair, blushing modestly as the printer politely starts spitting out the hitherto-missing invoice and its four copies. Alex congratulates me with surprised respect. At noon we are chugging across to Russell on the ferry. I buy a raffle ticket from the Maori ferry-pilot's young assistant in aid of the Volunteer Firefighters' Association and sip the good strong tea he's made me. He tells me we're unlucky today—no dolphins are to be seen leaping in front of the ferry in good fellowship. At 4 pm I am walking back to my roadside motel, begrimed by diesel fumes and cardboard dust, my ponytail ragged and my jeans chafing.

But, oh, 5 pm finds me inside Kawiti Caves, an ancient limestone system five minutes drive from the main road into town. I am viewing the 150-year-old coals of a fire that was kept burning in that cave for several years by a Maori woman who had run away from her brutal cannibalistic husband and his family. I imagine myself trying to cope with the echoes and darkness, the eels and bats, the wetas and glow-worms, and the swirls and gurgles of the *taniwha* (water monster) in the tiny stream that swelled with the rains to flood the entire cavern. That she coped, escaped and survived to tell the tale is testified by the presence of the lovely woman who is guiding me through the cave—the other woman's descendant by several generations. At the other end of the cave, she lets me walk alone through the bush that has changed little since the Jurassic period—no cans or plastic bags or incongruous signs here—just fallen logs lush with moss that glows like emeralds, soaring kauri trees and huge circular boulders. And the intense hushed green. Halfway down I hear, or imagine, the slither of the *taniwha's* tail behind me. Too much a child of my sceptical generation to allow myself to turn and see it, I nonetheless break into a slightly faster trot, breathing a little harder, my heart beating a little faster.

Twenty-four hours later my bags are being carried to my room at the Heritage Hotel, Auckland. A cocooned, cushioned, cream and gold boudoir that is one hours drive and an hour's flight from yesterday's cave—but I know I am further away than the clock and calendar can convince me.

I met so many delightful Kiwis during my time in New Zealand! They were always indulgent and hospitable to the girl from the big country 'across the ditch'. I met Roger, who pulled the truck I was riding in over so that I could jump on an ice-coated puddle by the side of the road, and detoured to show me the best view of the snow-laden Southern Alps. Hamish drove me back to Invercargill, just an hour into our day, as I developed a migraine, and waited so kindly and bashfully (I hadn't known he was a childless bachelor) while I threw up at the side of the lonely road. Later he let me in on the secret of the best sites to go gold panning in Central Otago on my next holiday. 'Beachy' took me to see the spectacular Pancake Rocks blowhole at Punakaiki on the West Coast. Peter loaned me his woollen jacket to prevent me slowly freezing to death as we made our way down the Kaikoura Coast in August, pointing out the seals strewn over the black rocks at the road's edge; and carefully manoeuvred to avoid the huge section of road that the sea had scooped casually away the morning before, taking out the bread truck that happened to be driving along it at the time. Mark let me finish early in Gisborne so I could go to the beach and see the harbour where Captain Cook first viewed New Zealand. Beautiful Gisborne, where the three rivers Turanganui-a-Kiwa, Waipaoa and Taruheru meet before they continue on their short trip to the sea. It's the furthest east I've ever been. The Pacific is jade and sparkling here, and the water seems so fresh and alive that I am reminded of CS Lewis's *Utter East*. It's the sort of harbour one expects the Dawn Treader to sail into at any time. I prance and leap in the water like a little girl.

My father's family emigrated from Mauritius to Australia when he was seventeen. Did he miss the tiny island in the Indian Ocean, faceted like a jewel with cultures and creeds, spices and scents? I am travelling there later this year, to learn more about that life, and to be taught to cook meals that are the equal of those produced by Grandmere and my inspired Tante Roseline. In Australia, my father swiftly became nationalised and lost most traces of his accent. Now I am in New Zealand. Despite my love and respect for the country and its people, I will never change my Australian nationality. For I enjoy the point of difference between myself and the rest, it makes me memorable. Kiwis love to tease, it seems to be a prelude to familiarity; so my unchanged 'Strine' accent provides an easy ice-breaker. As for being a social scapegoat for all Australia's disgraces as viewed abroad, well, isn't it a good thing to take away the imputation of sin from among the people?

Would I ever go back to Australia? I can't say yet. My heart wants to stay here, where it always has a dim consciousness of ancient forests and caves, stark beaches, and the mineral springs that well up through the earth that is so rich and brown here. When I dream of New Zealand, my mind's dreaming agent turns the country into some land of fantastic legend; peopled with antipodean banshees and goblins, and black-eyed, brown-skinned pisgies. The air is white and gleaming, and the water is an icy aqua colour that glints and sparkles. And every now and then the *taniwha* in my head gnaws its lichened teeth on a vein in my brain; so that a migrainic ring of shimmering light pops into my vision. It sends great pain, and great inspiration.

I yearn for Australia always, yet when I go back during holidays the ache and longing are unsatisfied by the things I see. Bureaucracy is on the increase, sapping the public's common sense. In Melbourne, the air is yellow with topsoil blown down from farming Victoria. The concrete of new developments is slowly eating up the bush. The memories of my childhood are under that concrete, and I don't want to come back to the city. So, for now, I remain in Dunedin, with ferns under my feet and paua shell around my neck. I taste the spices of Mauritius and feel the warmth of the Indian Ocean's sun. But I still have the scent of eucalypts in my nostrils, and I am holding a handful of Australia's red earth.

Natalie Delary-Simpson has been living in Dunedin since 1997 and from 1999 to 2002 she worked as a trainer and QA at Mainland Products. Both with work and out of personal interest she has travelled around New Zealand many times.

MEETING AN AUSTRALIAN

My husband was appointed as Australian Ambassador to Lebanon in 1998 and we arrived there early in 1999. The subsequent three years were among the most glamorous and exciting of my life. As an Australian expatriate with a diplomat husband I got the opportunity to meet many interesting people from a wide range of society. However, because of our privileged existence in a country that boasts Roman ruins, Crusader castles and Ottoman opulence, there was often an immense gulf between the kind of life we know as Australians and what we came to know in Beirut.

Somebody once described the downtown area of post-war Beirut in 1990 as the world's largest open air archaeological dig in an urban environment. Certainly it would be true to say that, if nothing else, one good thing to have come out of the destruction wrought in central Beirut by the disastrous fifteen year civil war from 1975 to 1990 was the opportunity opened up for historians and archaeologists to discover the past.

Modern day Beirut sits on top of layers and layers of Phoenician, Roman, Greek, Byzantine and Arab treasures. Over thousands of years, Lebanon has served as a crossroads of cultures. In present times, both the American University of Beirut (AUB) and the Lebanese University hold the rights to dig in the very heart of downtown Beirut and, within weeks of my arriving in Beirut in February 1999, I was invited to have a look at the dig site.

There I was able to sift through shards of pottery and assemble handles and rims of cups, vases and stoneware jars from the past. I enjoyed the monthly talks that were arranged by AUB's Friends of the Museum and these talks proved popular with scholars, students and people like me who were simply wishing to learn. Sometimes, as a native English speaker, I was called upon to take notes of the lectures in English. My subsequent meeting with a wonderful historian and archaeologist inspired me to write something about my experiences.

Having returned to Australia, friends sometimes ask me what it was like living in Beirut. Was it dangerous? Was I scared? For me it was, overall, totally absorbing.

Lebanon is a country of amazing paradoxes, both material and religious. Mornings can be spent visiting refugee camps that lack water, electricity and sewerage but evenings are whiled away in ballrooms built for thousands and decorated with chandeliers, where tables groan with food, and champagne is more readily available than drinking water is for the underprivileged. Also by way of contrast, it is possible to tee off on an expensive golf course situated right alongside a squalid Palestinian refugee settlement.

I once described Lebanon as being like several broken jigsaw puzzles all waiting to be joined. Sadly, as has been highlighted in the past three years of the *intifada*, the Middle East, and Lebanon in particular, are not known for religious tolerance, in spite of having been home to Christians, Muslims and Jews for centuries.

I look back on an amazing three years in which more people—both famous and ordinary—walked across our personal stage than I could possibly enumerate.

One such person was 86-year-old Leila Fleyfel (nee Ghanem), who I met with her husband Louis, over my very first lunch in a Beirut restaurant.

Leila's story is typical of many Lebanese and I was fascinated when she told it to me in a broad Australian accent. It was all a bit disconcerting until I discovered that Leila had been born in Geelong in Victoria in 1914. She was the twelfth child born to Lebanese immigrants to Australia. In the late 1880s, Leila's mother had been sent from north Lebanon to live with her sister in Egypt because of a deteriorating economy in Lebanon. That sister's husband had a good job as one of the engineers doing maintenance work on the Suez Canal. Leila's mother had been educated in Beirut and it was the expectation of her family that she would marry a Lebanese man and return to Lebanon. However, in Egypt she met and later married Leila's father and bore him two children. Both infants died in Egypt before the young couple took up the opportunity to emigrate to Australia.

The couple boarded a ship bound for Sydney. However, when the ship berthed in Melbourne, Leila's father recognised a Lebanese friend working on the wharves. That friend persuaded Leila's father to get off the ship and join him. The search for work took Leila's parents to Geelong where he found a job with a provedore company supplying stores to the trading ships which, at the time, were plying the profitable England-Australia wool trade route.

Leila's early memories were a bit confused as she relayed them to me at her advanced age in 1999, but she still remembered a little room off the kitchen of their house in Geelong where she and her sisters and brothers lived. She told me that, as the youngest child, she was the one who stayed the longest time with her parents and although they did not teach her how to write Arabic, they taught her enough Arabic words that she could understand her mother's feelings of homesickness when her mother would stand at the grate of their fire from time to time and dream of the homeland she loved but would never see again.

After leaving school in Geelong, Leila trained as a nurse at St Vincent's Hospital in Melbourne. After the commencement of the Second World War, Leila was quick to join the Australian Army and was sent to Palestine in 1941 to work in military hospitals there.

On her return to Australia at the end of the war she met a newly-arrived immigrant from Lebanon, Louis. Louis Fleyfel and Leila are first cousins. They married in Australia 52 years ago, against the wishes of Leila's sister. ('Mother would never have allowed it if she had still been alive,' said Leila.) Leila's biggest regret was that she and Louis never had children. As a result of blood tests carried out after their marriage, they were advised not to have children. Unfortunately, in Lebanon as in many other countries where inter-marriage is common, or where there is marriage among small village family groups, this practice has resulted in an increased incidence of deafness, blindness and mental disability in children. The orphanages in Lebanon are filled with unwanted children, many of them with birth defects.

When I met her, Leila carried her campaign medals around in her handbag but she would wear them on her lapel with pride on Anzac Day. At the outdoor service at the Commonwealth war graves cemetery in Beirut I offered her a chair because I thought she might be feeling the heat of a warm spring morning. But Leila refused with imperious disdain, saying that she preferred to 'stand up for the boys'.

We spent several Sunday lunchtimes with Leila and Louis. As well as being owner of several prominent Melbourne restaurants, Louis had been Honorary Lebanese Consul in Melbourne in the 1970s. He was the consummate host and loved entertaining. Their gorgeous villa, built high in the hills above Jounieh to the north of Beirut, was apparently designed, and to some extent built, by Louis himself. One special Sunday in 1999, between 60 and 70 guests—many of them Australian-Lebanese—sat down to a sumptuous Lebanese banquet. There were hot and cold *mezzes*, salads, lamb, chicken and beef, suitably washed down with an ample supply of Australian red and white wine. The dessert? A piece of the five-tiered cake to celebrate the 50th wedding anniversary of Leila and Louis. They were married in Melbourne on 28 March, 1949, only weeks after Louis had arrived in Australia to begin life anew in his adopted country. The more I talked with Leila, the more fascinated I became by her story about being married to a business tycoon like Louis. At 86, her memory let her down at times but she was obviously a driving force behind Louis's success.

Leila died in 2002 and, unlike her mother, is buried in her ancestral village in north Lebanon.

Apart from Leila, another woman who impressed me during my time in Lebanon was Rabab el-Sadr. In Lebanon I met many devout Muslim women who have given their lives to promoting the wider cause of disadvantaged women and children. One such woman, Rabab el Sadr, runs an orphanage in Tyre in southern Lebanon which is designed to give girls from under-privileged and broken families a chance in life. Many of the girls are orphans from the Lebanese Civil War and, without the help of the El Sadr Foundation, these girls would have limited prospects. Also, because of the low income of their families, many of the girls are not motivated to learn academic subjects, and so the emphasis in Rabab's school is on vocational subjects like hairdressing, hotel management and agriculture. Rabab, who is a serious, quietly spoken and well-educated Shia woman, epitomises humanitarian values.

Another equally impressive Muslim woman I met is head of the Women's Humanitarian Organisation (WHO). A Sunni Muslim, Olfat Mahmoud is dedicated to improving the way of life for young and old at the Bourj El Barajneh Palestinian camp in West Beirut. Because of an insufficient number of schools and teachers to cope with an ever-growing population, children in the camp are denied the full-time education that we in Australia take for granted. On one of the several visits I made to the camp, Olfat explained that, for the most part, Palestinian children do not have the opportunity during term time to do anything other than the school syllabus. Moreover, since schools have to double up on class sizes during the school day because of limited classroom facilities, Olfat has been the driving force behind the creation of an after-school activities program in the camp. Money to run the schools is provided in large part through the United Nations Relief and Works Agency for Palestine Refugees to which Australia contributes, as well as to non-government organisations, of which WHO is one.

Our posting to Lebanon was my husband's final overseas posting; he retired upon our return to Australia. Now we can look back over the highs and lows of embassy life, the laughter and the tears of family separation, the pain of the death of my father and so much more. Most of all, we treasure the friendships made within the diplomatic, expatriate and local communities, and we feel privileged. Like Leila's mother, I sometimes stand at my fireplace in Australia and yearn for the warmth of the Mediterranean experience. It taught me so much about the Lebanese, about myself and about the world.

Marion Fennessy is the wife of a retired Australian public servant. Over a span of 25 years she has travelled with her husband on postings to Seoul, Ankara, Wellington, Warsaw and Beirut. She is now happily residing in Canberra.

FANTASMAGORICAL AND FARAWAY

In July 2002 my family—husband Michael, 43, myself, 41, daughter Eden, 13, son Ben, 11 and our two cats—relocated to Helsinki in Finland for a two-year period. Michael works for a company called Datex-Ohmeda, the parent company of which is Instrumentarium, one of the oldest and most successful of Finnish companies. Among expats in Finland you are either N or NN: Nokia, or Not Nokia. Obviously we are NN, which makes us almost an oddity.

Ah, Finland. What can I say about Finland? Where on earth do I start and, once I start, can I stop? It is, for a European country, a relatively large one and has just over five million inhabitants, which also makes it one of the most sparsely populated. It has 187,888 lakes (who was the poor bugger given the task of counting?), which makes me wonder if every time someone pisses against a tree the count goes up. It is gorgeously green in summer, then in winter with the snow blanketing everything takes on an ethereal, stark beauty. The coastline is very picturesque with islands dotted about; the crime rate is very low so it is extremely safe; it is one of the cleanest countries in the world; and the public transport is an absolute dream: frequent, reliable, fast. So why have I found Finland to be such an extraordinarily challenging place in which to live?

It's a well-known fact (well, I know about it at least) that expatriation is hardest on the wives. The husband gets the stimulation and sociability of his job, while the wife gets (in my case, at any rate) a country with a foreign language, disgruntled children, loneliness, unfamiliarity, frustration, disorientation and the absence of family and friends to bolster her spirits. In my pre-Finland life I worked as a freelance book editor, which was an ideal world as it enabled me to enjoy a well-paid, intellectually invigorating job and still be at home for the kids. In my freelance capacity I was sought after and well respected. I went from being someone who could cope with a full-time job, running a household and the demands of two teenage children to being someone who broke down into hysterical sobbing on the floor in front of the washing machine because it had no perceivable symbols or an English-language instruction book. It was quite a shock to the system.

(PS: I've figured out how the washing machine, the clothes dryer and the dishwasher all work now, so the white goods and I are on pleasant speaking terms.)

If you look at a globe of the world, Finland is diametrically opposed to Australia. Between you and me, that's about how far apart we are culturally as well. Shortly after arriving, Michael and I went for a four-hour walk in a national park; it was only supposed to be a one-hour walk, but we got lost! During those four hours we said hello in both English and Finnish to everyone we met, and we met a lot of people. Not one single person, *not one*, replied or would even look us in the face; and that, I feel, illustrates pretty well the dichotomy between Finns and Aussies.

Australian   =   gregarious, fun-loving, warm, generous, open, funny
Finn   =   polite, reflective, formal, reserved, controlled, silent

It was something I, as an Australian, found very difficult to endure or understand and it took some getting used to.

There are, I believe, only around 60,000 expats in Finland, a tiny number. You do get sharp looks from the people near you when you speak English and they realise you are not a native, and I have to say there is quite a measured resistance to foreigners. Finns simply want Finland to remain Finnish, inhabited by Finns. Narrow minded? Possibly, but anything different to what you are used to can strike you as being parochial.

I took Eden and Ben to some pet stores shortly after arriving, which caused me to start seriously wondering about the Finns. You would of course expect to find cute puppies and fluffy kitties and cuddly wabbits and widdle mice running around plastic wheels, but that's far too mundane for a Finnish pet shop. Here they (or at least the ones we visited) are full of metre-long lizards, hermit crabs, macaws, bearded dragons, prairie dogs, corn snakes in every conceivable size and colour, terrapins, chameleons and—wait for it—big, fat, ugly, hairy tarantulas. Don't get me wrong, I actually like spiders, but am I missing something here? Does cuddling up to these critters raise your endorphin levels in the same way that cuddling up to a newborn kitty would? Adrenalin levels definitely; endorphin levels—I don't think so! I can hardly wait to go to the pet expo.

It took me a while to get the hang of the driving on the right-hand side of the road thing, especially in a manual car trying to change gears with my right hand. The first few trips were harrowing, but my kids were extremely supportive so it was okay: 'Do you even know *how* to drive?' 'Do you even know where you're *going*?' 'You stalled the car, you *loser*!' 'Isn't that a *red* light?' 'Are you *sure* this isn't a one-way street?' 'Are you even *allowed* to turn right here?' and so on and so forth, showing just how greatly they appreciated my efforts. I still occasionally get into the car on the right side and wonder where on earth the steering wheel's gone, then sheepishly get out and hope no one notices me going around to the other side of the car.

One of the first things you learn in Finland is to *carpe diem* while the sun is shining, because once the very long winter arrives it means instant houseboundedness, month after fabulous month of it. With this in mind, Michael and I took advantage of a gloriously sunny day to go to the 'beach' (read 'lakeside'), a word that should be very loosely applied. Picture the scene: gorgeous gritty grey dirt posing as sand, centimetre-high waves that literally knocked you off your feet, sparklingly clear water that you couldn't see more than five centimetres into, weeds, floating plastic bags, slime underfoot, power lines stretching from island to island—I could go on and on, but I don't want to make anybody jealous.

In the beginning I was constantly flummoxed at the supermarket in my searches for familiar food items. In this country you simply can't buy self-raising flour, pumpkin, custard powder, tinned spaghetti, jelly crystals, decent cheddar cheese, sweetened condensed milk, lamb that doesn't cost an arm and a leg (and an eye and an ear as well) or genuine, tasty sausages. The Finns just don't do sausages as Aussies know them— there goes the outdoor barbie—but instead have as Pretenders to the Great Sausage Throne variously shaped and coloured par-boiled 'things' that to our palates taste yuck!

Many times I took home items that turned out to be completely different from what I thought they were going to be by the pictures on the packet; talk about false advertising. On one occasion I bought what I was fairly confident was puff pastry, as the wrapping depicted fluffy-looking turnover thingies. When I opened the packet at home I found the very thick pastry pre-cut into pieces seven cm wide and 15 cm long. What on earth are you supposed to make with something that size: eye pillows? A lot of the flour here has, in capital letters right across the middle of the packet, the word '*sunnuntai*', which means 'Sunday'. Excuse me? Does that mean you can only successfully cook with it on Sundays? Will anyone tell on me if I use it on Tuesday or Friday? Good grief!

As opposed to many European countries such as Germany, Italy or France, here English is very widely spoken, a fact about which I am eternally grateful. Coming to Finland makes you feel like an ignoramus, when you are confronted by people who speak another one, two, even five European languages. (To be fair, though, what need does the average Aussie have of other languages when English is so ubiquitous in the Southern Hemisphere, and where and on whom would we ever practise?)

Finnish is a Uralic language that is not Scandinavian and is not related to Indo-European languages, so apart from a few words such as '*taksi*' and '*hotelli*' there is not much that is recognisable or upon which you can make an educated guess. Many Finns told me that I shouldn't attempt to learn the language if I was planning on being in the country for less than two years; to my credit, I did sign up for a course. A couple of months later, when I finally admitted what I had suspected from the start—that I would never speak Finnish—I quietly surrendered. I can count to one thousand, I know colours and days of the week and months of the year, I can say 'hello' and 'goodbye' and 'please' and 'thank you', and I can get by in the supermarket. It's enough for me.

I have read that Finnish is easy because, unlike English, it is pronounced phonetically. You only have to know that there are ten different ways to pronounce the English word ending 'ough' to get the thinking behind this. But Finnish is a language that I'm sure was invented by Venusians or by someone seriously under the influence of psychotropic drugs. I challenge anyone to find words such as *itsestäänselvyys* (truism), *salamyhkäisyys* (mysteriousness), *viihdekirjallisuus* (light reading), *pääsisäänkaynti* (main entrance) or *yllytyshullu* (toy) easy to pronounce. Just attempt to phonetically wrap your mouth around those words without biting your own tongue off or loosening a few teeth!

Winter in Finland for a Sydneysider who has seen snow perhaps four or five times in her life is something else! Of course, the year we arrived Scandinavia had one of its coldest winters ever, with the Baltic Sea freezing all the way to Norway for the first time in forty-eight years. The ice in some places was over two metres thick. I will never forget my terror at driving during a blizzard for the first time, although by the end of winter I was complacently fanging around like I was born to it.

I always thought I didn't mind frigid weather, but it does get just the teensiest bit tiresome when every time you walk out the door you have to spend twenty minutes putting on your layers, and this is just to walk to your letterbox! The ice-cream man comes down the street in his van every fortnight, even in winter (work that out), but you haven't got a hope in hell of getting your boots, jacket, scarf and gloves on before he disappears down the street in a puff of exhaust. I still don't understand how people can be out in the street at night when it's well below freezing drinking alcohol. The mere thought of chugging something cold down my throat when I feel like a polar popsicle just leaves me, well, cold!

Once during winter, on a day when it was –21°C, I went for a loooong walk with Julie (American) and Sylvia (English), two friends I'd met through the British Women's Association. I don't believe I have ever been so cold or so miserable in my life. You know the kind of cold I am talking about: the kind that has your nose streaming, then the snot dries hard on your woollen scarf and scratches your face to pieces. The kind where you think your toes have frozen off and departed company from your feet. The kind where your facial muscles are so numb you can no longer talk sensibly. At the end of the walk we stopped at a café; my hands were so deficient of sensation I literally couldn't make them work. I peeled my scarf off my face and tried to order coffee, but they couldn't understand me because I couldn't speak coherently. I tried to open my purse to pay but I couldn't get my fingers to prise the money out. Thus, during the simple act of an after-exercise coffee, I managed to both look like an utter moron and sound like a babbling ninny. No bloody wonder Finns give expats odd glances!

I did, however, manage to learn some valuable life lessons for surviving winter along the way:

1. *Don't* drive too close behind other cars because the studs from their winter tyres just might come pinging off and put *big* chips in your windscreen.

2. *Immediately* wipe off any water that gets between the car doors and the frames after you go through the car wash. Water freezes at zero, dummy, and the doors will *freeze shut*, preventing you from exiting the car in the normal manner.

3. Put the winter tyres on *before* the advertised date of 1 November. If you don't, and you get caught in an early blizzard before that date with your non-grip summer tyres still on, *don't* expect to be stopping at any red lights or for any pedestrians. Wheeee!

4. Put the anti-freeze in the window washer bottle *before* the temperature drops below zero. C'mon, use your brain! It snows, then it turns to slush, your windscreen gets filthy and needs washing every five minutes and it is *very difficult* to do this when the water is frozen in the hose!

5. Standing around at Meadowbank Park in Sydney at 7 pm in the middle of winter watching your son at soccer training is *not* cold. Standing around the harbour in Helsinki on New Year's Eve when it's -25°C, now that's cold. Really cold. Really, *really* cold. Really ... okay, you get the picture.

6. Further to the last point, *don't* fool yourself into believing even for one second that you can just duck out to the local supermarket to grab bread and milk when it's -18°C wearing only a thin jumper and no jacket, gloves or hat. You *will* freeze your tits off on the two-minute drive to the shop. Trust me on this one.

7. Check *before* you go tearing out of the house at 3.15 pm for the fifteen-minute drive to school to pick up the kids, who get out at 3.20, that the front-end loader hasn't been down your street earlier in the day clearing the snow and dumped a one-metre wall of rock-hard, icy snow right across your driveway. Although, having said that, this sort of experience is very useful for testing out the four-wheel-drive capabilities of the company Peugeot.

8. Despite manufacturer's claims about how much grip your boots have, *don't* walk up (or down for that matter) a steep street that is

covered in black ice and expect to retain any shred of dignity whatsoever. Anyone slipping over and thumping down on their arse in the middle of the street looks like a complete idiot and *must* expect to be laughed at.

After we had been here for a few months, after we had struggled to deal with unco-operative bureaucrats, the language problems and buying food in the supermarket, we laughed when we read something on the internet. One American was questioning another American on what it was like living in Finland, asking advice about taxation laws, buying a car and whether or not he could get American football on TV. The reply? 'It's life, Jim, but not as we know it.' Never before were truer words spoken.

At the international school my children go to they are both in classes consisting of twelve students, so if you don't find a friend in the class it makes for a lonely existence. Michael loves it here and would happily extend his contract (aaarrgghhh!). Ben, my tranquil but quirky child, has been fairly stoic about the whole experience. However, the dearth of friends has meant he has spent far too long in front of the computer, often into the wee small hours (on the weekends only I hasten to add). I went into his bedroom one afternoon at 2 pm to ask him if he was planning on getting up at all that day. He was fast asleep, but he quickly sat up and said: 'It's on my to-do list!' then promptly lay down again and went back to sleep. Eden, my capricious but wickedly humorous first born, will miss precious little about FF. I have trouble thinking of this country as anything other than FF, because when we told the kids we were expatriating here Eden, always shy about letting others know how she's feeling, said: 'I'm not moving to fucking Finland!' Out of the mouth of babes.

I will miss Finland when the time comes to return home. I will miss meeting witty, intelligent women from all around the world. I will miss the glorious riot of colours as the leaves begin to turn in autumn. I will miss standing on the ferry to Estonia or Sweden in the middle of winter and watching it plough through solid ice. I will miss hiking in the forest while the snow falls gently on my face. I will miss walking on the frozen Baltic Sea out to an island and back again. I will miss finding baby hedgehogs in my garden with the first flush of spring. I will miss sitting at the outdoor table of a café in summer drinking beer and watching the world pass me by.

If nothing else, I have learnt the quintessentially Finnish art of being silent, by no means a bad thing. Thank you, Finland.

Lisa Foulis had, prior to expatriating to Finland, spent her entire life living in Sydney. She worked in publishing, now, due to the lack of a work permit, Lisa is a tennis-playing, lunch-taking, book-reading kept woman. Even after extensive travels, she still considers Australia to be the best country in the world in which to live.

Expat in trouble

I knew things had taken a turn for the worse when I awoke with multiple fractures and an armed guard sitting beside my bed. One eye was welded closed. Through a small sliver of vision I could see a leg with full-length bandaging slung from a hoist, a spaghetti junction of tubes where my knee used to be, a sling-held arm lying on my chest and a Second World War issue wooden rifle looming over my shoulder.

My first instinct was to turn to the uniformed sentry seated beside my bed and ask him if he knew what had happened, where I was and would I be walking again anytime soon. This turned out to be a mistake on two fronts; firstly, turning my head delivered a cattle-prod jolt of pain through my head (broken collar bone I would later learn) and secondly, the noble sentinel was snoring fitfully and salivating on the edge of my pillow.

I took the only option available and passed out.

Until now, my eighteen months in Dubai had been little short of perfect. As an ambitious but very junior journalist I'd escaped the clutches of a suburban in-your-letterbox newspaper and landed a job with an English-language daily in the Middle East.

While living in Perth, I'd traversed the Nullarbor by plane, coach and hitchhiker's perseverance in the quest for a job with a national daily but to no avail. My lucky break came courtesy of an ad sales girl at my suburban newspaper, the *Midland and Kalamunda Echo*, who scored a job as an air hostess with Emirates Airlines.

Community newspapers had been a valuable learning experience but I was beginning to dread the prospect of looking for a news angle at school fetes from here to retirement. Living in a one newspaper city, my chances of a call-up to a major daily were beginning to look as remote as my long-awaited call-up to the Australian cricket team.

It was with all the forlorn hope of schoolboy looking for 20 cents in a public telephone change-slot that I half-heartedly asked the Dubai-bound Vanessa from sales if she would be so kind as to fax my resume to newspapers around the world as she travelled. It was a long shot.

A year of Wednesday nights taking notes at shire council meetings later, I received an unexpected telephone call. The accent on the other end of the line sounded as if it knew its way around Oxford. The accent said it was calling from Dubai in the United Arab Emirates and wanted to know if I was still interested in a reporter's position with *The Gulf News*. The *What News*? From the Union of Associated Arabs? Where? Of course I was interested.

Six months down the track from this conversation with Francis Matthew, editor of *The Gulf News*, and another three-day hike across the Nullarbor to meet him for an interview, I had at last grasped my job with a daily broadsheet. Long Shot had come in by a nose.

Based on my television-derived insight into the Middle East, I spent the months ahead preparing, at the age of 27, for a life of abstinence, chastity and hard work. It therefore came as something of a shock to find myself, in March 1998, living in a version of Utopia seemingly dreamt up by drunken twenty-something town planners with a wicked sense of humour. It was the Middle East—but not as we know it.

My job seemingly entailed covering an endless procession of desert trips, dhow cruises and promotional product launches with free cocktails. My income was tax-free. The nightlife (lack of drugs notwithstanding) was unparalleled. The sun shone year-round. The beaches were long and white. The population was diverse, colourful and full of great cooks. All the expat males seemed to be in their mid-twenties and in positions of seniority they could not aspire to in a Sydney, London or New York head office.

And the Western women, almost all whom bore no grudge at the label 'trolley dolly', had been screened by the airlines prior to arrival to ensure they were young and attractive.

I was in the air hostess capital of the world where a highway stretched as far as a horse could run, lined with towers housing hundreds of sexy, international single girls living abroad for the first time. I was also the owner of a 5.0 litre soft-top 4WD Jeep Wrangler, drinking copiously and complacent. I was happy.

The United Arab Emirates (UAE) is a federation of seven ancient emirates wedged between the vast dunes that is the Empty Quarter of Saudi Arabia to the west and the Arabian Gulf to the east. Iraq is a Scud missile's journey to the north. The lesser sheikhdoms comprising the UAE, namely Fujairah, Umm al Qawain, Ras al-Khaimah and Ajman, survive on relatively meagre oil royalties and bear more physical resemblance to outback Australian towns than they do to the glistening architectural delights of Dubai, Abu Dhabi and, to a lesser extent, Sharjah.

Fifty years ago, before oil exploration began, Dubai, part of the Trucial Coast as it was then known, had no hospitals, schools, bridges, deep harbours or buildings standing more than a few storeys. Today, it is home to six-lane highways, the world's only seven-star hotel and the most astonishing water fun park ever conceived. Three world-class golf courses have miraculously sprouted in the desert, one of which is fully illuminated for a night-time round.

Dubai, more than anywhere else in the country, or indeed the whole of the region, is the decadent millionaire with new money. It is has all the brashness (and class) of Beckham and Posh and their purple wedding throne.

Barely a day goes by when it isn't courting the tabloids—spectacularly staged world record attempts being the favoured method of saying, 'look at me'. Dubai lays claim to such honourable world records as world's longest gold chain (in honour of its magisterial gold souk), the most Roll Royces ever given away in a raffle (in recognition of its status as a filthy rich oil kingdom) and, my favourite, the world's longest sofa (apropos to nothing I can think of).

But like any superstar courting media attention, things occasionally go wrong. Like the (inaugural?) world record attempt for the planet's longest cake. As the kilometre-long cream sponge curdled under the unrelenting afternoon sun, a rumour begun to circulate among the five-deep throng of Pakistani and Indian labourer onlookers restrained behind police barricades. The prospect of sponge cake was already close to irresistible for the salivating masses. When word got out that the keys to a new Mercedes were hidden in one of the slices, it was pandemonium.

The barricades were toppled and hundreds of men launched headlong into the failed record attempt. Tables toppled, icing flew, sponge was sifted through thousands of fingers and police batons came crashing down. No key was found. And nor did my story on the debacle appear in next day's edition of *The Gulf News*. Unlike Beckham and Posh, the UAE didn't just court the media—it controlled it.

As far as the government was concerned, Dubai was near enough to perfect and the media should focus on the great achievements and events of the city state (the Summer Shopping Festival, dental care and a captive breeding programme for Arabian leopards). It should not mention AIDS, institutionalised racism, 12-year-old locals driving and crashing high-powered 4WDs on the roads, or kidnapped five-year-old Bangladeshi children strapped to the back of racing camels. These were mirages that officially did not exist.

For most, however, the blanket ban on media coverage of anything negative only added to the allure of the place. Anything bad that happened (like the scores of Indian labourers transported in a locked cattle truck— nothing new in itself—being asphyxiated when drums of toxic industrial adhesive stored in the same cabin-cum-coffin toppled onto them) became part of the mysterious believe-it-or-not folklore to be joked about over a pint. And there were plenty of pints.

Life away from work, or mine at least, revolved around Fridays (for many, the only weekend day off), Thursday nights, beach clubs, frigid airconditioned cinemas where local youths in their all-white dish-dash (tunic) would to talk to their friend in the third row on their mobile phone, shopping centres selling everything from Iranian sweets to Bentley motor cars, 20 cent street kebabs, lavish five-star dining (at a reasonable price!), all manner of land and water sports, camping and four-wheel driving in the desert, furtive appointments with my Indian whiskey bootlegger and watching the very occasional public execution. (The hundreds of bars, pubs and nightclubs, all attached to an accommodation hotel, sold liquor freely. Takeaways were bought at one nondescript official, non-signposted outlet in Dubai (called **MMI**). Each Westerner had a ration book and monthly allowance for alcohol purchases based on his or her income.)

But like any good movie plot, paradise came with a twist. It is a thin veneer separating the comfortable existence of all expats from a script reading more like *Midnight Express* than *Blue Lagoon*. There are myriad ways the unsuspecting outsider can slip through the cracks and descend into a legal system fraught with inconsistencies, bias and often incomprehensible rationale and severity.

Dubai is a city that has acquired its riches and grown so fast, it resembles many youthful superstars—flashy, impressive, and stunningly good-looking on the one hand; superficial, immature and ignorant on the other. It has built an awe-inspiring infrastructure and established itself as a financial centre of the Middle East that will outlast the importance of its rapidly diminishing reserves of oil. It is developing from the top down and has yet to mature in many ways.

The legal system broadly determines the outcome of most cases on the basis of a racial hierarchy. Indian and Pakistani labourers make up no less than 85 percent of the UAE population but in the eyes of the 5 to 10 percent of the populace with a UAE passport, they merely form the amorphous backdrop to a life of luxury. Legally, these workers are at the bottom of the pecking order, subject to vague labour laws that allow for exploitation. Above them are the Western expatriates. Next are other Arab nationalities and at the top of the tree, the UAE locals.

If an Indian has an accident with an Omani for example, the Omani usually prevails in court. A Westerner with a Pakistani, the Westerner wins, a Jordanian with a local, the local emerges on top, and so on.

Crucially, the system also operates on the premise that somebody has to pay when something goes wrong. Should you be driving along one of the expansive highways and happen to be the car under the bridge when some hapless soul decides to jump from it, you're in trouble. Irrespective of fault, the driver is liable to pay *diya* (blood money), to the family of the deceased because fate dictated that the driver killed the bridge-jumper. The non-negotiable amount was recently increased to AUD$85,000 (UAE dirham 200,000). Failure to pay can mean jail until the money is found. It is even rumoured that some opportunistic suicidals target their final jump to land on a late model Mercedes, BMW or similar.

Drugs are the nemesis of the legal fraternity and sentences for possession of even minute amounts of cannabis or hashish result in a minimum jail sentence of four years. The tough stance on drugs is well publicised and their usage subsequently minimal. But what is not so widely known is that a recreational bong or leisurely joint smoked by the holidaying expat back in their own country can result in a very bad trip indeed. Should you return to the UAE, and for whatever reason be subjected to a blood test (as a result of a car accident for example), the detection of drugs in the blood is an automatic four-year reservation in the city's harsh prison.

As a reporter, I had cause to visit Dubai's prison several times. It is no correctional facility. There is no airconditioning throughout summers that simmer in the mid to high forties, there is little or no recreation, bar a baking sand pit with a torn fishing net feigning as a volleyball net. The food consists of a watery camel soup and some camel pieces. For the monthly prison visits, visitors are corralled into a birdcage-like structure. A giant tarpaulin screen and a two-metre moat of concrete and wire mesh divide the visitors from the inmates on two of the birdcage's four sides. When the screen is lifted, loved ones jostle for position and a screaming match ensues as each person tries to make themselves heard for the next 12 minutes over the scores of others. As the tarpaulin descends when time is up, men inch lower to the ground, eventually lying prostrate on the ground as they shout their last words to each other.

It was in these circumstances I met a 25-year-old American from Louisiana. I'd written stories on the law regarding drugs and as a result he had written to me to seek publicity for his case back in the US. He had crashed a motorcycle, awoken in hospital under armed guard (a situation I would later relate to personally) and been blood tested. Two weeks earlier he had smoked a joint with his mates back in the States during his annual vacation.

As the screen began its morbid descent during my final visit, his last words to me across what might as well have been a million miles of concrete were, 'You've gotta do something. I've been in here two years, man. I'm just a fucking engineer'. He served another two.

Serious car accidents have their own distinctive smell. It's a kind of metallic aftertaste with an disturbing mixture of overheated radiator steam and the coppery trace of blood. The fear and underlying panic also seem to settle on the olfactory sensors. The smell is the enduring memory I have of the head-on collision that changed my perspective on life in general and Dubai in particular.

It was a school night so I had opted, on this rare occasion, to stay in and catch up on some sleep. My friends, always susceptible to a quiet lager shandy on a hot day, had other ideas and rang me at midnight to join the birthday celebrations of good friend and Australian 'trolley dolly', Mehernaz. My late start to the evening ensured that by the time I got to the watering hole known as Rockbottoms (it wasn't quite, but you could see it from there), the gang were well-enough acclimatised that I was never going to catch them up. I opted to go Skipper for the evening and nursed a pint of Guinness while the others installed tomorrow's hangovers.

Clambering into the Jeep that night was Mehernaz and Samantha, a sharp-witted Emirates duo, and a young professional lad named Chris. With the top down, we made our way to the main bridge crossing The Creek, uniting the old side of town known as Deira with the flashier side known as Bur Dubai.

There's every chance the detour signs were once in place, but by early am they had long since been knocked down. It thus came as quite a shock, having taken my usual entry ramp onto the bridge, to see two headlights bearing down on us. In the collision that ensued seconds later, the front end of the Jeep Wrangler was pushed into the front seat and the chassis snapped clean in half, with the girls in the back seat left staring down at us from a 45 degree angle. Well, they would have been staring had they been conscious.

Moments before the crash, both had been standing and holding the roll-bar while serenading the city with a rousing singalong. Now they were dangling limply, suspended by seatbelts clipped into place seconds before impact. They were lucky.

My recollections of the aftermath are of cries of 'I can't feel my legs' from my right, a frightening silence from behind and the gradual clamour of onlookers, mostly labourers, who eventually lifted me from the wreckage. An ambulance arrived at some point, reassurances were made that everyone was alive and then I awoke in hospital as my appointed guard slept with his head resting beside me.

Any temptation to grab his rifle and shoot my way out of the country was tempered by the inconvenience of a broken leg, broken arm, broken collar bone and broken nose. In the coming days, I would learn that my friends had suffered to a similar degree, with some 17 broken bones between us. The driver of the other car, an Iranian, escaped with a broken foot—a small victory for the Range Rover.

As a humble reporter on a local paper, my medical insurance was not what it might have been and so, as the others were transferred to more salubrious wards in modern hospitals, I remained in the Al Rashid Hospital, which after a few weeks would feel like Al Catraz Hospital. The various surgical procedures went well enough. But the after sales service was a little lacking.

Regular complaints about hospital nuances like unrecognisable foodstuffs applied here as much as in any other hospital in the world. But shower time best encapsulated the ambience of the hospital. At sunrise (the first of the days five prayer times), I was lifted from bed and lowered into an early prototype wheelchair, while a fence picket wedged under my bum supported the length of my shattered leg.

I was wheeled into a grimy shower recess and took my place in the assembly line of infirm, industrial and car accident victims (the latter of which there was no shortage, with the UAE at the time boasting the highest per capita road toll in the world). Like strapped and bound offenders facing the firing squad, we winced involuntarily as the shooting started. The fire extinguisher wheel was cranked open and the line-up was blasted with a fire hose torrent of cold water. Eventually, the escape from Al Catraz was made.

Months of painful physiotherapy followed. Physio was hard work but something more gruelling lay ahead. Court beckoned. My case was flimsy, my legal team flimsier. Australians also ranked below Iranians on the legal league ladder.

From the start, any similarity between the court's version of events and reality was tenuous. The police presented drawings that revealed two cars had side-swiped each other before crashing into railings on the bridge. Closer examination of the evidence, namely two cars with their windshields touching and sides unscratched, might have revealed otherwise. I didn't complain, with this scenario striking me as easier to defend in court than driving up a one-way street the wrong way.

The real hurdle in my mind was the blood alcohol reading of 0.02 my pint of Guinness had elicited. Below the legal limit in almost any other country (it was then .08 in my home town Perth and .05 in the eastern states), it was an unknown quantity here. Alcohol legally did not exist and therefore drink driving was a legal impossibility—or so my defence had assured me.

What really happened in the court room I'll never fully know, the proceedings being conducted in Arabic. Each week I would go through the imaginary version of the accident with a scholarly English-speaking local lawyer who cashed a sizeable portion of my modest monthly salary. Each time I appeared in court, my knowledgeable Armani-clad lawyer was absent (probably on the yacht I was funding). In his place was a slovenly, obese behemoth with no English, ill-fitting robes and acute narcolepsy.

His ability to sleep and drool at the same time was as scary as his rapport with the judge. My Arabic skills were limited to little more than counting to ten but it didn't take a firm grasp of the language to see that he was making a very ordinary impression on the man who would decide whether I spent an extended spell in prison. The judge made Arabic sound as mellifluous as French poetry when he addressed the Iranian's legal team. Addressing my inept ogre, he dug deep to deliver a guttural version of the language that made my healthy leg tremble.

For six months my passport was held by the police and my court case repeatedly adjourned. For each appearance in court, I had to pack my toothbrush in case today was the day sentence was handed down. The Australian in trouble overseas is quickly made aware that the consulate will not be providing a SWAT team to storm the courthouse perimeter and come to the rescue. Whenever I went to court, a consular representative attended. But aside from being a passive onlooker, there was little they did, or could do.

The final verdict came as a complete surprise. For six months I had been making regular appearances in court and not once had I been asked my version of events or asked to produce witnesses to the fateful February night. The Iranian on the other hand had made frequent approaches to the bench and enjoyed a certain geniality with the judge. I simply limped in, took a seat next to Humpty Dumpty, endured the occasional head-shake and look of contempt from the judge and gripped my toothbrush till my fingers went numb.

It became clear I was never going to expound my 'sideswipe defence', complete with the police drawings as supporting evidence. The day did finally arrive when I had to approach the judge but it was only to hear him deliver his verdict—in Arabic. I stood non-plussed as he growled at me with obvious disapproval. My firm grasp of numerals was causing heart palpitations. 'Arabic Arabic, Arabic Arabic Arabic (nine) Arabic Arabic,' said the judge. 'Nine years, nine lashes, nine consecutive life sentences?' I pondered.

When it became clear I hadn't resumed my seat, collapsed or done whatever I was expected to do at the end of his tirade, the judge addressed the packed gallery. An Indian labourer volunteered his services and provided the first translation of proceedings in six months. 'It would be easy to jail you for a year,' the Indian gentleman told me without any obvious sign of malice. 'But in finding you guilty I shall demand you pay a fine of 19,000 dirhams' (or a few months salary), he said.

It was over. Everyone had survived the accident, the injuries were healing, friendships that could have deteriorated had grown stronger and we could all move on. But the Indian gentleman had other ideas. Approached by my lawyer to interpret for him, he said: 'Congratulations, no jail is very good news'. I couldn't work out why it didn't sound like it was coming from Humpty, who for the first time looked almost fully awake. Maybe his joy was lost in the translation. 'Now we must begin to prepare for the civil case', the interpreter informed me.

Civil case?

'Yes, civil case' he continued, reading my mind. 'I am very confident that should there be a civil case we can keep the costs to a bare minimum.'

It was time to try my hand as an expat in London.

Craig Francis grew up in Kwinana and has worked as a journalist in Collie, Perth, Dubai and London before moving to Hong Kong where he is now the online editor with CNN International. His wife, Lisa, has enjoyed and endured, in equal amounts, the lifestyle of the nomadic expatriate Australian. They have a baby boy, Tom.

NARROWBOATS

If you must live in England, then you may as well try to live somewhere special and enjoy your home because, with the vagaries of the English weather, you are likely to be spending some time in it. People often shout at me when I'm in my home, imaginative things like 'Hey Aussie!' If some sporting event in which Australia is inclined to annihilate the competition is on, the hailings may be a little longer, though probably no more articulate. The people shouting might be sitting outside a pub, or just walking along, but they are always cheerful. That may be because my home, 15 tons of steel, 50ft long and 6ft 10in wide, is cheerfully painted, or it may have something to do with the 3ft x 5ft Australian flag that I fly.

If, for whatever reason, you find yourself living in England, and you don't feel you can cope with poky English houses with their peculiar plumbing and piddling showers or, worse still, furnished (in the loosest term) rented flats, why not get yourself a narrowboat.

I'm in for the duration so I bought mine. But you can rent them. You can find them for rent on websites, through brokers or in the classifieds at the back of the magazines for canal boaters. You could get a 70-footer and share it (and the rent) with your mates, and you can moor it right in the centre of all the major cities, or right out in the countryside. And, providing you have remembered to fill the water tank, you can enjoy power showers to your heart's content because the boats' water systems are pressurised. I bought mine as a bare shell, and am fitting it out myself. I thought six months would do it. The canal population, however, which is unique in the realms of English neighbourhoods in that they are friendly, welcoming and helpful people, fell about laughing. So in truth I'm looking at a six-year project. I hope.

Some say I'm not a regular Aussie because I don't sound like one and because I have spent relatively few years of my life there. But, since leaving Australia at the age of eight on my parent's 'Australian Citizen/ British Subject' passport (as it then was), I have resolutely only ever had an Australian one, though never one issued in Australia itself. Over the years this has meant standing in line and paying through the nose for a French visa, and standing up to an English husband who simply could not understand why I persisted with this nonsense, when I ought to have grabbed the chance to have one belonging to the imperial masters of the world. But this document tells me who I am. It reminds me that my family has been continuously born in Australia since the first member of the first branch arrived in 1812.

I'm not the only Australian making the best of living in England in this way. There are a number of us and our boats are often identifiable. Many fly the flag; suspect a boat painted in a green and gold livery, or more obviously, bearing the name Wombat or Uluru. Indeed, it was an Australian who introduced me to this way of life. That was when I was still Private Secretary to the Dean of Windsor, Senior Domestic Chaplain and confidant to the Queen. At that time I was still firmly ensconced in the goings-on within the walls of Windsor Castle and a world away from where I am now. And I wouldn't trade this one for that again. My friends had just bought a little second-hand narrowboat, cosy for the two of them but magical. They got a bigger one as their family increased in number, then with regret moved ashore when the lure of the canal waters on the other side of the gunnel began to intrigue their toddlers. Not that this ever worried the families that lived and worked on these canals from the nineteenth century right into the 1960s, raising huge families in tiny one-room cabins at the back end of their cargo carrying barges.

My own family, however, was shrinking. Having cruelly ripped an English rose of a husband away from his roots and off to Dubai for ten years, he decided that, actually, the expat lifestyle suited him, and took himself off again, leaving me to co-ordinate our daughter's doctors and care workers in London. She lives independently now, but it will be a while before I can relinquish my need to stand in her corner to shout a bit and push her case from time to time on her behalf.

It was about that time I felt a sense of being trapped, and not just by the massive walls of Windsor Castle. So at the age of 45 I enrolled at the University of London. Two degrees later I was a more relaxed self on the canals that stretch across the countryside for 2000 miles, should I care to explore the full extent of them, earning a living as a Punch and Judy 'professor'.

The boat helps me feel that my time here is not permanent. Not that that was an issue I identified, until I returned to Australia in 2000, for the first time in 36 years, and was bowled over by the country, my own country. Only on the narrow canals in England, I realised, do you find the same sort of helpful, delightful, friendly and humorous people that I found up and down the entire east coast of Australia.

I have just started continuous cruising. That means that I no longer have a permanent home mooring. It means that I no longer have plug-in electricity, a land telephone line, localised sewage disposal, and water and diesel to hand. I no longer have the security of a private towpath and lock-up car park. Or regular neighbours to walk to the pub with on a Friday evening or for Tuesday quiz night, or muck-in barbecues.

It also means no mooring fees. The deal with British Waterways, the governing body, is that you can stay for free almost anywhere for two weeks, then move on about ten lock-miles. Locks and regular miles added together give you lock-miles. And at that rate it would take about twelve years to cover the whole of the canal system. It means taking the boat to the pub and mooring right outside. Which means not having to walk home afterwards. It means being spoilt for choice of pubs because there are so very many of them. Entrepreneurial publicans built them in the nineteenth century, at very regular intervals, in the path of the canals to refresh the Irish navigators or navvies who were digging them. It means taking the boat right up to one of the many sanitary stations provided, instead of trundling along the towpath with a 20+ litre cassette in a wheelbarrow. Besides, it's still legal, in an emergency, to dig a hole in the countryside and bury the processed workings of your inner self. There are even more points for fresh water. Then there are the supermarket chains that are snapping up derelict canalside industrial sites to build their out-of-town monoliths; they have discovered that restoring the quays not only attracts canal boaters to stop and shop, but the boats also provide an attraction for townies to come and indulge in a little nostalgia, and while they're about it, do the week's shopping before going home to their little houses and rented flats. Anyway, I've just had a phone call, there's a barbecue on Wednesday in Northolt; that's less than two hours by boat from here, I can pull up alongside and stay over in my own home; difficult to beat that for convenience.

Continuous cruising means a whole heap of neighbours, transitory ones, some moving in the same general direction, some backwards and forwards, our paths crossing from time to time. And each time you meet again it's like meeting up with an old friend; maybe you saw them just last week, or it may have been two years ago. And if, for some astonishingly unlikely reason, you should find yourself with a dud neighbour, you simple slip your mooring pins and move on. There's the retired couple on their two boats, his and hers, his an historic boat that he has spent fifteen years restoring from a wreck; there's the young BBC documentary maker, a tree surgeon, two joiners, plying their trade; a classical violinist, an IT consultant, a taxi driver, a travel writer. There's the chap recovering from cancer. There's the Irish couple, I'm not sure what they do apart from produce children, nine at the last count, all welded into their little life jackets and bouncing about the boat with a sure-footedness unimaginable for a land-based child.

Next week I rendezvous with the fuel barges, a pair of boats still working in the old way, with the traditional 'motor' and its engineless butty. The husband and wife team sell 'red' (tax-concessioned) diesel and coal, and live in two tiny cabins, just as in years gone by. These days meeting up is less haphazard—we liaise by text message. Last week an incredulous television journalist reported from a quarry which, because of its location next to the Grand Union, has decided to move its gravel by canal. It's a slower method of transportation, though immaterial to this non-urgent load, but more importantly, one work-boat will carry the equivalent of 47 lorry loads. In anyone's terms, that's a phenomenal saving in fuel, road space and environmental impact.

I'm moored in West London at the moment, at the end of Ladbroke Grove, right by the famous Portobello Road in Notting Hill. I tucked myself in between a load of other narrowboats, close by a pair of defunct gasometers. The skeletal Victorian steel-work outlined against a thundery sky was an astonishingly beautiful reminder of the industrial era, when the canals were the epitome of efficient heavy duty transportation. Cycling back along the towpath with the Sunday papers a couple of days later, I realised that both gasometers were very much full. When did that happen? Though fascinating to observe them decreasing as Notting Hill cooked its Sunday roasts, not being a fan of gas appliances, I probably won't hang around here for much longer. There are plenty of other places where I can pull up for blackberries and hazelnuts, both just now coming into fruit. Just two of the seasonal goodies within arm's reach of the boat, all along the canal side.

Of course, you mustn't mind being able to stretch out and touch both sides of your home in one reach. On a 50ft boat, my living accommodation measures just 35ft x 6ft. But though small, it doesn't equate to a poky flat in any way. For a start, I'm surrounded by open space, above and all around. The canals may run right though England's industrial heartlands and city centres, but they are buffered all along by trees and hedgerows, green lungs to filter out the sounds of the city and its choking carbon monoxide. Exit the London underground, round a corner, and disappear down into the cut. Down there, just a few steps from the hustle and bustle, you can sit out on deck with a sundowner, listening to the extraordinary range of the blackbird singing his heart out from a vantage point in the treetops; watch for the turquoise flash of the kingfisher swooping low beneath the overhanging branches, spend hours mesmerised by the stealthy fishing technique of the heron, and feel chuffed when you find you can hold your breath for as long as the cormorant. Right in the heart of London. Anyway, a small home means less housekeeping.

Though not maintenance. Naturally enough, not even the canals offer a free lunch. Here we are dealing with two elements that are not compatible: steel and water. Depending on the means by which you separate these two elements, the boat will need to come out of the water every couple of years or so for the bottom to be cleaned down and reblacked. Incidentally, narrowboats have bottoms; they have tops and roofs, sides, left and right, fronts and backs, and they are tied to their moorings with ropes. This, of course, is immensely helpful for non-boaties and immensely embarrassing for yachtie types who will get used to being giggled at if their boats have port sides and starboards, bows and sterns, and are tied up with sheets and painters.

A little flat? I think not. I would much prefer to be woken in the morning by the sound of a swan scraping the algae from my hull, than by the sound of rush hour traffic. If you have to live in England, this is an extraordinary way to go about it.

In an ideal world, I will find a way of earning a part-time living in Australia, preferably in that wondrous mountain forest area on the southern Queensland border that I discovered for the first time in 2000. The ideal arrangement would be splitting my year between there and my delightful UK home, until such time as my daughter is confidant enough to let me introduce her to the land of her ancestors. In the meantime, my son is getting married in Jamaica in November. The boat will go into a boatyard, where there will be people around to keep an eye on it. And I shall relax and enjoy the wedding, unlike my bricks and mortar-owning friends whose holidays and even weekends away are fraught by the threat of squatters.

Stephanie Fuger was born in Melbourne and moved to Switzerland with her family when she was eight. She returned to finish school in Melbourne before moving to Beirut via Switzerland. After hitchhiking across Europe, she settled in England, long enough to establish her own family, before moving to the Middle East for ten years. She began studies at the University of London in 1993 and completed a first class honours degree in Drama and Theatre Studies and a Masters in Media Arts. She now combines family and travel with Punch & Judy performances, reflexology, and thinking about writing.

GUIDED BY THE SOUTHERN CROSS

Here I am, a landlubber by birth, sitting at the helm of a fourteen metre catamaran and staring at an unbroken 360 degree view of the Pacific Ocean. After nearly twelve months at sea we have traversed half the globe, and are only months away from home—the Great South Land. Having lived abroad for over twenty years it seems appropriate to be taking a circuitous route home. Long trips at sea provide abundant time for reflection. During the past year many hours have been spent ruminating on such matters as the similarities between an ocean and the desert, or one's kinship with unknown ancestors who also crossed these oceans on their journey out to Sydney during the 19th century. My thoughts turn now to life as an expat Australian: how did I get where I am (wherever that may be) and how did my Australian roots help me along the way?

It all started in 1980 while sitting on the back of a horse in the Moonbi Ranges, between Armidale and Tamworth in New South Wales. Cattle prices had slumped by two cents per kilo on the very day we had taken our first load to the market. Robert, my husband at the time, and I were managing a property for a friend while he was taking an extended overseas trip with his family. I was not looking forward to the phone call I would have to make that night advising him of the price we had received for his cattle. However, when the moment arrived, I was surprised to discover that he was barely perturbed—he had hedged his cattle on the futures market. Not only did I have no idea what he was talking about, but neither could I have guessed how the futures market was to become the stepping stone to life as an expat, and the platform that shaped my own future.

Upon our friend's return from abroad both Robert and I found jobs in the futures market in Sydney, but left Australia two years later to satiate Robert's travel bug. Ironically, I had not been too keen to travel at first, but more than twenty years later I am the one who has made my home abroad, whereas Robert returned to live in Sydney almost a decade ago.

Arriving in London in the summer of 1982 enabled me to secure a job quickly. It was just before the opening of the London International Financial Futures Exchange and the whole financial services industry was looking for experienced hands in that field. By 1986 I had moved to JP Morgan where I was to enjoy a fourteen year career, eventually moving to New York as Global Head of Futures and various other challenging and rewarding assignments.

Three factors contributing to this success can certainly be pinned on my Australian background: love of the outdoors, a self-deprecating sense of humour, and an ability to adapt. There are other reasons too, such as being in the right place at the right time and enjoying plenty of luck—perhaps better described as good fortune. Truly the most fortunate aspect of my life is having met, worked with, and lived among so many intelligent, interesting and wonderful people.

Had you asked me at the age of sixteen what I wanted to be, it would have had something to do with the outdoors. We were reared in the outdoors. This was partly because four energetic children growing up in a small three bedroom house (with no TV room—in fact, no TV!) were constantly being told by Mother Dear to 'Go and play outside'. Therefore, it came as something of a surprise to discover that, not only did I work in an office, but I loved it. This was possible because I had found a way to get outdoors every day. I became the bane of lunch-time traffic—a jogger.

Although an avid sportswoman from childhood, it was not until working in Sydney that I took up running in earnest. A happy discovery of the futures business in 1980 was that lunch hour actually meant one and a half hours as the Exchange conveniently closed from 12 noon to 1.30 pm daily. Along with some fellow traders, I began running in the Botanical Gardens each day. This established a pattern that continued until I quit working on Wall Street a couple of years ago.

Running in London took me up and down the Thames, weaving figures of eight around the bridges: Tower Bridge and Southwalk, or London and Waterloo. I also explored every corner of Hampstead Heath over the course of ten years. My job in London was a regional one wherein

I had to cover clients all over Europe. This meant many two day visits to practically every European capital over the course of about five years. I was determined to see more of them than simply the airport, the hotel and a few office blocks. Imagine going to Geneva and catching no more than a glimpse of the lake, to Basle and not seeing the river, or Budapest and not making it over the bridge to Castle Hill. By sneaking my running shoes into a corner of my overnight briefcase, the hour between dawn and breakfast was enjoyed hot-footing it around the canals of Amsterdam, past the little pissing cherub in Brussels, through Les Tuileries, along the Seine, trying to find the city centre of Luxembourg or discovering Frankfurt's green belt. Trips to Tokyo enabled me to follow the footsteps of many avid city runners there who circumnavigate the Imperial Palace—a gruelling run.

And so to New York. I pounded the pavements between Wall Street and Battery Park, up the East River one day and up the Hudson the next. The environs of the World Financial Centre had been given a facelift during the nineties and it became my favourite place to run: the expanse of the river, the ferries, the far shore of New Jersey, the Statue of Liberty and the fabulous New York City skyline. It was a wonderful way to stay fit and at the same time keep in touch with the great outdoors. I hated to run in a gym. That childhood in the outdoors commanded me to get outside and experience the weather, face the elements, breathe the air. The worst days were when it was below zero and the three day snow had formed ice all over the footpaths. It was so cold you could taste blood in your throat. The snow ploughs would cause mounds of ice to form on every corner so crossing a street became an obstacle course where you'd put in more practice for hurdles and high jumps than you would for running.

I cite running as a factor for success because getting outside every day, facing the elements and generating some endorphins made me feel so alive. It totally cleared the head. I always came back from a run with at least one or two problems solved, or some completely new idea that could not have been generated had I remained seated on the 42nd floor of an air-conditioned glass tower. Fitness and being in good shape were almost a side benefit.

Australians are renowned for their self-deprecating sense of humour. Without this, I would not have survived my very first job abroad. I was working in a London dealing room in The City—Mincing Lane to be exact.

This was the commodities end of town where the barrow boys eventually rose to prosperity in towers of concrete and glass of their own. I was the only female trader amongst a group of approximately thirty cockneys and a couple of toffs. The toffs and I got a hard time. They were greeted each morning with a chorus of 'wha wha wha' (this was meant to mimic the Etonian accent and required a double chin for additional visual effects) while I was usually greeted with 'G'day Sheila, where ya goin' today ... up ya gum tree?' I believe we can blame Rolf Harris for such supercilious banter. One day a sign appeared on the wall taking off the toffs. It read 'air hair lair'. If you say it slowly and lean on the last word you will get it. These endearingly jovial east enders (actually they were more likely to be from Kent or Essex than the East End) were the sharpest, wittiest, most irreverently fun-loving bunch I have ever had the pleasure to get to know. You know that within two minutes of a world catastrophe hitting the headlines at least five jokes will be circulating... that dealing room was an incubator for them. I can't relay any here as those I remember would offend at least someone. Nowadays, this lighthearted banter might be labelled 'sexual harassment' in some form, which is a shame as we had plenty of laughs. Letting off steam certainly helped to ease the tensions of a high pressure job. After all, I gave as good as I got (as any Aussie would do) and enjoyed it as all part of a highly intellectual game of wits. Now I recognise that we've all had to relinquish a little frivolity because some people, unfortunately, don't know where to draw the line.

Anyone who travels has to be adaptable. One of the things you have to adapt is your vocabulary—unless of course you don't mind constantly repeating yourself. If you say 'Where's the lift?' this will work in London but in New York you will be answered by a blank stare. Once you correct yourself to say 'elevator' you will be directed expeditiously. If you need a euphemism for 'toilet' then 'loo' works in London but until you discover 'rest rooms' in New York you will be squeezing your legs together for a long time. I quickly learned that saying I came from 'the bush' earned me incredulously blank stares, as if I had said 'cabbage patch' or something. Neither does 'almost in the outback but still this side of the black stump' help when you can't describe where the black stump is. Eventually I just said Sydney on the basis that, if ever I went back, that's where I would make my home.

The extent of these language differences came home to me after we had lived in America for a couple of years when my son and daughter—all of five and three years old respectively—explained to me that they spoke three languages: English, Australian and American. As teenagers, they have refined their languages further. Now their accents seem to change depending on which continent they are on.

As for me, at this stage I am simply confused. I can't remember in which country I am supposed to say 'tap' or 'faucet', or whether the accent I just heard was South African or North London. Is it in England they say 'papaya' instead of 'paw paw' or just in America? And where is it that they eat 'courgettes', or could it be 'aubergines', rather than zucchinis ... is an 'aubergine' an egg-plant and not a zucchini at all? But just to show how muddled you can become if you have been away from home too long, I recently lost $100 on a bet that the Southern Cross was not the Southern Cross. Worse still, the bet was with an Argentine who probably believes that the Argentines are the true antipodeans, and that the Southern Cross is theirs. They don't even have it on their flag! No matter how many times I've eaten humble pie it doesn't get any sweeter, but at least I don't get indigestion from it any more.

Adaptability is a Darwinian concept. His theory of evolution is often shortcut to 'survival of the fittest', which presents an erroneous impression that brawn succeeds over brain. Actually, he professed that 'fittest' meant an animal's ability to adapt, thus putting intellect on a higher pedestal than physical strength. Whichever way you interpret it, adaptability in New York definitely requires one's animal instincts to predominate. At the height of a typically humid and oppressively hot New York summer, I once became a wildebeest in a mad mob making our frantic way across the Downtown Serengeti. There I was, standing in the blazing sun outside the entrance to the subway, snorting and pawing the ground with a stiletto, heating up both inside and out. My ears, highly sensitised by the accumulation of jungle survival skills, pricked up at the first subterraneous rumble of a train approaching. Suddenly, the whole herd was in stampede as a mad rush ensued down the stairs, through the barricades and onto the train. I managed to wedge myself in between the closing doors, with my bag and left foot still on the outside of the carriage. All this is to avoid the heat on the subway platforms themselves, which, in summer, goes well over 100 degrees Fahrenheit.

Australians think New York is a dangerous city. I did too until I got to know it. Now I feel safer there than I do in London. We can give Rudy Giuliani some credit for that. A few years ago I nearly scuttled Rudy's statistics by almost becoming another victim of a mugging. Descending to the subway near Trinity Church, I suddenly saw a figure coming up the stairs with a hand extended in my direction and talking loudly at me. I thought the hand was about to grab me and I freaked. Screaming isn't my thing, so instead an incoherent sort of aarrggh sound started escaping from my mouth. All those day dreams about a karate-kick to the genitalia deserted me and I was left with this impotent aarrggh sound. Suddenly, I was close enough to look my assailant in the eye. At that moment I realized the figure was my sister who lives on a property in the mid-west of New South Wales! Admittedly she had been staying with me for a few weeks, and perhaps we had said we would meet somewhere near Trinity Church, but anyway, I bet I am the only person who was nearly mugged in New York by her own sister.

One thing I have not been able to adapt to is the fact that fruit is never in season—or, it is always in season, depending on how you look at it. In New York you can get anything you want any time of the year. It won't look ripe, it won't be juicy and whether it is labeled 'mango' or 'papaya' it will taste like styrofoam, but, no matter, you can get one. I do long for those sun-ripened peaches and nectarines we used to buy from the endearingly toothless Mr Lucky at his farm on the Macquarie River flats of Dubbo. If you dropped one, it would squelch into a sticky mess. In New York it will bounce right off the pavement, get run over by a limo, roll on down Second Avenue, and still look perfect.

We are now turning our sailing boat, *Tortuga,* north for a final fling in the Pacific islands before heading due west for the Australian coast. We're leaving Tonga behind, Fiji is ahead, and only two additional stops stand between us and the Great Barrier Reef. It's been quite a journey so far. We left France mid July 2001, cruised half the Mediterranean, crossed the Atlantic, the Caribbean, passed through the Panama Canal and into the Pacific.

So what's a landlubber from almost the outback but still this side of the black stump doing in the middle of the Pacific on a boat called *Tortuga?* *Tortuga* is Spanish for turtle, so named because half the crew, including my partner, Eduardo, is Argentine. Standing on the sideline of a soccer field in New England ensures you will meet an abundance of expats, peppered with South Americans. Thus, an antipodean connection was made between an Aussie and an Argentine, fuelled by rivalry on the world sports arena. We've had our ups and downs over women's hockey, where our girls won the gold in Sydney but subsequently lost the World Cup to the Argentines. As for rugby, we are both looking forward to the opener of the World Cup: Australia v. Argentina. Clashes on the soccer field have been restricted to our own progeny. Perhaps this is a good thing...

My Argentine turned out to have sailing in his genes, and an adventurous spirit as keen as my own. His friends (also Argentine) who are sailing with us are similarly endowed. Thus, an adventure began that has actively demonstrated to our children, who are enjoying the trip with us, one of life's most valuable lessons: not only can you dream big dreams, but you can make them come true too.

Our adventure will end when we sail through Sydney Heads in December 2003. What a moment that will be! We'll get there even if our navigation equipment fails. After all, there is at least one person on board who understands something about celestial navigation, and with the Southern Cross as our guide, where else would we end up?

Stephanie Hanbury-Brown (nee Newby) left Australia in 1982 and settled in London until 1991, when JP Morgan transferred her to New York. She has held various senior management positions at JP Morgan, including Global Head of the Futures Division, Head of International Private Banking, Chief Operating Officer of the Global Equities Division and Head of eCommerce. Although continuing to reside in Connecticut in the US, she stopped working full time in 2000 to spend more time enjoying her two children, Adam and Holly. Stephanie grew up in Bathurst, Berridale and Dubbo and received a BA from the University of Sydney.

MOIEN FROM A SMALL COUNTRY

'Where am I?' asked a bewildered American friend as she arrived at the airport in Luxembourg. In case you are feeling similarly confused, Luxembourg is a tiny country about the size and population of the ACT, wedged in between Belgium, France and Germany. The local language is Luxembourgish, which is a German dialect, and *'Moien'* means 'Hello'. The local children speak Luxembourgish in preschool, but primary school is mainly in German and they also start to learn French. High school is mostly in French, and the students begin to learn English. Luxembourg is a constitutional monarchy, with the Grand Duke Henri as the head of state.

I have now been living in Luxembourg for a year, but in some ways you could say the story began when I was fourteen. My high school in Canberra organised a month-long school trip to France and Germany. As I was learning French, I was billeted for two weeks with Frédéric's family in Strasbourg, in eastern France. After my visit, Frédéric and I continued to write occasional letters to practise our French and our English. It was after this trip that I became particularly interested in language. I first dreamed of becoming a diplomat because then I could live in different countries and learn different languages. I then considered becoming a teacher of English, but finally decided to train to be a speech and language therapist. After Frédéric finished his studies, he moved to Luxembourg to work as an accountant.

Like many young Australians, when I was 25 I decided to spend a year travelling around Europe in between doing temporary jobs as a speech and language therapist in the UK. Frédéric invited me to visit him in Luxembourg, and so after travelling in the Netherlands and Belgium, I found myself at Luxembourg railway station. I had no idea what Frédéric looked like now, but fortunately my huge blue backpack identified me. That was nearly five years ago.

Over the next weekend, Frédéric showed me all around Luxembourg city, and then I continued on my travels, and onto my next temporary job in the UK. Frédéric then invited me to spend Christmas with his family, and then at Easter we met again in Paris. Frédéric had never been to the UK, so in the summer he came to visit London and Scotland with me. Eventually we started going out.

Going out with someone who lives in a different country is somewhat tricky, but we met up for weekends at places somewhere between Luxembourg and the UK, such as Brussels, Paris and Bruges. I later obtained a job as a speech and language therapist based mainly in British schools, which gave me time off during the school holidays. This meant that every six weeks I came to visit Frédéric in Luxembourg. We had many long discussions about how we could live in the same city. I thought that it would be a brilliant idea if Frédéric applied for a transfer to London (or even better, to Sydney), but he was settled in Luxembourg where he enjoyed his work and lifestyle and had no desire to move. As he pointed out, I had been the one travelling around the world.

My dream had been to travel overseas for a year, and then go back to Australia and hopefully find a position as a clinical educator linked to a university, to become involved in training speech and language therapy students. Luxembourg was unlikely to provide this opportunity so I studied for a certificate to become qualified to teach English as a foreign language to adults, and then started applying for jobs in Luxembourg. Trying to obtain permission to live and work in Luxembourg was like an enormous obstacle course, where you had to collect innumerable pieces of paper, some of which were quite obscure, as well as a chest x-ray. I know now almost every government department, including the strangely named 'Ministry of the Middle Classes', which issues business permits. After three years of administrative hurdles, lost files, and having my initial application for a work permit refused, I finally received permission to live and work in Luxembourg.

Now I work as a freelance English teacher at a private language school. In the first week I learned that I would need to teach a course in 'Advanced English for Banking and Finance'. This was terrifying for someone whose money management consists of stuffing receipts and bank statements into an envelope called 'Money Stuff'. At the same time

I was also asked to drive to a course that was held on the outskirts of the city, and I panicked: 'But I've never driven on the right side of the road before!'. Nevertheless, I learned to drive on the right, and Frédéric helped me with the banking and finance terms so that at least I could give the correct answers to the students. After 'English for Banking' came the unexpected challenge of 'English for Hunting Wild Animals in Africa', when I was asked to teach an individual course for a man who wanted to become a hunting guide. I didn't even know that you were allowed to hunt animals in Africa, and I wasn't sure whether teaching him English meant I was putting endangered species at risk.

I have found that I really enjoy teaching English. It enables me to meet a whole range of people from many different cultures and backgrounds, and I enjoy the challenge of how to present language in such a way that it is easy to understand and so that people learn to communicate. I think I would now miss teaching if I returned to working full time as a speech and language therapist.

However, leaving my profession has been very difficult. My specialty was working with children, and I miss the regular contact with them. After six years I had achieved a relatively senior position, and I received double the salary that I do now. I now hope to work again as a speech and language therapist with English speaking children in Luxembourg, as there is a large British and American community here. Once again there are many administrative hurdles, but so far the Ministry for Education has accepted my Australian qualifications, the Ministry for Health has given me permission to practice, and the Social Security Department has given me a provider number. I'm now just waiting for the bureaucrats at the 'Ministry of the Middle Classes' to change my business permit.

So, what is it like living in Luxembourg? Sometimes I say that I experienced more culture shock when I spent two years living in Parkes in country NSW. At other times Luxembourg seems very unfamiliar.

The multilingual aspect of Luxembourg is fascinating. I marvel at the way many of the other teachers at the language school can speak at least five or six languages, and switch between them without thinking. Forty percent of people living in Luxembourg are foreigners, and so it is very cosmopolitan. Frédéric and I speak a mixture of French and English to each other, sometimes switching from one word to the next. I have started to learn Luxembourgish, but since the Luxembourgers all speak French, I don't have much opportunity to practise, for the moment. Many people commute each day from France, Belgium and Germany to work in Luxembourg; in just half an hour you can be in another country. The city of Luxembourg is built on enormous fortifications, and there are still underground tunnels that you can visit. The city is very green, with lovely parks, and as it is not very big, it is easy to get around. There are many cultural events such as the summer festival, jazz and blues festival, and almost every day there seems to be a concert somewhere. Luxembourg prides itself on being in the centre of Europe, and so it is easy to visit other countries. After Christmas it was −14 degrees Celsius in Luxembourg, but Frédéric and I had a lovely holiday in Athens visiting the historical monuments in our t-shirts, and eating traditional honey cake on terraces. A few weeks ago we went bushwalking in the Austrian Alps, and encountered landscapes and characters that could have come straight out of 'Heidi'.

Frédéric and I have moved into a new apartment block, and since everyone was new at the same time, I was very keen to invite the neighbours over for afternoon tea or dessert to get to know them. Frédéric's friends and family thought this was a very odd idea indeed: 'But you wouldn't want strangers to come to your home. If they came, they would just come to see what furniture you had and criticise your flat. Why do you want to talk to the neighbours anyway? It is much better if you keep your privacy'. Eventually, however, the mad Australian won out, although I reduced my invitation to just the closest four apartments. Two couples agreed to come around for dessert one evening, and as it was around Anzac day, I served Anzac biscuits and pavlova. The pavlova was a great success, but I guess the Anzac biscuits looked a bit boring in comparison. In the end the neighbours ended up staying until after midnight.

I often complain to Frédéric that there are too many rules. Appearances are much more important here than in Australia, and so Frédéric and I have had many discussions about my clothing. In Australia my taste was eclectic, sometimes I wore more tailored clothes, sometimes I wore my long hippy skirt with flowers and tiny bells. Here my hippy skirt has been banned, and wearing shorts to go to a fair is not appreciated, while clumpy sandals are definitely out. You need to make sure you wear dark colours in winter and light colours in summer.

Food is very important, and there are also lots of rules here. At Christmas I wanted to cook a traditional Australian Christmas dinner; roast turkey, baked potatoes, pumpkin, sweet potato, corn on the cob and cranberry sauce. First the turkey was vetoed; it was too common for Christmas dinner, so we needed to have a cockerel. (How do you cook a cockerel?) In addition, it was impossible to consider having dinner without a starter, so we needed to have Coquilles St Jacques (a sort of shell fish in a type of tomato soup). However, once these rules were adhered to, Frédéric and his family were ready to participate in the exotic Australian Christmas lunch and even tried the strange habit of pulling Christmas crackers and dutifully wearing the paper hats.

When you are greeting people, the Australian 'Hi!' is not enough. Between friends, men kiss women and women kiss women. (The men shake hands). If you are with a partner, his friends and family are your friends too, so at a wedding I found myself being kissed by lots of people I had never met. French people kiss twice (once on each cheek), Luxembourgers three times, and the Belgians four times. So what do you do if a Belgian meets a French person in Luxembourg? There are also rules about which side to start kissing, so if you are not careful, you might end up banging heads. Usually in companies, colleagues shake hands, but in one company where I was teaching English, a student would arrive late, and instead of sitting down quietly, he would first go around and kiss all his women colleagues (and shake hands with the men). Fortunately as the teacher, I got to shake hands.

It has taken some time to meet friends. I have been playing netball with a group of mainly English women, and I have been out a few times with them, and also with some of the teachers where I work. I think that you need to be proactive, and keep inviting people to do things yourself, rather than waiting for the invitation to come from them.

It is only a few days until I fly home to Australia for a visit. My upcoming trip makes me think about how I miss my family and friends, and Australia itself. I also wonder about what my career path might have been if I had returned. On the other hand, living in Luxembourg has given me opportunities I would have never dreamed about when I left Australia five years ago. I might not be a diplomat, but I have the chance to live in another country and learn other languages, while meeting people from many nationalities. I have enjoyed discovering new skills in teaching English, and there might even be new directions for my career as a speech and language therapist. Most importantly, if I hadn't visited Luxembourg, I would have never ended up being with Frédéric.

My last trip home to Australia was nearly two years ago, and Frédéric came with me. He couldn't quite believe that he was really on the opposite side of the world. He is very keen to return again for a holiday, maybe next year.

So for now, it's *'Addi'* (goodbye) from Luxembourg.

Karen Heins was born in Canada to Australian parents in 1973, but moved to Australia when she was two, living in Adelaide and then Canberra. Karen trained to be a speech and language therapist in Sydney, and after graduating, spent two years working in Parkes in country NSW. In 1998 she left Australia to travel around Europe and has worked in Wales, and Newcastle-upon-Tyne and Kent in the UK before moving to Luxembourg a year ago.

KEEP THE KANGAROO FLYING

Okay, maybe moving to Jerusalem in the middle of a violent *intifada*, or uprising, isn't something most people would consider. But when you're married to an ABC foreign correspondent who's made a career out of covering nasty little wars—and the occasional royal funeral—it makes perfect sense.

Jerusalem was our third overseas posting. During our two years in Moscow and four in London, Chris had spent a lot of time on the road, covering conflicts from Chechenya in the former Soviet Union to Ireland, Kosovo and Bosnia. Meanwhile I'd stay safely out of danger wherever our home base was at the time, watching the news every night to see the world through Chris's eyes, waiting for satellite phone calls to let me know how he was, when he'd be home next.

This posting was going to be different. For a start, this time round we had Jerome, our nine month old son to consider. And bizarrely enough, with a conflict right on the doorstep, Jerusalem seemed to offer a golden opportunity to combine career with family life. Chris would be able to dash up to Ramallah to film the latest confrontation between Palestinians and the heavily armoured Israeli army, or zip downtown to the devastating scene of the latest suicide bomb attack ... and still be home in time to read a goodnight story to Jerome.

Jerome's three grandparents flinched when we told them the news. Taking a baby to what was essentially a war zone? What the hell were we thinking? We weren't quite so worried. Of course, there would be some dangers but then again we could also get skittled by a bus, crossing the road in Sydney.

The *intifada* had only been going a few months when we arrived. A few suicide bombers had struck, but most of the really nasty stuff was confined to the West Bank.

The drive from the airport on arrival was the first eye-opener. Met by Tim Palmer, the ABC's radio correspondent, he explained that we'd be taking the long route from Tel Aviv to Jerusalem. 'There is a shorter route across the mountains,' he said casually. 'But it's on the Palestinian side and they've been shooting at Israeli cars recently. It's a no-go area unless you're in an armoured car.'

At that stage, only a few of the correspondents and some of the diplomats drove armoured cars. The ABC, as one of the smallest international news outfits, simply had a few flak jackets and helmets. Protection amounted to big 'TV' signs, marked out roughly on the roof, rear and sides of the car with insulation tape.

These markings identified the car as a media vehicle—essential for those who didn't want to be mistaken for an Israeli by a Palestinian on a lonely country road in the West Bank. Or, indeed, as a Palestinian by some young Israeli at a checkpoint. (Later on, the ABC car was also adorned with a huge yellow kangaroo road signs—just in case there was any doubt about the international nature of the car.)

The ABC flat in Jerusalem turned out to be in the middle of town, a few minutes walk from the Ben Yehuda mall in one direction and the bustling central market in the other. Brilliant, I thought naively, not realising that these sites were traditionally two of the most popular targets for suicide bombers.

Jerusalem seemed much like any other Western city on first acquaintance—if you took out the sight of soldiers everywhere, sub-machine guns casually slung over one shoulder, and the obvious cultural differences. But things were relatively quiet for our first few months, at least in terms of what happened later.

Jerome and I spent hours wandering the hilly streets soaking up the sights and sounds and smells. We became used to the wail of the siren echoing across the hills and valleys of Jerusalem signifying the start of Shabbat on Fridays. I no longer looked twice at pale-skinned men in furry hats and eighteenth century frock coats, or women with shiny nylon wigs, all clearly bought from the same supplier.

Then the tension ratcheted up a few notches. Talks broke down yet again. Israeli soldiers closed down parts of the West Bank. Still, wave after wave of suicide bombers snuck through the Israeli checkpoints. No longer did I assume that any loud bang was the sonic boom from an Israeli fighter jet streaking on a routine run down the Jordan valley. It was just as likely to be another bomb going off down the street. Sometimes I could stand on our balcony and watch the black plumes of smoke shooting into the air.

Israelis were dying almost every day—as were Palestinians, for that matter. But the Palestinians were out of sight in the Occupied Territories, while we were walking along the same streets, drinking at the same cafes and shopping at the same stores as the Israelis. It was all getting too close to home. We decided to move out of the world's most dangerous square mile, further out of town to Abu Tor, a hilltop area overlooking the walls of the Old City and the Mount of Olives.

Right on the border between Jewish West Jerusalem and Arab East Jerusalem, Abu Tor is a popular spot for expats to live. Well, expats and religious nutters of all persuasions who want to live within sight of the Mount of Olives—not to mention the odd liberal, left-wing Israeli who doesn't mind Arabs living next door.

Our street was originally part of the Green Line, the old border of 1967. Now on one side of the rutted road were large, modern Israeli apartment blocks and renovated old stone homes with balconies dripping with bougainvillea, high walls and security systems. Israeli Star of David flags flew from many homes.

The other side of the street was unmistakeably Arab. Flat topped white houses were home to large extended families. Walls were fly postered with pictures of suicide bombers, posing for posterity before their moment of martyrdom. Women with covered heads beat carpets on the balcony railings. Children in bare feet played in the sand, only darting aside to let the cosseted Israeli kids in airconditioned cars glide past on their way to swimming or ballet lessons.

Rubbish collection occurred like clockwork on one side of street; on the other, and all the way down into the Palestinian areas proper, rotting garbage piled up for weeks until desperate locals would set fire to it, creating an even worse stench. Skinny cats lurked like burglars everywhere.

One of the houses still had a shell hole in it from the 1967 war and the site of our apartment block was once a sniper post. Heavily guarded tour buses drove through regularly, and on national days young soldiers ran through the neighbourhood yelling patriotic slogans. On days like these, the Palestinian neighbours stayed indoors.

It was another world from central Jerusalem. For the first time, we were in daily contact with Palestinians. Our apartment block was on the Arab side of the street, but was actually owned by a couple of wealthy Jews who somehow bought the land and built a striking modern apartment block, now home to a motley collection of aid workers, journalists and diplomats. It stood out like a sore thumb from its neighbours. As did we.

People stared as I pushed the blonde-headed, blue-eyed Jerome down the street in his stroller. And I was aware that it wasn't just the fact that I was out walking in the blistering summer heat. The Arab kids sometimes chucked pebbles at us and the adults never smiled. I could sense that they were trying to work out where we fitted in. Neither Jerome nor I looked Jewish. But we were certainly not Palestinian.

For the first time since moving overseas I was aware that I wanted people to know that I was Australian. I stuck an ABC logo and a few kangaroo road sign stickers on the stroller and hoped for the best. I also made sure to keep my legs and arms covered in deference to our Arab neighbours' sensibilities.

In the midday sun I didn't wear a hat (religious Jewish women wear hats) and as tensions and the death toll continued to rise, I had no intention of being mistaken as a Jew. This was not hysteria or anti-Semitism, just commonsense. The first words of Arabic I learnt were 'Hello' and 'I am not a Jew.' Along with Jerome's first words of English, he learnt how to say 'Thank-you' and 'Hello' in Arabic and to identify the Al-Aksa mosque and the Dome of the Rock, both of which were clearly visible from our balcony and became two of his favourite shapes to make with Play-doh.

Soon, the Palestinians on our street got to know us by sight and the pebble-throwing stopped. One teenage girl, Diala, baby-sat occasionally and the children loved playing with our dog. Some days I felt like the Pied Piper as I walked down the street with a gaggle of Arab kids following behind, demanding to push the pram or hold the dog's lead.

So it was a double shock when one day Chris and I were returning from a walk with Jerome in a backpack. We were just climbing up some steep stone stairs to our road when something whizzed past Jerome's blonde head. It was a lump of brick, thrown with force and big enough to kill him outright. Chris yelled but whoever threw the brick had run away into one of the courtyards.

We returned home and enlisted the help of an English journalist who spoke fluent Arabic. He went down to what became known locally as Brick Lane and explained to everyone that we were Australian. We were journalists. We were not Jewish. We did not appreciate having bricks thrown at our son.

I forced myself to walk down Brick Lane a few days later, not being able to bear the thought of being scared to walk in my own neighbourhood. That time, men rushed to help me carry the stroller down the stairs. Women nodded and smiled cautiously. They knew who we were now, and seemed to accept us.

One day, after a Saturday lunchtime barbecue with the ABC Jerusalem crew, in fine Australian tradition we broke out the bat and ball and started an impromptu game of street cricket. The Arab kids started off hanging shyly round the edges, but before long were fielding and batting furiously.

An Israeli neighbour, originally South African and a keen cricket nut, heard the ruckus and came down to find out what was going on. He was itching to join in but instead watched nervously from the sidelines. It was the closest I ever saw the two sides of the streets come to engaging at all socially, but by then this state of affairs seemed normal to us.

Expats occupy a weird place in such a divided region. It was possible for us as outsiders to have a Shabbat meal with Israeli friends, or to travel into the West Bank to celebrate Eid with Palestinians, but the two sides never met. By the same token, one night at a Passover Seder, the meal was all but forgotten as we watched TV with our hosts to see news of the carnage wrought by a suicide bomber. Yet the next day I helped collect milk and medicines for children in a Palestinian orphanage. As outsiders and Australians, this was not our fight.

One has to accept many things as an expat. By then, I was used to chucking the supermarket shopping on top of bullet proof vests in the boot of the car. I was used to seeing the settlers (Israelis who've moved into Palestinian areas) carrying submachine guns with them wherever they went—even on a jaunt into town to the shops or the zoo.

I'd even become used to being searched for explosives each time I entered a shop, or visiting friends at consulates and having the underneath of the car swept with mirrors for bombs. But I felt a real jolt of fear the day I realised that one of the Israeli parents I met regularly in the park now carried a gun as he supervised his children playing on the swings. What the hell were we doing here?

Leaving the house could be a life and death decision, although it was possible to minimise our exposure to danger. That meant no nightclubs (not too hard a sacrifice with an early waking toddler son), no cafes, no restaurants, no public transport. Basically no place where other people congregated.

I didn't even take Jerome to the supermarket anymore. Two of my regular supermarkets had been targeted in a small way with a bomb in a watermelon and a bomb in a beer can, both of which went off like damp squibs and caused little damage. Other supermarkets—and shoppers—had not been so lucky.

The problem was that unlike a regular war zone, there was no predicting where or when the next bomber might strike. One neighbour was beside a bus that exploded. Another suicide bomber detonated his load just outside the gates of the French school where many expat children go. The bomber's head ended up in the playground. Now they have built a higher fence and many of the expat children who haven't yet been evacuated are sent to school in armoured vehicles.

As for cafes, I have to admit that sometimes I did succumb to the lure of an expresso, although I was a little less susceptible after one close shave with a suicide bomber—fortunately overpowered by an alert waiter.

Not even a trip to the local park was without risk. Several Israelis were stabbed—some to death—in one park where I used to spend long lazy afternoons playing with Jerome. A pipe bomb was found in another park not too far away from our house. And if it was dangerous for Israelis, it was certainly no picnic for any Palestinians grabbed by the police for acting suspiciously, or simply being in the wrong place at the wrong time.

Home was the definitely the safest place to be. Or it was, at least until our windows were shot out by some sort of mechanical catapult from one of the Palestinian villages down in the valley. Fortunately, we weren't there at the time. But the German diplomatic family upstairs were and it was sheer luck that their son wasn't playing on the rug where the boulder landed.

Enraged, the Germans contacted the head of the local Palestinian political organisation and demanded that our apartment block not be targeted. The Palestinians promised to do a doorknock and letter drop, explaining that although the block was Jewish-owned, the residents were all expats. It seemed to work. Well, it was either that or the ten-foot green and gold flag of Matilda, the boxing kangaroo, that thereafter fluttered proudly from our balcony.

Victoria Heywood has recently returned to Australia. She is co-author of *International Careers for Australians* shortly to be published by Global Exchange.

Cultural Discoveries

Roses are red, the sky is blue, and I love you, are my only memories of St Valentine's Day as a boy. Having been a student at an all boys' school, I have few other memories of Valentine's Day from that time. My experiences in adult life have been more romantic, giving roses to my loved one, wining and dining her and letting the evening progress from there.

My expectation was that Valentine's Day in Japan would be similar to my experiences in Australia, where receiving an expensive gift from a woman you'd seen on a few occasions previously would tend to indicate interest. When I received a large box of handmade Belgium chocolates from a young Japanese lady who I had shared dinner with on a few occasions, I thought that this indicated a little more interest than passing social contact.

Being a romantic at heart, I wrote a letter in reply to the gift that I had received. Later in the week, I had a telephone call in appreciation of the letter and was invited to dinner. Naturally, I was pleased that I was going to see this woman again and felt confident that our courtship was progressing smoothly. We met for dinner, had an extremely pleasurable time, shared intellectual discourse, and decided to leave when the departure time of our last train was approaching. We lived in opposite directions, and as we departed I was given a letter without any comment. I thought that this was a little odd, I opened the letter and was shocked. It was a Dear John letter. That was the last time that I ever saw her.

I learnt later that there was a large cultural difference between us. In Australia, and many other areas of the world, Valentine's Day is a romantic occasion. In Japan it is a little different. There are two kinds of Valentine's gifts in Japan, true romance, where handmade chocolates are given to men, the other *giri* (duty), where women give their male acquaintances a gift because of a cultural obligation. The gift I received was given in order to fulfil a cultural obligation that I had no idea about, and the thank-you letter that I wrote appeared to be a little too forward, one of several cultural differences that I have subsequently learnt.

Actually in Japan there are two Valentine's days, 14th February is Valentine's Day, and one month later, 14th March is White Day. Valentine's Day is the day when women give men a gift, and then one month later the women wait in anticipation for a gift from the men. Watch out if you give a lower priced gift to a woman! Let me tell you from personal experience that it will take a lot of effort before she forgives you.

Following my initial unsuccessful experiences with romance in Japan, I decided to concentrate on other activities. In Australia, I preferred an active lifestyle, and spent a lot of time outdoors. I guess that this was due to being a country kid at heart, as well as my four-year involvement in the school's Army cadet unit, followed by an involvement with the Australian Army, that further encouraged an active lifestyle. A love of the outdoors and a good homely upbringing led me to being an independent bloke. Naturally, I appreciated time on my own. This is difficult to achieve with over 127 million other people in Japan, 12 million of them in Tokyo. So I found it necessary for my own sanity to get away from the congestion and pollution of Tokyo as often as I could.

I was able to escape from the bustling city of Tokyo in less than two hours. Through a need to escape and an interest in hiking, I met several other like-minded people, and in the outdoors it did not matter whether one was Japanese or not.

Is it the beauty of the natural environment or escaping from a busy city that makes people more sociable? In the countryside and in the mountains I found that people were a lot friendlier than they were in the city. Actually, I found the same to be true in Australia: while walking down the road in the country people would greet each other, and more often than not would extend a short greeting into a conversation. On return home to the city I found that people would look on you as being weird if you uttered 'G'day' towards them, crossing the road in avoidance.

Often in rural areas, people are welcoming, much more so than in cities. I think that this friendliness stems from valuing neighbourly harmony, devotion to family, and believing in the importance of long-term relationships.

There was a long spell between the abrupt end to my Valentine's experience and my next romantic moment. Some two years after arriving in Japan, while studying Japanese earnestly at the local International Exchange Association, I met Yoko, a young graduate school student. My friend and fellow student of the Japanese language, Alex, who was also a post-graduate student and knew Yoko as they had studied in the same department, introduced me to her. Both Alex and Yoko were far from home like me; Alex was from the Philippines and Yoko was from an area near Osaka. Another area of common interest between us was that we all had a horticultural background. Yoko and Alex were post-graduate students studying horticulture, majoring in plant tissue culture. Alex made a good choice in introducing Yoko and I because, through our common interests and a love for the outdoors, our friendship blossomed.

A common way of meeting an eligible marriage partner in Japan is through a matchmaker, who knows of both people and will arrange a meeting of the prospective couple together with their parents. Traditionally, the matchmaker also plays a large part in their courtship and subsequent marriage. Some time ago, when Japan's society was more traditional, this method of meeting a prospective marriage partner was austere in that the young couple had little say in the matter.

Today's demanding and less active social schedule has created another problem for romantic encounters, as Japanese youngsters are either too busy or reticent to meet a prospective consort. The *omiai* (matchmaking) party assists young people in meeting an eligible partner. There are many types of *omiai*, none of which are cheap. The commonest is a dinner party where the same number of young women as young men attend, introduce themselves, participate in social discourse, and then secretly rate each other at the end of the party. If the organiser finds that any of the ratings correspond the couple are informed and arrange their next meeting by themselves.

Not long after meeting Yoko, while training earnestly in karate, a fateful collision changed my life. It was a winter's Sunday night—I was feeling on top of the world, my new romance was exciting, my fitness level was near its peak, and work was going well. Just after karate class, and an enjoyable dinner with my fellow *dojo* (karate club) members, this life-changing event occurred. While riding the 12 kilometres home to my tiny single-roomed apartment, along a four-lane dual carriageway, I was hit from the rear by a semi-trailer carrying hazardous materials. I did not know that I was in danger until I saw my legs flying through the air. Noticing that my flight path was along the road, in front of this mass of steel, I let out a loud, piercing scream. Fortunately, I was thrown to the side, onto the footpath out of further harm's way. In fact, I flew over 15 metres before hitting steel railing and landing on my back. It was a cold, dark night and nobody was on the street. I thought to myself that my back could be injured, so I did not move. Slowly, I tried to move my fingers, first my left hand, then my right; fortunately, they all moved. Then I tried to move my toes, they seemed to be okay, but I couldn't be sure as I had shoes on.

Gradually some bystanders appeared on the scene. I think they heard me scream only moments before, although it seemed like it had been hours. They came closer uttered *'daijyobu desu ka'* (are you okay?), saw that I was a *gaijin* (foreigner) and did nothing. Actually, I am not sure if they didn't do anything because I was a *gaijin* or that they did not know how they could help. I learnt later that the average person has very little understanding of first aid. I think that I was in shock as I had become extremely cold, freezing cold, and wished that one of the bystanders would be kind enough to place their jacket over me, but they didn't. I reached for my rucksack, where my karate *gi* (uniform) was, and was told not to move by the bystanders. Being trained in first aid I knew that it was important to keep warm and proceeded to cover myself as much as possible. In the distance I heard the wailing of ambulance and police sirens, at that instant the truck driver came and said *'gomen nasai'* (I am extremely sorry) and asked *'daijyobu desu ka?'*.

The ambulance appeared on the scene, with the ambulance officers looking more like construction site workers than medical workers with their hard hats on. The ambulance officers placed a normal stretcher beside me (I thought they would have used a scoop stretcher, as there was a possibility of a spinal injury), and began to talk to each other. It appeared that they expected me to get onto the stretcher by myself. Eventually they managed to lift me and place me onto the stretcher. I was carried into the ambulance, where they proceeded to ask questions for the next twenty minutes, all this time the ambulance was stationary! We eventually reached the emergency entrance of the hospital. It had been an extremely bumpy trip. Fortunately, the hospital staff proved more professional as I received a prompt and thorough assessment.

The night duty doctor was meticulous, assessing my condition seriously, from head to toe, including X-rays and a CAT scan. At that time my Japanese language ability was elementary, being immobilised in hospital was an opportunity in itself, as I had to use the local language. A period of hospitalisation is difficult at the best of times, not being able to communicate with doctors and nurses about my condition made it even more stressful. Medical vocabulary is complicated enough in one's own language but through the use of dictionaries, gestures and body language the medical staff managed to inform me of my injuries. I had sustained internal bruising to the liver, stomach, and kidneys, as well as external bruising, abrasions and a deep cut near the ankle. When the head nurse brought my cycling helmet to me, I felt a sudden chill go down my spine. The helmet had been severely damaged during the collision, receiving a cricket ball sized hole to the middle right side, yet I had not sustained a head wound in the slightest. I am thankful to the Bicycle Federation of Australia and the Cat Eye Company, as it was in Australia where I learned the benefits of wearing a helmet. In Japan, only young school children wear a helmet while cycling. However, the helmet that they wear is more like a hard hat.

My new companion, Yoko, provided great support and assistance during my hospitalisation and afterwards when aggressively negotiating with insurance companies. I came through this difficult period satisfactorily because of the assistance of Yoko. Our relationship had strengthened unbelievably. Some six months after the accident I gathered enough courage to invite Yoko to a weekend away in Kanazawa, the home of a beautiful Japanese garden, where I proposed to her. Without hesitation, she replied positively with *matte ita* (I have been waiting for you to ask).

Meeting the parents of your spouse to be, is no different in Japan than Australia. I was looking forward to meeting Yoko's parents but was somewhat concerned. I was apprehensive about whether I would be able to communicate effectively and how they would take the idea of having a *gaijin* as a *giri-no-musuko* (son-in-law). The day came for us to meet. At first we were all nervous then her father asked if I liked *sake* (alcohol made from rice) and I replied that I worked as a wine promoter and enjoyed a drink or two. Feeling more at ease, the atmosphere developed into one of acceptance and friendliness. It was at dinner, on the day before we were to depart and make the long trip back to Tokyo, when the atmosphere altered. Yoko received a lecture warning her about marriage to a *gaijin*, which included pointing out that there were cultural differences, language barriers, problems with children in the future, and the eventual relocation to a new country. The concluding comment was that should this be what she really wanted, then her parents wholeheartedly supported her. I did not understand the final remark, only that it sounded like they opposed our decision after an enjoyable three day visit. However, I soon learnt that I was well regarded by Yoko's parents. The parcels that I often receive from them is an indication of their approval.

Two and a half years after I proposed to Yoko we were married in Australia. The wedding was attended by both of our families and guests from Japan as well as all over Australia. Before the wedding, our families had a great time together, talking, wining, dining and sightseeing. Yoko made an *utsukushii hanayoume san* (beautiful bride) and made me extremely happy as a friend, ambassador, and a very welcome member of both of our families.

Being a *gaijin* in Japan is often difficult, however, as a person married to a *nihon jin* (Japanese person) life tends to become a little easier. Most citizens look more favourably upon a married man, especially if he is married to a local, and the government officials are often more lenient. Unfortunately for those who marry and wish to stay in Japan, the possibility of obtaining the same rights as a local is near impossible. If the marriage should end in divorce, and children are involved, then it can prove difficult in obtaining visitation rights, and often the foreign partner cannot stay, being forced to return to their country of birth.

Fortunately, I have not experienced any of these devastating outcomes, however I have had other experiences. Often older men will stare, looking both of us up and down sleazily In this society, it is considered as something that just has to be tolerated. Also, young women see married men as stable, loyal, and fair game, trying to seduce a man who wears a wedding ring in many enticing ways.

My past six years in Japan have been a wonderful learning opportunity and I am most indebted to all those who helped me on my journey so far and for having met Yoko. In a year or two Yoko and I will be moving back to Australia to continue our endeavours in regard to wine, horticulture, and nature through ventures in education and tourism.

Tony Kennedy was born and raised in Melbourne, where he gained a deep appreciation of nature and the outdoors. Educated in horticulture and wine marketing, he promotes travel to Australia and Australian wines to the Japanese. His six years living in Japan has provided an opportunity to observe and reflect on Australian society from the outside. He looks forward to returning home with Yoko, his new wife, where they will endeavour to promote greater cultural understanding.

HOME IS WHERE THE HEART IS

There is nothing like returning to a place that remains unchanged to find the ways in which you yourself have altered. Nelson Mandela

The room was heavy with silence and concentration as each of us focussed on answering the exam questions in front of us. It was no wonder that at 8.46 am the focus was broken when we heard an unbelievable load crashing noise, like large sheets or metal pipes tumbling onto the floor above us. Having seen the renovation work going on in the lobby of the Marriott Financial Hotel, I assumed, just as many of the others in the room did, that the noise was associated with the renovations. Most of us looked at each other questioningly, but since the penalties for breaking the silence during exam conditions were severe, nothing was said. We continued on with the exam.

The sound of a second crashing noise at 9.03 am, almost identical to the first, was enough to send our proctor out of the room to find out what was going on. She returned and calmly informed us that we needed to evacuate the room because there was a fire. That was it. We knew nothing more about it. I gave only peripheral attention to the fire, assuming it was nothing serious, as nobody seemed alarmed. The big news at the moment was what this meant for the Series 7 exam. I had spent the entire last month studying for this exam, because without passing it, I was most likely out of a job at Credit Suisse First Boston. And now we were being evacuated, meaning the exam would have to be re-taken. What an inconvenience! Descending two flights of stairs in the fire escape, and out onto West Street, I quickly forgot about this inconvenience, and slowly took in what lay before me on the street, and what I saw above me. On that day, Tuesday, September 11 2001, it seemed like the whole world had gone mad.

As I looked behind me I could see an enormous fire gripping the upper levels of World Trade Center I (WTC) (the north tower). My mind rapidly tried to grasp what was going on, and my immediate thought was that a bomb had gone off up there. But as I continued to walk south down West Street, away from the WTC, I took in what could only be described as carnage on the street. How was a bomb up there related to what I saw down here? To my left, the entrance to the building a block south had been blown apart and the burnt out hulk of a vehicle lay in its lobby. To my right canvas medical sheets covered what were presumably the remains of two human bodies lying in the middle of the street. As I looked back again I noticed a single large tyre lying on the pavement and wondered whether or not that tyre belonged to an aircraft.

My work colleagues and I continued to walk south, mostly single file, towards a barrier marking the evacuation area. None of us spoke as we continued to slowly process what was going on. The piercing sounds of fire truck sirens blaring by were muted in my mind as the enormity of these events and my danger sunk in. If a bomb had indeed exploded on this street, might there be the chance of another explosion at any point in time? To reinforce this fear I saw scattered pieces of human flesh on the road and pavement. I recall wondering just what sort of irreversible damage these images would have upon my relatively unexposed and untainted mind.

Finally I reached the barrier and stood there for a while, taking in the sight of WTC I on fire. One of my colleagues shrieked in horror and pointed to the sight of someone rapidly falling towards the earth. 'Oh my God that person jumped!' A shiver ran down my spine knowing a person's life had just come to a horrifying end. What sort of conditions did those trapped victims face up there? I found myself next to Annie, a work mate, and she appeared frightened and distressed. Her boyfriend worked in an adjoining building, and so naturally she feared for his safety. She also wanted to get up to her apartment and call her mother, since our mobile phones were not receiving any signal. Annie only lived two blocks away, and I went with her to the 30th floor of her building. The fact that it stood some five blocks directly south of the WTC was not lost on me. As she got on the phone to her mother, I tuned into CNN and listened to the unbelievable report that not one but two jet aircraft had crashed into the WTC towers. It also reported that another plane was thought to be in the control of terrorists and heading towards New York City. Looking out towards the harbour of New York from the view of Annie's 30th floor apartment, I realised that more potential danger existed. I dragged both of us out of there immediately and onto the street.

From where we were at Annie's building I could see where United Airlines flight 175 had entered WTC II (the south tower). It was like a massive tear in the building. Just then we bumped into another work colleague, Greg, and we decided that it was best to move as far away as possible from the scene. Walking south again, we ended up in Battery Park. Probably only 10 minutes had transpired since leaving Annie's apartment, and as we turned around to the sound of a tremendous rumbling noise, I witnessed something I thought I would only ever see on the big screen. In front of my eyes WTC II collapsed upon itself, spreading around it a massive plume of ash and dust. My heart at that moment went out to those poor people still trapped inside that building. How many people had died? Surely thousands! Equally upsetting was the sight of people in the streets around me crying, shrieking, sobbing; some potentially lamenting the loss of people they knew.

Even before I had time to absorb the momentous destruction of a 110 storey building, I watched with horror as the plume of ash headed inexorably towards me. My rational side told me that the plume really was just ash and smoke, and therefore harmless. But around me panic had erupted, and people started running anxiously away from it. You couldn't help but go with the flow of the human mass. But within seconds the plume had engulfed us, and visibility was reduced to mere metres. Overhead I heard the sound of another aircraft, while people around me panicked and stampeded. Handbags were left lying on the pavement. Some people jumped into the harbour, eager to be off the island. For at least 30 minutes the dust hung over us and blocked any view of what was really going on. The fear of the unknown is often the greatest fear, and what I feared at that point was not knowing whether or not another plane was on its way.

I was still with Annie and Greg, and despite the general panic and stampeding going on, we waited patiently for the dust to clear, as we knew it would. Covered in ash we then started walking north up the island and eventually away from 'ground zero', as it has come to be known. I recall calling my mother from Greg's apartment, and the sound of how upset she was on the phone almost made me cry. I guess she was that relieved to hear I was still alive. She could not have known how close I had been to all of that action. In the days to come I found myself keeping considerable distance from New York's landmark buildings, such as the Empire State Building or Grand Central Station. The sound of a large truck hitting a pothole on the street would remind me of the noise of the planes impacting and a certain kind of fear would grip my body for that instant. The very next day I came into work, not knowing what to do with myself, and those of us who worked in the mid-town area were faced with prank bomb threats that forced several buildings on Park Avenue to be evacuated. It was enough to send some people over the edge and out of Manhattan. I resolved to myself that the occurrence of another major terrorist attack in this city would see me somehow on my way home to Australia. To live in fear is not a way to live at all.

Mine is the story of a 30-year-old Aussie from Brisbane who has been over here in the US for more than four years. I live on the Upper West Side of New York City in a brownstone walk-up one bedroom apartment. Mercifully I have a balcony which allows me to smell the fresh air of the noiseless courtyard I overlook and affords me the luxury of cooking the occasional steak on my George Foreman fat-free BBQ. I work, metaphorically speaking, on Wall Street, as an associate at the investment bank, Credit Suisse First Boston (CSFB). We do billion dollar mergers and acquisitions, and advise on the best means to raise capital for our corporate clients. I have been at CSFB for two years now, starting my job one week before witnessing the September 11 tragedy. I want to share with you the trials and tribulations, the highs and lows, of my life overseas in the US, and without question what transpired on September 11 was the nadir of my time here. Hopefully by the end of this story I will have conveyed to you that there is much to learn from an expatriate experience, particularly about one's own country and its people. Ultimately I have learnt that home is where the heart is, and my heart lies in a warm-spirited, unique southern land called Australia.

Despite later anthrax attacks and high terrorist alerts, the immediate fear of living in New York City eventually subsided. There existed in the city around that time an extra sense of community and warmth, and in many ways I was proud to be a part of the rebuilding process. But there was still further pain for me to endure here, as I watched the US economy dip into a recession and I felt the impact of a slow market on the investment banking industry. CSFB has so far carried out seven rounds of layoffs, culling the excess headcount fat that had built up during the 'dot com' boom. Because I work here on a H1B visa, my ability to stay in the country is directly tied to being sponsored by my employer. I have been fortunate not to have been 'let go', unlike many of my peers around me. However, for at least a year and a half I have dealt with the insecurity of not knowing whether my job would continue. Despite these difficulties and uncertainties, there are many high points of my life in the US.

These emotional and economic lows of my expatriate experience in New York have been countered by many redeeming facets of the New York lifestyle. I enjoy an active, if not hectic, social life which is sometimes more vibrant during weeknights than on the weekend. The city has abundant energy coupled with an unparalleled range of nightspots and restaurants. For an Aussie who loves his sports I have been able to get into running (I finished the New York Marathon last year), cycling, triathlons, squash and soccer. Free community and cultural events are constantly on offer, such as Shakespeare in the Park, Symphony in the Park and Monday night movies in Bryant Park. The dating scene is very active, and operates in a similar fashion to the hit show 'Sex in the City'. On the surface I can say, with little modesty, that most American women are charmed by the Australian accent (which is curious because it appears to have the opposite effect in the UK).

Another high point of my time in the US was the rare privilege of being accepted into Harvard Business School. I completed the Boston-based two year MBA program prior to my employment with CSFB, and it was the reason why I found myself in the US in the first place.

Apart from the aura surrounding its name, there simply were some remarkable aspects about being at Harvard. The 800 plus students had all converged on Harvard to take two years out of their lives to learn more broadly about business and management skills and to take their careers to the next level. Interacting with the broad range of talent and intellect was a humbling experience. Some notable classmates included an heir to the

Heinz Ketchup family, Chris Heinz (who at one point was dating Gwyneth Paltrow), and Mary Lynch, a daughter of the famed Fidelity fund manager Peter Lynch. I even had occasion to meet Monica Lewinsky at a Halloween party. She was good friends with a fellow classmate, and found herself the centre of attention at the Halloween event. One of my mates introduced himself wielding a gigantic cigar in his mouth!

Various leaders from the business community were also invited to the school as guest speakers. We had as visitors the likes of Meg Whitman of eBay, Jeff Bezos of Amazon.com, Jack Welch from GE and Warren Buffet, the billionaire CEO of Berkshire Hathaway and famed value investor. I recall Mr Buffett's opening words as he moved up to the podium to speak, 'Testing ... one billion, two billion, three billion ... '. I saw Mr Buffett in 2000, perhaps at the very peak of the 'dot com' era, and he, unlike many of the other speakers who visited us in Boston, was very outspoken against the internet bubble and predicted a wave of consolidation for the industry.

My time in the Northern Hemisphere has afforded me the opportunity to do what any Australian loves to do ... and that is to see more of the world. During my time at Harvard in particular, I had large chunks of time that I could use to travel to exotic locations. Always one for a challenge I decided, at the end of my summer break in 2001, to travel to Kenya and Tanzania and climb the mighty Mt Kilimanjaro, Africa's highest point at 5900 metres. A year later I was back in the mountains again, this time trekking the Annapurna circuit in Nepal with my sister, Angela. And only recently I took on one of the highest peaks in the US, Mt Rainier, a stunning volcano lying several hundred kilometres outside of Seattle.

Not all of my vacations have involved challenging mountains. I have also travelled around Western Europe and to more exotic places like Turkey, Russia and Morocco. Most recently I joined a small band of Aussies from New York to watch the fourth Australian cricket test match against the West Indies in Antigua. One of the highlights of that trip was watching a reggae band featuring Richie Richardson and Curtley Ambrose, both former West Indian international cricketers, on guitar!

The connection I have had with other Australians in this country has also been another positive of my time here. There were only 10 other Australians in the MBA program with me at Harvard, but we made an impression at the school all out of proportion to our size. The Anzac club hosted the notorious Priscilla Ball which required the male party-goers to come along dressed in drag. I was not an attractive looking woman wearing a yellow sequined dress and sporting a five o'clock shadow!

In New York the Australian Consulate, in connection with the Australian American Association and the Young Australian Professionals in America (YAPA), have done an excellent job of unifying the Australian community in the New York area and providing them with access to a wide range of social, cultural and informative events. There are estimated to be around 15,000 Australians in the greater New York area. Through YAPA I recently met the Queensland Premier Peter Beattie at an event hosted in a Soho held specifically for Queenslanders. Annual events celebrated here include Anzac Day celebrations, the AFL finals (up the Lions!) and the Melbourne Cup, which all afford an excellent opportunity for like-minded Aussies to gather and maintain their links to home.

While I have made many friends with Americans and other internationals who reside in New York and elsewhere, my closest friends here are Australian. And I think for good reason. The Australian culture is distinct because we are a sincere, straight-forward kind of people with an easy-going attitude to life. Many Americans, and New Yorkers in particular, are often uptight and one never quite knows how one stands with an American. (There are exceptions such as my good friend, Mark, from Atlanta.) I have found that the society is conditioned to saying the right things and behaving in a politically correct manner, despite what thoughts lie beneath the polite veneer. It just doesn't mesh well with the way an Australian has been bred.

And how do Americans perceive Australians? They certainly love our accent and our positive, easy-going nature. They see our success in the global sporting arena, in sports like tennis and rugby, and they watched the Sydney Olympics with much fascination. Our recent participation in the war with Iraq had many Americans singing our praises, and many of them took note of John Howard's visit here earlier this year to see the President at his ranch. Almost every American I come into contact with either wishes to travel to Australia or has in fact been there, and the universal conclusion is that it is a wonderful place with wonderful people. Which always makes me ponder what I am still doing here?

I have outlined above many of the redeeming aspects of taking part in an expatriate experience, despite my fearful encounter with terrorist activity on September 11. I view the work opportunities and potential for a higher income as other important factors for me remaining here after completing my MBA. And I do believe the experience has made me a more balanced and well-rounded individual with a greater appreciation of world affairs. But increasingly I look longingly to the golden shores of Australia and plan my exit strategy for home. I miss the incredible quality of life and the low stress environment that all Australians enjoy, and I see it more clearly as the place I wish to settle and bring up a family. Australia is the place where my own family lives along with some other special people that I no longer want to be apart from. A phone call home once or twice a week is no substitute for the beauty and warm spirit that I unfailingly recognise as my home. And that is where my heart is.

Paul Kromwyk has been in the US since mid 1999 and currently lives in Manhattan. In his first two years he lived in Boston completing an MBA at Harvard Business School. He has also worked in Sydney, Milan and London but comes from Brisbane where he graduated from the University of Queensland.

THANKS TO THE HUELGA

'The little one is pregnant,' Senora Maggi comments to the assembled company. We are enjoying *sobremesa* (the after dinner social interlude) with Chilean lunch guests, friends of the Bolivian family with whom we are boarding. I am not only *embarrazzado* (pregnant), I am embarrassed. I can hear Maggi discussing my condition with people I have only just met, as though I were not there, while I listen mutely, unable to marshal sufficient words in Spanish to speak for myself.

My husband and I are theoretically improving our career options in Latin America by studying Spanish at the Instituto de Idiomas in Cochabamba. Actually, having left our last posting in Lesotho and with no other prospects in sight, we are between jobs. Our host Ancicetto, a civil engineer and descendant of past presidents and ambassadors, forced by health to relinquish the higher altitudes and aspirations of La Paz for the lower altitudes and lesser economic options of Cochabamba, is in a similar position. We are providing hard currency to finance the education of the family's two sons who are studying in the US. But we are not the only boarders. Carlos, the medical student, who could not get into medical school in his native Colombia, is probably supporting us all.

Living with a Bolivian family is supposed to enhance our acquisition of the Spanish language, but today's experience merely reinforces my already severe doubts about the efficacy of the immersion theory of language learning, among other things. The Chileans are speaking such rapid and attenuated Spanish that I can hardly understand a word and the few Spanish words I have accumulated have completely failed or deserted me. Learning Spanish is supposed to take my mind off being pregnant, not to remind me of it (though whether I should take my mind off being pregnant in a foreign country is another matter).

I do not need any Spanish to know that Maggi's indiscrete comments are purely a conversational gambit or ploy to revert attention to herself. My skills lie more in the direction of intuitive leaps, as my language instructors have informed me. Not that I need an intuitive leap to predict that Maggi will regale us with the trials and tribulations she endured during each of her three pregnancies. Senora Maggi enjoys holding court and I have heard how her cravings sent Anicetto out into the night on avocado buying errands of mercy so many times before that Spanish is quite superfluous.

I am not suffering any cravings or symptoms, on principal, but I am suffering from hunger. The big meal of the day is at lunchtime when everything closes for two hours. Lunch is a three-course meal, but 'big meal' is a misnomer. The first course is usually a watery vegetable soup made palatable by copious amounts of the local herb *quilquinia* and lots of hot peppers. Dessert is fruit. If we are lucky there is meat: blood sausages, cutlets whose transparency has been camouflaged with breadcrumbs, *aji de lengua* (tongue with chillies) or *escabeche di pesca* (pickled fish). However, meat is often unavailable for a week at a time.

Bread is also frequently unobtainable, even though Wali the maid queues at the bakery in town at five o'clock each morning. The freshly baked hard bread rolls are the staple food of the household, eaten with butter at breakfast, soup at lunch and jam or cheese at high tea, which the family shares with cats, daughter, daughter's boyfriend, maid and medical student, all sprawled together on the double bed in front of the television. In the absence of bread, there is always cake. Flour shortages inevitably result in an abundance of highly priced cake at the expense of cost-controlled bread.

High tea may be sufficient for the elegant Maggi who has tottered around the house all day in her high heels, and possibly embroidered some Japanese figures on the table linen she sells to earn additional income, but it is not enough to sustain me. After walking to the Institute in the morning, returning to the house for the two-hour lunch and siesta period and repeating the two-mile round trip in the afternoon, also on foot, I am ravenous. Instead of high tea, we eat a light supper of soup or eggs or leftovers, but I am so hungry an hour later that my husband and I resort to sneaking out of the house late at night when the curbside *hamburguesa* (hamburger) stands open for business. Despite the meagre meals and exercise, I am gaining weight.

On Friday nights we forsake the diet regime and feast on *pisco* (Bolivian brandy) sours and pizzas at the Institute, after everyone else has attended Mass. The Institute, run by the Maryknoll order of Catholic clergy, provides language training for a select group of students, selected more for political than religious grounds. There is a constant procession of new arrivals at the Institute, ostensibly for *repaso* (review of language skills). They are Jesuit and Maryknoll priests, Irish nuns, Witnesses for Peace and Amnesty International workers; fugitives from persecution or repression who tell horrifying stories of *desparecidos* (persons who have disappeared) in Chile, murders in Guatemala, civil war in El Salvador and Nicaragua and racial inequity in Bolivia. It is 1983. Liberation theology is challenging traditional power structures in Latin America with often-violent repercussions. Pinochet is still in power in Chile, there is a military dictatorship in Guatemala, the Sendero Luminosa are committing atrocities in the Andes, and in Nicaragua the Sandanistas have overthrown Samosa, who has fled to Paraguay.

We are neither Catholic, clergy nor political, merely development workers with good connections, who, have received special dispensation to attend classes. I wonder about the wisdom of insinuating myself, a somewhat flamboyant symbol of fertility, in the midst of the Catholic clergy, forgetting that maternity is the norm in Latin America. But maintaining a low profile with an expanding stomach proves difficult. The child will be the first born at the Institute and the brothers, regarding the stomach as communal property, take the liberty of patting it each day.

Cochabamba's number one obstetrician agrees to take over my care, but a week later leaves town to undergo bypass surgery in the US. As he does not return for the duration of my pregnancy, I inherit his son Joaquin, a handsome, arrogant man who speaks slightly more English than his patrician father but who is equally patronising. As a non-Spanish speaking transient, pregnant with her first child at the exalted age of 36 in a predominantly Catholic culture, I am considered both foolhardy and a medical risk, and am expected to be grateful for any mercy. I am forbidden to attend relaxation classes. Like his father, the son cannot abide the woman who runs the classes, and threatens to refuse care if I attend classes.

I am in no position to argue, but, being used to having some say in my health care, I do, fiercely. I bring my English language pregnancy textbooks to each appointment to back up my halting arguments in Spanish, and fail to have any of the expected complications. Behind my back, Maggi monitors my progress via regular telephone consultations with el doctor Joaquin.

My brothers send baby presents, which never arrive. The parcels are presumably at the house of the postman who has been arrested for stealing mail, along with all the other mail he has accumulated in the past two years. The postman is inexplicably released but there is no corresponding release of the impounded packages. It is the same with our suitcases, still languishing in Brazil where they have been awaiting shipment for the past four months. I am reluctant to tempt fate by buying baby clothes, but we have nothing for the child and prices are rising daily as inflation decreases the value of the peso. Our fellow students at the Institute surprise us with a baby shower and present us with pale yellow knitted garments for the impending arrival.

The baby is already a week overdue when my friend arrives from Africa. She alone knows the sex of the unborn child, having dispatched the results of my African amniocentesis test, which we received many months later in illegible condition. I am duty bound to produce this child during the three days she is in town. I spend all day in the markets buying intricately embroidered tapestry coca leaf bags and *chulos* (alpaca wool hats with traditional llama motifs and ear-flaps) from Indian women clad in bowler hats and voluminous layers of skirts. I spend all evening at a local bar listening to folk music and drinking wine.

Next morning there is a *huelga* (national strike). Strikers blockade all roads out of town, burning old truck tyres and slinging bricks at cars that attempt to bypass the makeshift barriers. We are becoming used to *huelgas* that—as the only form of social protest available to the masses— occur almost weekly. Today the *heulga* is somewhat inconvenient. I have woken up with a hangover that turns out to be contractions and the strikers stand between me and the nice modern hospital five miles out of town where I had hoped to deliver our child.

Joaquin considers flying the Red Cross flag on his car in an heroic attempt to run the blockade, but instead arranges my admission to the Clinic of San Francisco near Cochabamba's central plaza. The clinic is located on the second floor of an old two-storied house. There are no elevators. Six men are carrying a large woman on a stretcher up the central wooden staircase. Climbing the stairs myself seems much safer. Joaquin hangs around all morning, seemingly in no hurry to leave, while nothing happens. Outside the door, I find out later, Maggi, Anicetto, their daughter Cookie and my friend accompany my husband during the vigil.

As siesta approaches, the baby develops symptoms of foetal distress. Five doctors are summonsed. Thanks to the *huelga,* which has disrupted their golf plans and confined them all to the city, they arrive within the hour. I am relieved that medical emergencies take precedence over siesta, but, having finally and belatedly appreciated the precariousness of the situation—that the lives of my child and myself depend on the skill of Bolivian doctors in this ancient, dingy hospital—I am also deathly afraid. Too terrified to ask which one of us will be saved, I cravenly remind them that it would be a pity to waste all the education already invested in me. The anaesthetist keeps me awake to reassure me with a spinal anaesthetic that does the opposite, while they successfully separate child from mother. The five-day hospital stay, including surgery, costs a mere US$125.

A few weeks later, a telegram arrives offering my husband a job in Thailand. Sadly abandoning language investment, non-existent career options and the Bolivian godparents, we take off to Bangkok with our daughter, her newly acquired Australian and US passports and the Bolivian legacy with which we have saddled her; sixteen embossed but incorrectly spelled Bolivian birth certificates and a Spanish middle name ensuring she never forgets her Bolivian origins.

Elizabeth Kugler left Australia 30 years ago and has since lived in the US, Lesotho, Bolivia, Thailand, Indonesia (twice), Poland and Kyrgyzstan. She is married to an American she met in Africa and they now live in Kyrgyzstan. Their Bolivian-born daughter lives in California. Elizabeth is hoping that as Australia is now sufficiently foreign to her that it will be her and her husband's next destination.

THE ODYSSEY AND THE ECSTASY

'Well, you finally made it', exclaimed my father on the day I made my final vows to serve God in a fully-enclosed monastery in Sussex, England, in 1979.

It was the first time he and my mother had travelled out of Australia and, despite his fear of flying, he was determined to come and see for himself the place that could hold me down for longer than five minutes!

I was born in Canberra in 1948, the fourth of eleven children—six boys and five girls; my father had been an only child and always expressed the desire to have enough children of his own to form a cricket team! Canberra in those days was very rural, surrounded by bushland and we lived in the main street, not far from the local school, shops and police station. It was very quiet and at night we could hear the occasional drunk serenading the night air from his lonely abode in the police cell. We had plenty of freedom to wander the countryside at all hours and got up to all sorts of mischief. We were a pretty wild bunch and had great fun stretching the limits of our parents' patience. We were a fairly devout Catholic family and both my parents tried to instil a sense of the existence and supremacy of God into our daily lives.

By the time I was a teenager, the prospect of venturing forth and seeing the world and how the other half lived became a passion. Just after my 20th Birthday, I finally set sail for England via New Zealand, Tahiti, the Panama Canal, Acapulco and New York. It was a fantastic adventure and the first time I had been away from Australia—and I was alone! When I arrived at Southampton five weeks later and travelled through the misty rain to London, cold reality sank in and I realised that with my lively, impulsive temperament, if I was going to survive unscathed in the big metropolis, I would have to tone down a little and seek some sort of support to cope with the various situations that might arise. So, as well as socialising about town, I frequented the local Church and gradually developed a deeper relationship with God.

Soon I felt an initial inclination towards possibly devoting my life to God in some form of a closer commitment, but I also had an overwhelming desire to see the world and I recoiled at the prospect of 'giving it all up' to follow *His* designs—especially in England! I therefore made a bargain with the Lord that if He would allow me to travel abroad and see the world, I would consider the idea of a deeper commitment on my return to Australia, in a year or so. He seemed to agree with this proposal and I happily went abroad to tour Europe with an Australian girl whom I had teamed up with, plus two other Australians. For three months we wandered around the continent in a dormobile, living among the locals and sharing their way of life. It was marvellous and very enriching. I returned to London and embarked on a spell of temporary work until my next trip which was to Greece by coach. I also flew to Israel on pilgrimage and later toured the UK. After 15 months of constant travelling I returned to Australia by ship, via South Africa and arrived back in Canberra—a well-travelled 21-year-old.

By then my pact with the Lord came back to haunt me! How was I to fulfil this inner conviction that I was called to devote myself to some higher purpose than gallivanting about and enjoying myself? I could not see the way forward and after much prayer and soul-searching, decided to join a group of Sisters in Sydney who were dedicated to spreading the Word of God through the mass media. It sounded very much my thing! However, after three months there, I could not settle and felt there must be something else in store for me. I returned to Canberra and wracked my brains as to what to do next. Inspiration came and I decided to go up to the Missions in New Guinea as a lay-missionary. I applied for a job in Rabaul as secretary to the manager of the Mission Station, a Father O'Neill. However, after several months of enjoying the social scene and going to several parties on the plantations round about, I discovered that the girl I was replacing had decided not to leave and there was not enough work for both of us. So once again, I returned to Australia, slightly puzzled as to how to fulfil my spiritual destiny.

I worked at Parliament House in Canberra on a Senate Committee and after 12 months there I suddenly experienced an overwhelming desire to return to England for a *long* time: 'This is my destiny,' I exclaimed to a colleague at work. I had no idea what the future held, but I packed my bags and this time flew to London in May, 1973. I was 24. I immediately started working and getting involved socially, but three weeks later, the old, niggling interior sensation returned—that I should do something more meaningful with my life, but what?

In desperation I decided to go down to a fully enclosed monastery in Sussex for a week-end retreat and ask their advice as to what I should do. After all, they did not know me and there would be no strings attached. I enjoyed the weekend very much and met some of the sisters and the Mother Superior. At the end, as I was preparing to leave, she said to me: 'I think you have a very strong vocation to the contemplative, *enclosed* life.' 'Oh,' I said. 'Yes, and you have been fooling round and kept God waiting long enough,' she went on. 'Oh,' I repeated. 'Have you thought of where to go?' 'No,' I replied weakly. 'Well,' she said firmly, 'you had better come here!'.

That was it! I had found my destiny! This was where I was meant to be! I was elated! 'I must return at once to Australia and tell my family,' I said. 'They won't believe it otherwise!'

So next morning I returned to London, booked a flight back to Australia, resigned from my job, paid a month's rent in advance at the house I was sharing with four other girls (one of whom was Australian), packed my bag and took most of my clothes down to the local Church where I told the priest: 'These are for the poor; I'm off to join a monastery!'

I also wrote a note to the Australian girl telling her of my decision, as none of the girls knew anything about it. When the others returned from work that day, saw that I had cleared out my room and left the Australian girl a note, they assumed I must have committed suicide and were amazed at the true story when told about it later!

After three weeks at home, I returned to England and went straight down to the monastery in Sussex. The big gates closed behind me, and my life as an enclosed nun began. What a shock to the system! From having been a free spirit who came and went as she pleased, I now embarked on a life lived in one place where I would be told where to go and what to do moment by moment for the rest of my life! Was it a challenge? Overwhelmingly so! I knew nobody there; I missed my family, my friends, my car, my social life, my country!

What a culture shock—to adjust to an English way of life in an enclosed monastery which seemed sometimes to have been frozen in the Victorian era! 'Children (newcomers) were to be seen and not heard,' whereas I was used to freely expressing my opinions on everything! I had to learn to eat an orange with a knife and fork in the refectory and in winter, we collected a jug of lukewarm water from the ground floor and trudged up to the third floor to our own rooms where we had a large tin bath, kept under the bed. We pulled it out, poured in the water and sat with our knees up to our chin as we splashed away on our nightly ablutions! That initial adjustment reminded me of a detox unit where one gradually manages to 'ride through' the cravings for material satisfaction. A very elderly sister tried to encourage me saying: 'The first 10 years are the hardest, after that one settles down and gets used to it—just like the prisoner sentenced to life: after 10 years he reaches a state of acceptance!'

However, once I started to settle down and get to know the Sisters, things began to fall into place. It was a very balanced and regular way of life. We were wakened by the rising bell at 6 am, spent an hour in Chapel for prayer and spiritual reading, had Mass at 8 am, followed by breakfast and then each of us went our separate ways to work until lunchtime. Some worked in the kitchen, cooking the dinner, some in the garden, growing vegetables, some round about the house, cleaning and dusting and some helped with receiving guests. It was all very busy and enriching ... there was a regular rhythm to the day. We met up after lunch for recreation when we had the opportunity to spend more time together, chatting and sharing. Then it was back to work followed by more prayer in the evening and finally retire to bed at 9 pm.

As time went on, I gained a greater understanding of the value of a close-knit community who could accept me as I am, with all my foibles and eccentricities. We younger sisters came to respect the wisdom and compassion of the older ones. They were excellent listeners and encouraged us when we started to flag in zeal, while our youthful enthusiasm and lively antics kept the older sisters young-hearted and on their toes. I found community life a great boon which more than compensated for the loss of the family I had left behind, and the great consolation was that we were all in the same boat! None of us had our families with us, so we all had to help and support each other!

Previously I had been so used to constantly moving around and doing what I wanted, at whim, that I had missed out on the peace and serenity of a life of stability and rootedness; which comes from living at a deeper level, where one's life is guided by inner, spiritual values and a close relationship with God. The support of a loving community to achieve this is, of course, vital.

Life in a monastery can sometimes even be quite exciting! On one occasion I was wakened at 1 am by the sound of a chicken squawking, followed by silence for ten seconds and then another squawk. 'I hope someone else hears this,' I said to myself; but nobody did. So, after the fourth squawk, I got up and went down to wake the Sister in charge of the chickens. *She* had to go and wake the Sister Bursar who had the keys and *she* had to go and wake Mother Superior to tell her that three of us were going out of the house. By this time, I was getting agitated: 'Hurry up! Or they'll all be dead!'.

Eventually the three of us ventured out into the dark, armed with a torch. As we passed the bonfire site, Sister picked up a pitchfork! 'Goodness,' I thought, 'I hope there's no violence!'. The chicken house was about 80 yards away and we had 100 chickens locked up overnight in a big shed. We reached the shed door and Sister shone the torch on the ground: lying there were four or five dead chickens! As we watched in horror, rooted to the spot, a little black furry animal darted into the shed through a warped section of the door, which should have been repaired a week earlier. This galvanised us into action and the three of us raced inside to find the animal, an escaped mink, grabbing a chicken off its perch, by the throat. He tried to drag it outside, but the two Sisters started chasing it round and round the shed, one with a torch, the other with the two-pronged pitchfork, and, of course, they kept missing it!

'For heaven's sake' I said 'this is ridiculous!'. And I grabbed a nearby heavy shovel that we used to clean out the chicken shed and banged the animal on the head. It made no resistance and died immediately, drunk on blood! It had a beautiful mink fur and I would have liked to have skinned it, but I was told to bury the animal instead. It was the first time I had ever killed anything, but it had to be done. We lost about ten chickens that night. Sister repaired the shed next day, first thing, and that was the end of that episode ... we never saw another mink again. From then on, I was regarded as the official 'watch dog' of the monastery!

After 24 years at Sussex, I transferred to another monastery at Minster, in Kent. It is a medieval Abbey, built in 1027, and is reputed to be the oldest inhabited residence in England. We have a small farm with sheep, ducks, geese, and chickens; and we grow our own vegetables. There is also a guesthouse where people stay for a time of rest and relaxation. We sing and praise God for all He has done for us and intercede on behalf of all those in trouble or who have no time to pray. It is a very peaceful and deeply fulfilling way of life and I thank God that, after all my earlier searching and meandering, He has called me from my much-loved home in Australia to where He now wants me to be. Although I love living in England, I have returned to Australia on several occasions to visit my family (including 35 nieces and nephews). As an expat I have never lost my affection for my country of birth; it will always remain part of me.

Sister Margaret Mary Martin is a Benedictine nun at Minster Abbey, Kent, UK. She was educated in Canberra and moved permanently to England in 1973 to follow her vocation as an enclosed nun. She has held various offices in the monastery and is currently Sacristan, as well as assisting in the guesthouse and maintaining the monastic gardens.

JUST A WHILE LONGER

Six in the evening and the temperature in London was just north of thirty degrees Celsius. This is a side of London that many Australians never see in their three month tour of Europe during the Australian universities' summer break, when London is in the throes of another long winter with the promise of spring still sometime off. But for the Australians working here during the English summer, the heat is a staple item on the menu of discontent, the great hordes lamenting the lack of a beach—a ready remedy for a hot summer's day in Sydney. The Brits in turn are convinced that most Australians complain ad infinitum about anything. There is a cruel inaccuracy in there somewhere. Surely this is a breach of the 'Rules of Colonial Relations' which clearly state that, among other things, the Ashes will always be retained by Australia and the English are responsible for the bulk of the complaining.

I had just passed the three-year point a few days before. Three years living in London. I was on my way, walking in the summer heat across the Waterloo Bridge towards the South Bank, to see an Australian friend. The recognition that three years had passed so rapidly caused an unexpected and nostalgic reverie in me as I sweated in my dark suit. This was perhaps why I looked with new eyes at the art deco grandeur of the Oxo Tower which came closer into view in front of me, and at the architectural brilliance of the Houses of Parliament and the Abbey to my right—bathed in the bright sunlight of a London summer evening. But it was more than just a reverie—the issue of 'what next' had been increasingly occupying my mind, in some way triggered by the passing of three years abroad. 'When are you coming home, son?', asks my Dad by phone at regular intervals. The Big Question is the timing—of re-entry—if ever—into the 'new world', my antipodean homeland. A question easy to answer in the first year or so but, then cumulatively, so much harder as a series of worlds have opened before me.

Worlds, cultures—experiences if you like—that were once part of languid conversation while eating fish and chips at Balmoral Beach on a lazy Sunday afternoon, or when looking at glossy pictures of Tuscan landscapes in coffee-table books. The experience I craved then, as now, was not possible on a shoestring tour of Europe with a 20 kg backpack. In that guise your status as 'tourist' permits only the most brief and remote observation of these other worlds—not the more meaningful experience of living abroad and all that comes with a life lived 'over here'. It's in the little things, like where to find the best pasta in Bologna at three in the morning, the warming hospitality of a midsummer party on the Swedish archipelagos, sipping schnapps at 3000 metres above sea level in the French alps before skiing down through the cloud layer, or London on a sunny morning down by the Thames on the day of The Boat Race.

While London is full of Australians pulling beers behind bars and filling in a couple of years before returning home, there are some that leave home in search of something else, adventure perhaps, or a broader cultural awareness than is gained from life on an island at the end of the world. By the time I left for London, Australia in general, and Sydney in particular, was starting to feel like a prison with bars, not made of steel but of isolation. The lives of those around me accentuated this—a North Shore schooling, university, then a job in the Sydney CBD—a life lived in a 20 kilometre radius. The sense of somehow missing out was overpowering. How could I truly understand Australia or what it really meant to be Australian without somehow gaining the external perspective I needed to re-define my own brand of patriotism?

So I took steps to break free from the comfort of the familiar and its dangerous myopia. A new life—a flat in Little Venice, a transfer with my company to our London office, with all the expat perks that ease only some of the pain of the transition including a West End location with a view down Shaftsbury Avenue. All this teamed with an aching ever-present loneliness that comes from being so far away from the life you know.

I knew precious few people in those early days with the exception of a Wollongong girl with little to offer in the way of friendship and who had, inexplicably, affected a home county accent. No-one to help make the experience of relocation real rather than a series of disjointed experiences as if my time here was akin to a prolonged visit to a museum—interesting but somewhat disengaged and even surreal at times.

There were also the novelties of the early days of the London expatriate experience. Getting up in the morning and going to work in a foreign city, weekends spent finding the good cafes and pubs around Paddington and Little Venice, the obligatory bomb scare in a pub in Hampstead—people filing out with bored, resigned attitudes, their conversations continuing uninterrupted. And of course the tube, London's underground rail system and its ongoing dance of incompetence. Riding the tube on the Bakerloo line each morning to Piccadilly Circus was its own self-contained adventure. A kaleidoscope of cultures getting on and off at each stop. Of particular interest to a single man living alone were the women, particularly the Italians with their almond eyes and air of suave mystery or the milk-fed Swedes—wholesome looking with a clinical Nordic beauty almost too long of limb for the cramped confines of the carriage.

On the work front there was the need to learn the new rules of London's corporate culture. I found that I gradually grew accustomed to the norms of a new and very distinct social milieu that is working life in London's square mile: working in organisations whose size and scope dwarfed all but the biggest Australian firms. Then of course there was the pub, it's role deeply woven into the fabric of London corporate life. In my first few months I was taken to the pub by a client in the middle of a Tuesday afternoon. We had just emerged from a meeting with the chairman of the company in question and, as the session had gone tolerably well, it was put to me that the only reasonable course of action was to cross the street and debrief over an ale. The key learning here is that Londoners will actually put away two pints of a particularly strong ale before returning to work. My training in weaker Australian lagers, typically consumed after work or at weekends, was shown to be inadequate. Two ales and several pages into a document I started to lose the thread of the discussion, much to my embarrassment.

During these early days it was convenient to look on Australia as a safety net, London being a temporary break in my 'normal' life which would resume once I had this 'living abroad thing' out of my system.

Few Australians actually leave home to pursue a career overseas with a defined return date in mind. But quite quickly an ongoing series of transient relationships and encounters gives way to a sense of 'being here'. Ties begin to form, some begin to bind. Local cricket matches in the postcard greenery of Barnes, the bars along the Thames in Putney, the clubs along St James' Square all become familiar. But mostly, it's the friendships among an eclectic blend of people, only to be found in a truly international city, that form a rich and binding tapestry. The question of 're-entry' to home, even at some point in the future, is then so much harder to get your head around. It's much easier to defer that one for a while.

I arrived at the South Bank, sweating more now and commenced the hunt for my friend, Kate, among the throngs of people sipping cocktails and drinking beer on the sun drenched concrete outside the Royal Festival Hall. Five minutes and a mobile phone call later, I found her. 'Three years as of last week,' I said by way of introduction. She looked at me with a blank stare for a moment before replying. 'Hi. Three years? I thought it was something like that. I bet that went fast.'

We spent the next couple of hours doing what we always do—sharing a common frame of reference for our London lives—dusting off the words that only have a meaning to Australians of our generation, laughing at the optimistic fashion decisions of London girls with size 14 frames and size 10 tops and skirts. And of course we talked, as we always did, about living here, about how difficult it was dealing with the bureaucracy of banks and any government body compared to back home. Applying for a new credit card, a national insurance number or using the National Health Service become things to dread. But we also reminded ourselves of why we were here—London in the spring, the theatre scene with a greater depth and breadth of work than those on offer in Sydney or Melbourne, the museums and galleries of which we were most fond, and the best stores in Jermyn Street and how these compared to the more conservative and homogenous business fashion of David Jones.

A few pints and a few hours later, we decided to make a move. Like many Australians, Kate held the view that the tube was sole destroying, so travel arrangements were always more difficult with her.

'We can take the Waterloo & City line together, you can jump off at Bank and get a bus,' I suggested. She pondered this for a moment.

'Only for you, and only because I've never been on that line before. It will be like a little adventure.'

Laughing, we moved off in the general direction of Waterloo Station. It wasn't until we were sitting next to each other, raising our voices slightly to be heard above the noise of the tube and the banter of a small group of German tourists, that we returned to discussing the three-year milestone.

'It's frightening how fast it goes. The time I mean,' I said to her.

'I know. A lot of my friends say that the longer you stay, the more stressful the whole idea of going home is.'

'I can believe it. Even though it's only been three years for me, it makes you think how long you will actually stay. I want to have some kind of plan for the future. Right now I want to buy a place, but it's hard to know where to buy when you have no idea where you will be in two years.'

'The price of relocation! The travel junkie's curse.'

'And you? What would tip the balance and make you consider going home?', I asked Kate. I didn't think she heard me because we sat in silence for a few moments as the train took the bends at high speed causing us to reach for the support pole in the middle of the standing area of the car. Then she said, almost to herself so that I had to strain to hear it, 'The loneliness. It can get so lonely here sometimes. Maybe it's living by yourself that does it.'

The emotional honesty of this caught me off guard but didn't stop me feeling a surge of affection for her. Not knowing what to say, I said nothing other than to make plans to see her again soon. We said goodbye as the train pulled into Bank and she went out through the doors that let in a burst of hot, stale tube-air. I reflected on what she said for quite some days afterwards. The expatriate experience can be emotionally volatile—moments of contentment and of excitement in experiencing the unfamiliar coexist with moments of loneliness and despondency when the tidal pull of family and the familiar looms large, and the question of 're-entry' is revisited. The time available for a roaming Australian building a life in London to make a conscious decision on 're-entry' is limited. At some point, the lack of a decision will have consequences of its own and the course of your life is likely to be dictated by serendipity rather than your own will. The timing of this decision and the forces that drive us to the decision are different for all of us.

In my case, I think I will defer that one for a bit longer. Just a while longer.

Robert Miller is a management consultant working for Ernst and Young in London where he has lived since relocating from Sydney in July 2000. His work involves consulting to the boards of major European organisations on human resource and compensation strategy.

UP FROM DOWN-UNDER

Despite more than a smattering of law graduates in my family, I chose to study Agricultural Entomology at the University of Sydney, graduating with honours, and stepping into Sydney's post-war workforce as a teacher. After seven years of teaching agriculture, I met an American professor from the University of Wyoming who took a liking to me and invited me to go to his university to study for a Master of Science degree. He offered me a graduate assistantship that paid US$900. This seemed great until I got to America, when I realised I would need to use some of my savings from Australia to get by.

In August 1957 I left Sydney on the Orient Liner *Orchades*. The sea voyage was three weeks—lots of beautiful girls and I was asked to show my slides of the many places I had visited throughout Australia. Both Australians and Americans on the ship found these interesting and I realised that I had an asset in the slides. Later I put these slide shows to great use in getting free meals and eventually a wife.

What a let down when I was turned loose in San Francisco. I was totally isolated and found that many people in shops and other places could not understand me. When they found I came from Australia the response was usually 'You speak good English.' My greatest difficulty was with words like 'Coke.' On one occasion I was given a slice of cake.

After travelling for two days on a Greyhound bus I arrived in Laramie, Wyoming (the old Wild West) where the University of Wyoming is located. While I was studying in the Department of Animal Science I became most interested in Agricultural Extension studies. The US has a highly organised system for communicating university research findings to farmers in a form that is useful to them. I realised this was what Australia needed and I saw my life time career taking shape. That year in Laramie was one of the best in my life. As opposed to the difficulties I first encountered with blue collar Americans not being able to understand me, educated Americans could not have been friendlier. Several drove me thousands of miles to see national parks and their ranches. However, while the accent problem I had first encountered was no problem with my university associates, I did find we spoke a different language. One of my professors asked me to his home for dinner. His wife had a young baby who was crying while she tried to prepare the meal. I said, 'Would you like me to nurse the baby for you.' This was greeted with horror. In Australia, nursing the baby implied holding it and rocking it gently. In America it meant breastfeeding the baby.

I entered the University of Wyoming in September 1957 and graduated as a Master of Science in May 1958. The dean of the graduate school had been away on a sabbatical during that year. So the day after my graduation I called to thank him for my experience at his university. He said, 'Didn't you commence last September?'. I replied that I had. He followed, 'This will never do, students cannot complete a Masters degree in two semesters.' I responded that with an Australian educational background I experienced no problems and as I had been given the diploma the day before, I did not intend to give it back.

Having determined that Agricultural Extension would be my life time career, I found that only two universities, Wisconsin and Cornell, offered a doctorate in Extension studies. I applied and was accepted by both, but Wisconsin offered me an assistantship so that is where I went. While many American students take six or more years to gain a PhD, I was able to complete my studies and graduate in two years.

In early October, the director of the Episcopal Church student centre on the campus asked me to give a lecture with slides about Australia. On arrival at the centre he approached me and whispered, 'I want you to meet Mary Schettler, she has a turquoise Thunderbird!'. It was one of those classic 1955 Fords. We were married at the student centre in the following January and lived together for the next 40 years.

Mary and I arrived in Australia in October 1960 and I commenced the search for a position in Agricultural Extension. I visited all Australian universities but none showed any interest in introducing such a course. The cultural shock for my wife was considerable. Because of rent control in Sydney there were absolutely no flats or homes to rent and we ended up spending the first year living with my parents. This was traumatic for an American woman who had left home after high school. Mary was also turned off by entering a butcher's shop with carcasses hanging on rails and sawdust on the floor. Eventually, she joined with the expatriate Americans and was elected secretary of the American Women's Club in Sydney. We finally bought an old Cape Cod style house in St Ives. After Mary put her decorating skills to work remodelling that home it was featured in *Australian House and Garden* magazine.

Our first daughter was born in Sydney in 1963 and while our life in Australia had become quite comfortable I had not found a position that challenged me. Then Rachel Carson wrote *Silent Spring*. The concern that the book created caused the US Congress to appropriate a significant sum of money to the Department of Agriculture to study the use of agricultural chemicals. The department sought recommendations from universities for someone to direct this study. The University of Wisconsin recommended me and I was duly appointed.

We returned to reside in America permanently in April 1965. Because I was not an American citizen the Department of Agriculture had to find a way to employ me. They appointed me to the Extension Service at Colorado State University. I was paid by the university but reported to superiors in Washington. I enjoyed my years in Colorado and travelled to consult in many other states and I could take my family with me if those trips were within driving distance.

The project with the Department of Agriculture was completed in two years. Then the US Public Health Service asked me to go to the Center for Disease Control (CDC) in Atlanta, Georgia to serve as a Chief of Information. As this was a senior position in the US Civil Service I had to become a naturalised US citizen. I carried the rank of GS-14, which is four grades below the top position in the Civil Service.

Unfortunately, my wife Mary was most unhappy in Atlanta. The locals were convinced that, as she came from Wisconsin, she must be descended from General Sherman, who had burned Atlanta during the Civil War. In fact on one occasion she was referred to as a 'dammed Yankee'. For that reason, when I was offered a position to direct a project that the National Library of Medicine had funded with the University of Pennsylvania, we left for Philadelphia and have lived here most happily ever since.

Being a member of the faculty (in America faculty refers to a member of the academic staff of a university, not a course of study as in Australia where one speaks of the Faculty of Science, etc) meant I was able to undertake private consulting assignments. To perform that consulting role I formed Educational Communications Inc. The role of that company was to develop training materials (manuals, sound-slide shows, films, videos and eventually interactive computer programs) for employees of major companies. The companies either used these materials in the US or sent them to their worldwide subsidiaries. In 1972 I left the university and devoted myself full time to growing the company. Employees joined the company and we organised the firm into two divisions. The Biomedical Division developed materials for the launch of new prescription products for major drug companies and the Engineering Division produced materials to familiarise service technicians with systems on new vehicles. We grew to 36 employees including technical writers, artists, and film and video technicians. The Biomedical Division produced materials for the worldwide launch of new antihypertensive drugs, cholesterol reducers and vaccines. Clients included Merck & Co, Abbott Laboratories, Wyeth Laboratories, and the Agricultural Products Division of Dow Chemical Co.

The American subsidiary of British Leyland was among the clients served by the Engineering Division. British Leyland was so impressed with the training we developed for their vehicles in America that headquarters asked us to form a company in the UK to develop training for their worldwide network of dealers. Rolls Royce Motors heard about the materials we were developing for British Leyland, and asked us to develop materials for their vehicles.

In all this work, both in the US and the UK, I was treated as a professional and fully accepted as an Australian-American. I was able to buy a home, built in 1803 on 12 acres of land overlooking a valley only 20 miles from the centre of Philadelphia. I often thought how difficult it would have been to acquire 12 acres of land within 20 miles of Sydney.

In 1988 my wife was diagnosed with Alzheimer's disease. Caring for her forced me to sell the company in 1994. At that time, the Australian government had established Australian chambers of commerce in some 15 US cities. The Australian Consul-General in New York asked me to serve as the executive director of the chamber in Philadelphia.

The *Australia Citizenship Act 1948* contained a provision that native-born Australians who became naturalised citizens of another country, automatically lost their Australian citizenship. This was a most extraordinary provision. Australians have come to occupy the most senior positions in the US and in such positions could exercise considerable influence on behalf of Australia. Examples are, the President of the World Bank, a US Ambassador to Israel, a former President of Ford Motor Co, the Chairman of Coca-Cola, the COO of Du Pont, the President of Merck Human Health and many others. In most cases these people had to become naturalised Americans to accept the positions. Instead of the Australian government working with these international leaders they rewarded them by taking away their Australian citizenship. The *Australian Citizenship Act 1948* was amended in 2002 so that Australians don't now lose their citizenship if they take another citizenship. However, that change was not retroactive and Australians who lost their citizenship under the old rules still have to go through the problems of applying for reinstatement.

Actually, the government attitude on citizenship reflected the public attitude that anyone who was disloyal enough to take another citizenship deserved to be cast out. My father was so disappointed that I, with my long Australian ancestry, had taken US citizenship, that he wrote me out of his will.

Because I had been forced to assume US citizenship to accept my job with the US Public Health Service, I was able to apply for reinstatement and eventually got my Australian citizenship back in 1997. Then the citizenship problem arose with my daughter who had been born in Sydney. In this case the bureaucrats were uncertain what to do. On my daughter's birth her mother had registered her as an American citizen by descent. So when she wanted to exercise her Australian citizenship she made application to the Australian embassy in Washington, DC. She was told that because she had never actually gone through any naturalisation procedure, she had never lost her Australian citizenship. She was told to apply for an Australian passport in New York. When she did that the immigration officer in New York told her that she lost her citizenship when I had become naturalised as an American. Eventually, after paying $550 to the Australian Administrative Appeals

Tribunal, she did get her Australian citizenship back, but why bother? The attitude in Australia seems to be that one must live in Australia to love and care about it and yet according to the Southern Cross Group's estimate 860,000 Australians live outside Australia.

As well as continuing to serve the Australian Chamber of Commerce in Philadelphia, I was elected as National President of all Australian chambers of commerce in American cities. In working with Australian companies and trying to help them license their patents or sell their products in America I have discovered a number of shortcomings in Australians' understanding of how business is conducted in America. I have written several short monographs to try to help Australian companies understand these differences.

Considerable advantage can be gained for new Australian businesses stepping into the US arena by tapping into the expertise of Australians who have themselves managed American companies. To assist such communication of local knowledge and experience, Ken Allen, Australian Consul-General in New York has established an organisation known as YAPA (Young Australian Professionals in America). The Sydney University Graduates Union of North America has names and addresses of some 1500 graduates living in North America. Many of the people in these organisations hold very senior positions, and so represent a valuable resource for fellow Australians entering the US business environment.

Philip C Minter, a dual citizen with deep Australian roots, migrated to the US, served at a senior level in the US Civil Service and on the staff of a major university before forming corporations in the US and the UK. He now serves Australian businesses though the Australian chambers of commerce in the US.

TAKING THE QUEENSLAND CURE

My father was determined to go up the ladder. My mother knew it and so did all of our relations. Together, they had communicated this phantasm to me before I was five years old. I can still see the vision, clear and crisp in my mind, as my father marches up the ladder, left arm out straight so that he can lean back and wave with his right. He's wearing grey pants and a spotlessly clean, white short-sleeved shirt. They were the same clothes he wore every day to his job as a supervisor on the factory floor. I knew very well that my father would go up the ladder; I just had no idea what it meant. As it turned out, neither did anyone else.

No one could have known that, over the next dozen years, we would go back and forth across three continents and own four homes on two of them. No one could have predicted that my father would become the head of a British public company, only to leave that job to start his own manufacturing company in the US, grow it to a company with sales of US$250 million and then sell it to Merrill Lynch, the mega investment banking firm in New York. Nor could I have known that by the time I graduated from high school, I would have attended no less than seventeen schools on three continents. I went to international private schools, public schools with only three classrooms, boarding schools and one big American high school. I would stay in one school for as little as two months or as long as two years. If self help books had been around at the time, we would have been reading all of them. As it was, the only thing that kept the three of us intact was a good old Australian sense of humour. A bit of a lark, that's all it was.

The Penn Elastic Company, owned by a British textile group, had a factory in Rocklea, a Brisbane suburb with some industrial pockets. The factory occupied an old grey quanset hut and the ceiling in that place had to be a mile high. When times were good and the factory was busy, they kept about one hundred and fifty people working around the clock on all three shifts.

My father started work there as a packer. He had to manhandle the eight foot long bolts of fabric off the knitting machines and into cardboard boxes. He was on shift-work. When his shift ended, he'd go and clock off and then go right back to work. He'd use that time to wander around the production floor and notice things that could stand a little improvement. He hit upon a way to reduce excess rayon, which would build up like clouds around the knitting machines, costing the company money to have it removed. His boss proposed that for every pound Dad could save, he'd get a penny. This was his first exposure to incentive compensation! Within two months he was earning more than his boss, and within six months he earned more than the General Manager. That had to stop; so they promoted him. No more big bonus cheques at the end of the month for us.

Instead, we got a company car, a green Zephyr which we washed and polished to perfection each Saturday afternoon. We would check out our teeth in the reflection from the paintwork. All three of us would line up and smile into the side door panels. If I squinted in just the right way, I could see Dad holding on to the ladder, smiling.

His ultimate dream was to be the General Manager of the plant in Rocklea. He knew he'd never get the job without overseas experience. The big break came when he was offered the opportunity to be Production Manager of one of the English subsidiaries. There were some real production problems at that site; if he did a good job and solved those problems, in two years he would return to Brisbane as General Manager in Rocklea. The company laid it on thick. They praised Dad for all of his achievements, his talent, his brains and, the real kicker, his choice of my mother for his wife. There were lots of coded messages here and my parents scrambled to decipher them. They said he had the right wife! This was the best news ever. Because, as everyone knew, a man could never get into top management without having the right kind of woman beside him. My mother had always been secretly terrified that she would hold Dad back. They meant every word they said. We were off to England for two years!

We sailed out of Brisbane occupying first class cabins on an Italian liner named the *Roma*. The whole family came to see us off. Not one single member of our family had ever been outside of Australia before. Not only did we have to say goodbye amid desperately long hugs and tears at the pier, we got to do it again about a mile down the river. There was a bend in the river, just before it went into the open sea, where my grandfather knew a spot where you could drive a car in through the low bush and get close to the riverbank. When we sailed around the bend, there they were! My grandparents, Nanna and Pop, my Aunty Dot and my cousin, George, all standing in front of their pea-green Vauxhall and all waving white hankies for all they were worth. The three of us were hanging over the rail of that ship, bawling our eyes out. When you take a giant step up the ladder, you leave behind a lot of the things that, it turns out, matter the most.

In November of 1998, almost forty years after leaving Australia, I was working on a consulting assignment at a major US petrochemical company. For the first time in my career I was working around several people who had completed overseas assignments. We had an almost immediate rapport and sense of camaraderie. I cannot tell you how much it meant to me to hear their stories and be able to tell my own. For the very first time in my adult life, I felt like an insider.

One morning, only a few minutes before I was to make an important presentation to some of the company's more senior executives, the head of human resources stuck his head around the door of my office. He was about to take retirement and wanted to stop in to say goodbye to me. I told him how much I was enjoying my assignment at the company and mentioned that it came as a delightful surprise to be working with so many people who had overseas experience or were themselves current expats. The international relocations had fallen under his area of responsibility, he said, and at times he handled hundreds of them. I wanted to know if he felt that the individuals and families had benefited personally from the international experiences. His answer completely shook me.

'If you move them somewhere just one time for a couple of years and then bring them back home, it works out great. They have an adventure and everyone has a good time,' he said. 'And what if you don't?' I asked 'Don't what?'. 'Move them back home.'

'Well, that's more complicated. If you've moved a whole family and the move was to another Western country, it's usually OK if they end up staying there. At some point the kids usually come home for their education, of course. And the family travels back and forth a bit.' He paused. 'In are a few cases, men who are on their own, or couples with no children, they love the international life and prefer to become world gypsies and go from assignment to assignment. If you bring them home, they get itchy to hit the road again.'

'What about the other cases?' I asked. 'What happens to the families?'

'Upon the second move? It's a disaster! The wife either becomes an alcoholic or gets so depressed that she is a walking nightmare,' he blurts out. At this point, I can feel my heart start to pound and my hands feel cold and clammy. But I know I must ask the next question. 'And what happens to the kids?' I asked, trying not to sound panicky. 'They're just a mess. You can pretty much write them off. They can never get their lives together after that!'

And on that cheery note, off he went, leaving me to scramble to get my wits together. To this day, I cannot remember anything that happened right after that. I must have made my way to the conference room and given my presentation in some kind of altered state.

His comments had hit me so hard because they exposed the family secret we had lived with since 1962. Upon the second move, my mother became so severely depressed that she was barely able to function. She has battled this debilitating illness ever since. Ignorance about mental illness and the natural Australian intolerance for anyone who whinges made the battle more difficult. Of course, no one in the company could know of her condition or she would be a liability, not an asset to someone going up the ladder.

The factory in England, which my father had been assigned to run for two years before returning to Australia as a hero, turned out not to be in England at all. Just a minor fact that the company forgot to tell us! It turned out to be in Fforestfach, a small town on the outskirts of Swansea, Wales.

Today it would be impossible to send people off on a foreign assignment with as little preparation or information as we had in 1958. Companies now provide training and information programs for the entire family to familiarise them with the new culture. The employees themselves are more sophisticated and have ready access to information. We were such numbskulls that it was pathetic. For example, although we arrived in England in the middle of winter, we arrived wearing clothes appropriate for a Queensland winter. The company told us that it would be winter when we arrived and told us to pack our winter clothing. In Queensland, my winter clothing was my summer clothing plus a sweater. I can remember standing at Victoria Station, London waiting for the train to take us to Swansea. It was the middle of February and I was shivering in a pink cotton dress and a white jumper!

For my mother and me, the two years in Wales were some of the happiest in our lives. We knew that we would be going home to Australia, perhaps never to travel overseas again, so we really made the most of it. Loads of theatre trips to London, short trips to the Continent and road trips to the Lake District and Scotland; we packed them all in. Back in Brisbane, one of Mum's greatest life achievements had been to get her driver's licence. In Wales, she got her own car. Dad bought her a brand new Austin A40 and she was off and running! Best of all, we made great and true friendships in Wales. The weather there may be a bit dreary, but the people aren't. After two years, the length of time we have consistently found that it takes to really settle into a new country, our friends felt like family. The good kind of family; warm and accepting.

At the end of two years, my father had done a great job and turned the factory into a top producer. Of the three of us, he was the least happy in Wales. He had to deal with employees who were not too happy having an Australian at the helm, and he had some rough days trying to win them over. He was really looking forward to returning to Australia, to the top spot in Rocklea.

We waited for the big boss in the London headquarters to send the word that we were going home. It never came. In the end, it was my father who had to raise the subject. All this time we had been thinking that they had their eye on him, were keeping track of his achievements, and most certainly keeping track of the calendar. Oops! They hadn't.

My father was not going to get the top job back in Rocklea. He had kept his half of the bargain but they weren't keeping theirs. Why? They really liked Norman, the man who had been put in charge on an interim basis. They didn't have the heart to remove him. After all, he and his wife were in their forties and had finally succeeded in having a baby. What? What kind of nonsense was this? And what about us? There was no job of equal or greater pay available back in Australia and Dad really didn't want to be stuck in the same job in Wales. They offered him the Presidency of the US subsidiary. It was a much bigger job with a much bigger pay packet. He took the job. The odyssey had begun.

Like Homer's epic, it has been a grand journey, filled with excitement, hardship and surprise. In trying to find the right road back to Australia, we travelled down many roads. We never intended to leave Australia. Forty years later, we still cannot admit, even to each other, that we have left permanently. We have been gone for forty years but we did it two years at a time. Regardless of this length of time, we are and always will be Australians.

In her strangely disturbing book, *Silent Thunder*, Kathryn Payne's study on the plight of elephants (Penguin Press, US, 1999), she describes very poignantly the suffering of elephants when they are moved from their natural habitats. When the animals are moved to new locations, they suffer what can only be described as a sense of loss and emotional isolation and, while they may go on living, they fail to thrive. I shed more than a few tears when I read the book, feeling that I had suffered a similar fate. Admittedly, I have suffered in splendour.

Ever the Australian, I give myself a good, swift kick when I start to feel sorry for myself. I ply my brain with all the old adages from home. Australia never raised a quitter! Stop whinging! Pull your socks up! What have you got to complain about! If none of these work, there is always the sure-fire Queensland cure for whatever ails you. Go and take a shower! Taking the Queensland cure always works. Except, of course, on Christmas Eve.

Sharyn Negus lives in Philadelphia in the US and is active in many organisations with an Australian focus.

WALKING THE LINE

The best thing about being an Australian living in America is that everyone loves your accent. The moment you start speaking, you are transformed from the ordinary 'Sheila' that you were Down-Under into some exotic creature. It doesn't matter what you say, people want to hear more of it. As soon as you open your mouth, your audience melts with admiration. Most people ask what part of England you're from and after being corrected and told that you're actually from Australia, their admiration expands into adulation. Even after living here for twenty years and adopting some of the local vernacular, I am still dining out on my Aussie accent.

That is not to say that the accent doesn't have its drawbacks. There is an irresistible urge on the part of Americans to mimic what they think they just heard you say. In some cases, your pronunciation is such a huge source of amusement that you are asked to repeat words over and over again. Often a discussion ensues aimed at demonstrating how erroneous Australian pronunciation is, given the spelling of certain words, most famously perhaps the potato/tomato discrepancy. However, in spite of that, they still want to hear you say those words so that they can fall about laughing or be smitten with the cuteness of it all.

Even weirder is hearing their take on how you pronounced something. The result is generally something unintelligible or else bearing little resemblance to what you have said. I was at a major league baseball game with front row seats a couple of years ago and could have reached out and touched one of the outfielders, a gorgeously handsome player called Tony. Part of the fun of sitting in these seats is that you can interact with the players, so I proceeded to yell out 'Tony, Tony I love you!' My friend who was sitting next to me was rather alarmed at what she perceived as rudeness on my part. 'Why are you calling him tiny?' she asked, 'He's 6 feet 7 inches and 220 pounds of pure muscle and anything but tiny.' It was at this point she said that she started to get a handle on the Aussie accent.

One of my most unforgettable experiences in the US was when my accent actually worked against me in such a way that I ended up in jail. I had driven the babysitter home late one Saturday night in a quiet upscale neighbourhood. On my way home, I came to an intersection that would have been a give way situation in Australia but was actually a stop sign. Since it was one o'clock in the morning and there was no-one on the road but me, I slowed down and proceeded through without coming to a complete stop. Unbeknown to me, a police car was hiding nearby to catch the exact violation I had performed.

I had travelled about half a mile after the stop sign before I realized that the flashing lights and loudspeaker blaring behind me were actually directed at me. Already I had given the appearance of fleeing from the scene of a crime.

My previous encounters with the constabulary in Australia had taught me that a bit of flirting with a cop generally mitigated the severity of the punishment. I was still unaware of why I was being stopped but I immediately got out of the car to prepare for a bit of Aussie bantering and hopefully charm the police officer into letting me go. What I didn't know was that in the US you never get out of your car when being pulled over because that represents a direct threat to the policeman.

He ordered me to get back into the car and informed me of my transgression. As soon as I began talking he assumed I must be drunk because to him the sounds emanating from my mouth were largely incomprehensible. He asked me if I had been drinking and I admitted to having consumed a couple of glasses of wine with dinner six hours earlier but assured him that I had had nothing to drink since then.

Next he demanded to see my driver's license and my registration papers. Unlike Australia, you have to be able to produce these documents on the spot, otherwise your car can be impounded. I have never been one to bother too much about cleaning my car so when I finally resorted to fishing around on the floor under piles of junk for the requested documents, the cop had already made up his mind about me. Unable to produce this vital paperwork, I was told to exit the car to face a sobriety test.

The first thing I was asked to do was to put my hands on my head, walk in a straight line and recite the alphabet. I was most unsuitably dressed to comply with this request because I was wearing stiletto heels, which I rarely did, and walking was a difficult and dangerous exercise. I informed him of this impediment which seemed to further anger him.

By now I too was getting rather annoyed, both because of his total lack of humour and the absurdity of the acrobatics I was being asked to perform. I decided to play the smart-arse and recited the alphabet at three times normal speed in my best Tassie working class accent. The officer was not amused and decided that I needed to take a breathalyser test. I vaguely remembered that one could refuse such a test and asked the officer if he could explain my rights regarding such a refusal. This proved too much for him and he proceeded to handcuff my hands behind my back. I was pushed into the back of the wagon, a towing company was called to impound my car and I was being chauffeured to the county jail.

At first it was all rather exciting. I had only ever heard the words 'county jail' in American movies and here I was being personally escorted to one. The glamour quickly wore off upon arrival, when I found myself in the company of a large crowd of drunk, drugged and generally unhappy people. I was fingerprinted, mug-shot and de-robed of all items that presented a suicide risk. I got my own cell alongside a lot of upset and angry women. My request to call a lawyer went unheeded and I was finally released after spending a few hours there and passing a breathalyser test with flying colours. I learned a lot from this experience, including the fact that my accent wasn't always a reliable ally and that the Aussie sense of humour was easily misunderstood by my newly-adopted countrymen.

On another occasion my accent actually got me out of a very bad situation. Americans are by and large a very orderly people and the queue or 'line' as it is called here, is a sacrosanct way of ensuring that everyone gets their turn in a fair and democratic manner. At the time I was still married and my husband and I decided to take our kids to a rock concert in downtown Washington DC. The line had started building the night before and snaked around several city blocks. People had been camping out all night and the area looked more like a refugee camp than the downtown area of the nation's capital.

We arrived approximately one hour before the concert was to begin. Our teenage daughter had already left and joined her friends and my ex-husband and I, along with our eight year-old son casually tried to melt into the beginning of the line.

Within minutes of trying to be nonchalant and cool about pushing in, we were informed by the people in front of us that we were cutting into the line and that this was totally unacceptable behaviour. They advised us to hurry off to the end of the line before they alerted the authorities, or colloquialisms to that effect. I don't know what possessed me to spin a story, except the certain knowledge that the people at the end of the line had no chance of getting in. If we were going to the concert, this violation of American justice was our only chance.

In my broadest Aussie accent I feigned surprise and said, 'Line? You mean in the US you have to get in line to go to a concert? In Australia where we come from, you just don't have lines, everybody waits outside in a crowd and then you push your way in from there.' The people waiting were at first amused by this chasm of cultural difference and were quite happy to strike up a conversation with all three of us.

However, the people behind us were not buying this story and no amount of charm, wit or over-the-top accent was going to convince them that we had the right to usurp their twenty-four hour wait in the line. By now the crowd around us had grown decidedly angrier. Since Washington at the time was known as America's murder capital, it wasn't particularly comforting to hear one of our adversaries announce that locals were shot for far less egregious crimes than the one we were perpetrating. They started threatening us with physical violence while we continued playing the dumb tourists with the funny accents. I must say we shamelessly used our son's presence as a kind of shield against the hostility. After all he sounded cuter than either of us and he was just a little kid with wacko parents.

As the doors for the concert opened, our neighbours proceeded to summons the security guards to inform them of our evil deed and hopefully to have us moved to the end of the line. The guards approached us and asked whether we had cut in line. In unison we denied any wrong-doing and in truth, if outward appearances counted, they worked in our favour because we looked like such a clean-cut and wholesome little family and quite incapable of such derelict behaviour. Thus the family with the cute accent was able to pull off a rare and dangerous feat in American line-standing.

There were a few lessons learned on that day. The first was to never cut in line again in the US. The second was that you can get away with a lot more by pretending to be stupid. And finally I learned that there is a lot of goodwill towards Australians which I hope I haven't squandered for the rest of you.

Marte Newcombe lived and worked in Hong Kong for a year in 1974 and from 1978 until 1982 spent four years in PNG. In 1982 she moved to Washington DC where she now works as a computer graphics instructor at Georgetown and George Washington universities and as a graphic artist and animator at NASA's Goddard Space Flight Centre in Maryland. Marte is a graduate from the University of Tasmania and the Corcoran College of Art and Design in Washington DC. She has a daughter working in London as an environmental economist and a son studying medicine at the University of Sydney.

PATIENTLY BUILDING BRIDGES

I had my first expatriate experience at the age of three months. As part of my father's commitment with the Royal Australian Air Force, our family left Australia's shores for the Butterworth Air Force Base on Penang Island in Malaysia. Later, I spent two of my early teenage years in a very different land, the United States. Now I'm living my third expatriate stint, this time as a foreign resident in China.

Australia's remote geographical location can make travel so much more alluring. The waters that separate us from all other countries provide not only a physical barrier, but also can also inspire feelings of isolation. As a child I remember being given the board game *Risk*. I never did learn how to play the game correctly but I would spend empty childhood afternoons looking at the map of the world on which the game was played. With its vast oceans to cross and land bridges connecting far-off destinations, I would imagine the seemingly endless possibilities of travel.

Australia is a fine country; it has wonderful natural diversity and the freedom and opportunity for people to live their lives as they choose. It is often puzzling to people of foreign cultures why a person from a developed country would choose to leave the 'luxuries of the West' in exchange for the poverty and hardships sometimes found in the developing world. My answer to this question is that I personally believe that every culture has a richness that cannot be measured in dollars and cents. To journey from the cities of Australia and be enveloped in a culture with rituals and age-old traditions is a fascinating experience.

I always felt that the best way for me to experience and learn from a foreign culture would be to live in that culture for an extended period of time. So when I decided to travel, I thought that working in a foreign country would provide the combination of adventure and stability that I was looking for. I made enquiries with Australian

Volunteers International regarding work placements overseas and I was pleased to find that their program had a range of opportunities that suited my needs. Most appealing for me was the way in which a volunteer could work almost independently within their host community. I felt that there would surely be difficulties that arise from being thrown in the deep end, but I hoped that these challenges would bring on personal growth. There was an opportunity to learn a new language and social customs, and at the same time I could use my education and experience to help other people.

My home for the past year and a half has been Nanning City, in the Guangxi-Zhuang Autonomous Region of China. When I arrived in China it would be fair to say that my knowledge of Chinese culture was very limited. The one thing everybody knows about China is that it has the largest population in the world, well over a billion people. As an Australian, it's hard for me to fathom such a large population. The region of Guangxi-Zhuang alone has more than twice the population of Australia.

It's easy to perceive China as a single large entity. Its massive population and corresponding development projects like the Three Gorges dam tend to make us lose sight of the rich cultural diversity within the country. Perhaps it's better to think of China as a conglomerate of many nations under one government. The Han culture is the dominant group, but there are approximately 55 other minority groups, each with its own language, traditions and culture. The Zhuang nationality is recognised as the largest minority in China and it is for this reason that Guangxi-Zhuang has been granted the special status of autonomous region.

My work in China involves teaching English at the Guangxi University for Nationalities. I enjoy the work and my work colleagues and students have gone out of their way to make me feel welcome. I have benefited a lot by living where I work, on the university campus. To be able to walk to the local market and see familiar faces along the way has helped me to feel that I'm a part of the community.

English teaching is now a very big industry in China. I recognise how important it is for my students' future career prospects that they are able to communicate in English. Even more important is the fact that students in regional China are given the same opportunities as their contemporaries in the more developed cities. There is a wide gap in the opportunities and living standards between the east and the west of China and also between the cities and rural areas. In a small way I'm doing what I can to help bridge this gap. As important as English is for these students' education, I feel concerned that China appears to be forsaking some of its history in an attempt to be a part of a global community. The minority languages that are central to the heritage and culture of China are being over-run by the dominant languages such as Mandarin and English.

During my free time I like to pursue my interest in the local culture. With China's breathtaking rate of development, traditional and historical customs are becoming increasingly rare. From my experience in China, I think the traditions are still most observed during the festivals. These festivals are celebrated according to the Chinese lunar calendar and the most important festival is the Spring Festival, commonly known as the Chinese New Year.

The Spring Festival is a holiday time throughout China and almost without exception people take the opportunity to get together with their families to welcome the New Year. I decided to use this holiday to further explore the people and places of Guangxi.

While travelling through Guangxi, I got a startling introduction to the customs of Spring Festival's eve. Using my limited Chinese vocabulary, I was attempting to purchase a bus ticket in the city of Yizhou, my next destination. As I was being informed that many bus routes had been cancelled because of the festival, a thunderous noise suddenly broke out in the station. As first I was upset at the further inconvenience, and then realised that the person responsible for the noise was the station manager.

I simply had to do what others in the station were doing, block my ears to the deafening noise while multiple sets of firecrackers were discharged. The others didn't seem to mind and I even began to appreciate the situation. It was nice to see people taking time out of the regular work routine to observe a tradition.

In the cities of China the use of fireworks is restricted, but in regional areas they are still a central part of the festival celebrations. At the stroke of midnight on the Chinese New Year I stood in my hotel in Yizhou and watched as the fireworks exploded in every direction as far as the eye could see. It wasn't the extravagant fireworks of New Year's Eve celebrated on Sydney Harbour—it was a more humble affair, but very still touching as I sensed that each and every family was celebrating the New Year. Though I stood by myself in the hotel and welcomed the New Year alone, I had a warm feeling in my heart as I witnessed something traditional and special.

At the break of day the following morning, the railroad workers opposite my hotel set off more firecrackers to welcome in the New Year. With sleep foremost in my mind, my warm feelings for Chinese traditions had disappeared as I craved something that is extremely rare in China, peace and quiet.

The festival can be a lonely time if you are far from your friends and family, particularly if it is a time of year when families come together to celebrate. The Spring Festival isn't long after the Christmas season and many similarities can be found between these two traditions. To an outsider, the most apparent similarity is the way in which the occasion is marked by a special meal. To be reminded of this and to remember my family at home in Australia and the distance that separated us left me with an empty feeling. Because of this fact, it was even more pleasing to find that the people of Guangxi were generous with their hospitality over the Chinese New Year. On several occasions I found myself having dinner with families who had been strangers only hours before. After we met on trains, buses or in the street, people would insist that I have dinner with their family and share in the special occasion. In the cities of China, a single traveller can be lost among the multitudes of people, but my experience of rural China left me with a feeling of acceptance. People were interested in who I was and why I had come to their town.

It has only been during the recent decades that China has once again opened its doors to the West. In the eastern cities of Beijing and Shanghai, foreigners are not uncommon. In a remote city like Nanning, foreigners are scarce but there is a small expatriate community. If you venture further into the regional areas then you are likely to be the sole foreigner, something of a novelty.

Progress has reached even the most isolated parts of China and it's not uncommon to see minority village houses topped with satellite dishes or equipped with DVD players. During the Cultural Revolution Western culture would have been distant and strange, but now it seems that almost everyone in China has seen the film *Titanic* at least twice. As a foreigner in a minority village, I had the impression that my presence wasn't seen to be as peculiar as it would have been 20, or even 10 years ago. The people of China are seeing their country's identity change at a rapid rate and things that are foreign are coming to be expected.

One day, I felt I needed a break from the endless hustle and bustle and decided to take a walk in the mountains. It seemed that over every mountain crest and in every valley I would come across a village. Wandering into these mountain villages can be intimidating. There aren't any streets to speak of; instead there is usually a public square connected to a labyrinth of alleyways. When walking these winding paths you feel that the town and its people are literally on top of you—open doorways of houses directly facing the narrow alleyways. In such a situation there is no way to introduce yourself gently. Turning a corner, you come face-to-face with somebody who could be seeing a foreigner for the first time. You can do nothing but smile and hope that your presence is welcomed. The reactions I received ranged from curiosity and shock to humour and friendliness.

China's large population makes privacy almost impossible. At home in Australia, I'm used to being able to find a quiet spot in a park to sit down and read a book. In the rural areas of China a foreigner sitting in a park will attract attention, and a lot of it. And if you're a left-handed foreigner writing a letter home then people will stare openly. I have to admit that sometimes the attention gets a bit too much. It is nice to be treated specially from time to time but the price is that you lose any sense of anonymity and privacy.

I have my good days and my bad days. There are days when everything seems new and exciting; there are days when things seem familiar and you feel in your heart that in some way you really do belong here. There are also days when you feel you need to be home, just to walk down to the shop in the morning and buy a newspaper that you can actually read. Living and working as an expatriate in a foreign country means finding a home away from home. I've been fortunate to find friends and work colleagues who are willing to take the time to get to know me and understand my differences. I'm always grateful to people who are patient with my attempts to learn Chinese.

Relationships are central to the way we live our lives, whether we live in Australia or in a foreign country. Trying to maintain relationships when communication is a struggle presents difficulties, but being a foreigner means being patient and appreciating the satisfaction when you overcome these difficulties. I will never lose my sense of being an Australian but I have made changes in my lifestyle to find a balance between Australian and Chinese cultures. I have developed as a person because of the experience.

Ian Parry is a volunteer with Australian Volunteers International in China. Ian left Currumbin in Queensland in January 2002 to work as an English teacher at the Guangxi University for Nationalities. This is his third stint as an expatriate.

BITTERSWEET VEGEMITE

I never cared much for Vegemite as a kid. I found it drab, tasteless and boring, much like the Sydney suburb where I grew up. Dundas—where I lived—had a migrant hostel, and I always found the sandwiches of the hostel's many Southern European children—brimming with salami and smelly cheeses—infinitely more interesting than my own.

I felt much the same way about our national bread spread in the first few years I lived away from Australia in England and France. Visiting Australians (of which there were many) would bring a jar and it would sit in the kitchen cupboard for ages before I realised it was way past its use by date. And then I had a child. Suddenly I couldn't get enough of the stuff.

Now that I live in the US—the land of peanut butter and jelly—I've come to see my son's Vegemite-smeared face as a sign of his national identity. The French may have their *tricolour*, the Yanks their stars and stripes, but for me the ultimate symbol of our nation is a Vegemite jar—red yellow and black like the Aboriginal flag.

Like many of my compatriots I left home for adventure and stayed away for love. A journey so common these days I'm sure there will soon be a Lonely Planet Guide. I've spent nearly a decade of my adult life outside of Australia, so I've come to understand the challenges many like me face—especially those of us bringing up children without our families nearby.

There may be one million of us born in Australia now scattered around the globe—but there are many more happy little Vegemites who have never touched foot on Australian soil. Which leads me to ponder this new national phenomenon—how do you learn to love a sunburnt country if you don't have a sunburnt nose from summers spent there? What if you don't know heat so hot you call it a stinker because it burns your nostrils? No matter how many Wiggles videos they watch, or how many times we read them Snugglepot and Cuddlepie—how will our children know what it is to be Australian?

My son is an Aussiecan—half Aussie, half American. He's spoken to in Spanish at home and at day care. He has Australian, American and Portuguese passports. He's truly a citizen of the world—so why should his mother's cultural heritage matter? Because it matters to me. Soon he'll be raising his eyes at me and muttering under his breath—'not ANOTHER Vegemite sandwich mum'—much like the Italian kids at my school used to complain about their salami sandwiches. I'm realising culture is an invisible skin—like sunscreen but it doesn't wear off. You wear it all your life.

So I've compiled a set of rules—a sort of rough guide for Australians living overseas.

1. **Vegemite tastes better abroad** – Now there is no scientific proof of this. And it may be an urban myth like the way the water is supposed to spiral clockwise out of the bathtub in the Southern Hemisphere and anti-clockwise in the north (for years I thought that one was true). It's just one of those things those of us living abroad simply KNOW. Admittedly you have to grow up with the stuff to understand. There's a certain illicit quality to Vegemite eaten overseas. At least it costs enough in foreign supermarkets to think it an illegal drug. A simple whiff of the stuff can transport me right back to the playgrounds of my childhood. I can smell the wattle and feel the soft white bread between my teeth. It's sheer nutritional nostalgia. There's a kind of melancholic taste to it—when you're feeling sick or sorry for yourself, tea and Vegemite toast is about as close as you can get to a hug from your mum when she's on the other side of the world.

    I guess I've become one of those born-again Australians eager to convert that very substantial part of the world that does not like Vegemite. I've succeeded with my husband—a Yank—after much proselytising. We've decided Australian citizenship should require a Vegemite test—with points for eating it, liking it and mastering the delicate art of getting the consistency right. I've had to stop many a foreigner from spreading it on a croissant or scone as if it were a hunk of strawberry jam.

2. **It may be a big country but it's a small world** – It's easy to spot the 'Australian look'—kind of outdoorsy and sun-worn—when you're away from home. It's a skill you develop like a radar. Then there's the traditional Aussie greeting ritual where you spend the first part of the conversation establishing who you know in common. If you don't know anyone in common you're just not trying hard enough. It's kind of like being a Mason or a member of the Lions Club but there's no secret handshake or lapel pin. I've never met an Australian outside of Australia who was a stranger. We're friendly folk. Warm and open much like the wide brown land we're from. Because for us all—away from our homeland—our world is about as big as our old copper one-cent piece (remember the one with the tiny feather-tail glider on it?). Even our celebrities and politicians share this feeling of their world shrinking to the size of a pinhead once outside Australia.

3. **We have the most colourful English in the world** – When you give birth to an Australian abroad, you come to realise fast that our rich and varied vernacular begins from a very young age. Over the years I've got used to what I call the bewildered look when I use an Australian word. You expect this look in non-English-speaking countries—but you get it a lot in English speaking countries too. My first visit to my son's American doctor went something like this:
Me: He's been a bit grizzly.
Doctor: Bewildered look.
Me: A bit whingy.
Doctor: Bewildered look.
Me: But he quietens down when I wrap him in a bunny rug and give him the dummy.
Doctor: Bewildered look. I'm sorry could you translate?
I call my son mate or cobber. When he hands me something I say 'Ta' remembering how my American friend—an exchange student in Melbourne—spent her first few weeks there puzzled by this word. The longer I stay out of Australia the more endearing I find our slang and the more ingrained I realise it is in me. I stop short of using 'stone the crows' but my husband looks askance at me often these days—it is as if *Bazza Mackenzie* moved in after our child was born. The thing is I'm not bunging it on. I can't help it.

4. **You can learn more about Australia outside it than in it** – Did you know, for example, there are two and a half times more kangaroos than people in Australia? (50 million compared to 20 million.) And there are five times more sheep than people? Even at todays small flock numbers of 100 million. These facts I learnt outside Australia. But it was at Gallipoli in Turkey and the Kokoda Track in PNG where I learnt more about what it is to be Australian than a life time in the country could have taught me.

    My grandfather fought at Gallipoli. I never felt closer to him than when I touched those rugged cliffs he climbed on the morning of 25 April, 1915. During the dawn service I attended there I wondered how he—how all those Anzacs—climbed into those trenches knowing full well they were going like lambs to the slaughter. Amazingly he survived and that's just the thing about us—we surprise ourselves sometimes—especially when put to the test away from home.

    I felt this too on the Kokoda Track. How did 6000 young men—outnumbered six to one—deal with the odds? They were nearly all under 20 and far from Australia's finest soldiers (who were off on the other side of the world in other battles). I found walking the track hard and I didn't even have an enemy other than my own will. And that's what I've learnt is key to the Australian character. Bravery despite the odds. Which leads me to my next point ...

5. **We're a tough mob** – I've met Australians all over the world—selling meat pies in Budapest, barramundi in Florida and 'Aussie hamburgers' (with beetroot) on Greek Isles. What's astounded me is their entrepreneurism. Their ability to not just survive but thrive. It's no surprise, I guess, given we live in the land that is home to the ultimate survivors—one of the oldest races on Earth, the Aboriginal people—50,000 years in one of the most unforgiving continents on Earth. No surprise too, given that many of us are descendents of criminals.

    I often wonder how my own convict forebears—Henry Kable and Susannah Holmes—survived that eight-month journey to Sydney from England on the First Fleet. Then they faced not only the physical hardships of convict life but also that dreadful first year when the colony almost starved to death. They didn't just survive, they prospered. Set up the country's first constabulary, ran a successful whaling business and bore 11 children, nine of whom survived to an old age. In their honour, my son's middle name is Kable.

6. **Dry continent—dry humour** - I think our sense of humour is intricately linked to our survival skills. We know how to have a laugh. We like to take the piss out of people—especially ourselves. Oh, and of course the Poms. Just as well considering no-one knows much at all about our culture—in fact Poms claim there's more culture in yoghurt than in Australia. Which I'd say is not true but at least we can play cricket.

    I've experienced some mammoth misunderstandings in my time away from Australia that I may not have found funny if I'd come from a country that took itself more seriously. I once sang a heartfelt rendition of our unofficial national anthem, Waltzing Matilda, to some French friends in Paris who thought the chorus was 'washing machina'. I once went to Lille in northern France for a story I was working on for the *Sydney Morning Herald*. A story appeared in the local paper about my visit—as an envoy from the Sydney Money Earner.

7. **Summer is not the same without Christmas** - The old crooners from the North may pine for a White Christmas. But for me summer is missing something without Santa Claus dripping with sweat and a big box of mangoes under the plastic Christmas tree. Christmas and summer go together like passionfruit on pavlovas. It's kind of how I feel about the northern European night sky. Try as I might the Big Dipper just doesn't do it for me like the Southern Cross. I've never seen more clear beautiful night skies than the ones I've seen from the Australian desert—huge swatches of black velvet covered with diamonds. Hard to believe we all share a planet but not the same night sky.

8. **Real Aussies don't lose their accents** - Many of us who have spent a few years in the Motherland know what it is to return home and be called 'the stuck up Sheila with the Pommy accent'. But those rounded vowels are soon flattened after a few months back home. What I really hate is when Australians move overseas and after five minutes away start to sound like the Queen of England or

George Bush. I'm not talking the odd 'cheers' instead of 'Ta' or 'tomato' instead of 'tomahto.' Sometimes you have to adapt to be understood. What I hate are those Australians who purposely cultivate a new accent and identity as a way of denying their Australianness. Drop your accent at your peril. Keep your lack of pretension and you will always be one of the extended Australian family. You'll be known as 'our Nicole', 'our Pat', or 'our Livvie'. (You gotta love Olivia Newtown-John—after all those years in California her nasal twang is as fresh as the day she left Newcastle.)

9.   **Our birds and beaches are more beautiful than any -** Don't let anyone tell you otherwise. I've been to beaches all over the world and my first reaction is always, 'you call that a beach?'. I'll go to a wildlife park in some ornithologically challenged corner of the world and I want to tell them the birds in my parents' backyard are more colourful than this. I grew up waking to magpies chortling in the morning and a sea of white cockatoos on our front lawn. Pink and grey galahs would tip over gently to drink from our swimming pool, and kookaburras would eat from my hand. Rosellas and lorikeets jostled for space in a cacophony of colour and noise. Now, I never think of the suburb I grew up in as drab and ordinary. It's not just hindsight giving it a rosy hue but comparison to other parts of the world makes my childhood suburban home a technicolour paradise. If anything is the sound of home—other than my mum and dad's 'G'day love 'ow 're ya goin'—it's the birds singing in the background.

10. **Our greatest export success is green -** I've found gum trees— eucalypts as they're called here—all over this planet. On the west coast of the US the trees arrived with gold seekers back from the Australian gold rush. They were planted in the hope they could be used as railway sleepers, telegraph poles or ship masts. Of course none of these plans eventuated because the wood split. Now they remain as windbreaks and reminders of get rich quick schemes that went awry. Many foreigners hate them. Call them weeds.

Gumtrees pop up in the oddest places. Out of the blue—there they will be—as spare and beautiful as a piece of Tim Winton prose. Often they'll be taller than I remember them back home. When I see them I want to ask how did you get here? How did you survive in this foreign soil? Much the same questions I'd have asked my Gallipoli grandfather or the convict Kables had I met them.

In the Californian county I now call home, in wine country just north of San Francisco, legend has it author Jack London brought eucalypts here to make furniture. That never happened and now his legacy is a 100,000 acres of them. There's a grove of stringy barks near my home. As I drive through them I always wind down the windows of the car. Once a gumnut fell in and hit me right smack on the head. A big giggle came from my little boy in the backseat—as cheeky as a little gumnut babe. As the scent of eucalyptus wafted in the car I told him to breathe deeply—to smell home. Then I realised it was my homeland not his. He'll have his own homeland smells that—unless we move back to Australia—will not be the same as my own. I was talking to the trees, not to my son, so I told them this:

> It doesn't matter where you put down roots you will always be Australian. You may shed your bark but you never lose your leaves and this makes you different from a lot of other trees. You are enterprising and you can survive anywhere. We're a lot alike—us Australian people and our trees. And maybe like Vegemite—some of us are just better abroad. Maybe we're better nurtured there—have more room to grow. Sometimes we're prouder, stronger, taller and more exotic outside our country than in it. Maybe if we were to go home we'd be chopped down like a tall poppy. Sure, we may be shallow-rooted, fast-growing, and piss some people off, but we're bloody hardy buggers. No doubt about that mate!

Helen Pitt is a journalist and has worked as a staff writer for the *Sydney Morning Herald*, the *Bulletin* and *New York Times Digital*. After stints in Britain and France, she now lives in Petaluma, California, with her husband and son.

SIMPLY OVERWHELMED

I'm an internationally renowned housewife. Okay, not really. The Danes didn't seek me out to enlighten them about my innovative Australian housekeeping skills. It was, in fact, my German-born husband they sought out and most definitely not for *his* housekeeping skills. He's an IT professional. However, while he's safely tucked away in academia, I'm the one trying to negotiate the peculiar and intriguing world of everyday life with the Danes. This is my first stint as an expatriate so I have been a bit naïve (and still am). I didn't realise how utterly different things would be here and hadn't really examined what I was leaving behind.

Before coming to live in Denmark I had the impression that it was a socially progressive, friendly place. I did expect bad weather and in that respect I have not been disappointed. However, making Danish friends is somewhat harder than I had once presumed and their social progressiveness looks somewhat diminished from my current vantage point. At any rate, I now see Australia in an even more favourable light.

Although I've always felt like I'm an Australian, I had never really thought about what it actually means to be an Australian. By contrast, the Danes know exactly what it is to be Danish. That's the biggest difference and the hardest one to deal with. Australians can be many different things and still be accepted whereas you must look and behave in a very particular way to be thought of as Danish.

We've been living in Denmark for two years now and my husband has managed to get by without speaking more than a few phrases of Danish. When he's at the university (and he almost always is) he could be at any university, anywhere in the world. There are many foreigners there and everyone is speaking English.

It is quite a different experience for me though. I have to deal with doctors, dentists, preschools, other parents, neighbours, banks and so on. I've had a crash course in Danish language and culture and it certainly has been a shock. How can people who look so familiar have such a different attitude to things?

That would be okay except that the Danish government isn't really into multi-culturalism and wants immigrants to blend right in. They are still grappling, unsuccessfully, with an "integration" policy of the type Australia abandoned decades ago. I'll be happy if the degree of my integration extends to learning enough of the bizarre Danish language to have a conversation with a Dane over the age of five.

I'm currently avoiding Danish preschoolers like the plague. I've recently had a very nasty experience that has put my integration program back several months, if not a whole year. While collecting my daughter from preschool I was accosted by two cocky four year olds who questioned me mercilessly. They quickly realised that their own command of Danish was more proficient than mine and this led to that all-too-common assumption about newly-arrived foreigners, that is, that I was mentally deficient.

Presented with the unexpected windfall of having someone around to whom they were linguistically superior, they proceeded to taunt me with names equivalent to 'willy' and 'fart' and even resorted to physical violence in the form of a hefty right hook to my knee-cap. My feeble attempts to reprimand them with broken Danish and stern looks was only met with a renewed round of jeers and insults so I limped away, in utter humiliation, to find a teacher so I could dob on them. Justice was finally served and I received a loud, if not heartfelt, apology. I am still recovering from the mental trauma and have nightmares about being left alone with a group of belligerent preschool Vikings.

The Danes are very proud of their Viking heritage even though the current race bears little resemblance to their fearsome ancestors. In an attempt to recapture the Viking spirit, children under the age of seven are encouraged to resemble characters from Lord of the Flies. The Danish philosophy for preschoolers includes spending most of the day outside, regardless of the weather, with no organized activities and as little adult supervision as possible. Bullies are referred to as 'leaders' and disputes are often worked out with the aid of props, such as, toys guns, swords and big sticks.

It can be quite disconcerting to the newly arrived Australian parent to visit a potential preschool and see a row of 20 prams, filled with babies (some crying), out in the snow, without an adult in sight. Also alarming is the sight of 3 year olds hanging from the tops of trees like spider monkeys. Another new-arrival friend of mine questioned the teachers at our preschool about the safety of such a practice but she was assured that the tree was not being harmed in any way. What a relief.

The great mystery is that, somewhere before adulthood, the Danes are taught to be peaceful and responsible citizens. My children are still preschoolers so I haven't witnessed how this miraculous transformation takes place. Perhaps it happens in school. One interesting thing I have learned about the Danish school system is that the Danes consider it more important to learn to get along with their classmates than to excel academically. Danes go through most of their school-life with the same classroom of individuals. They are not divided up according to their academic ability. The slow kids get extra attention and the smarts ones have to amuse themselves somehow.

I think this method of schooling demonstrates some interesting quirks of Danish society. The first is the difficulty foreigners face in being accepted into Danish society. Danes are used to being with the same people all the time and not having to deal with incorporating strangers. They are friendly enough on the surface but developing anything deeper then a casual acquaintance with a Dane is quite a challenge.

This 'egalitarian' method of schooling also shows some characteristics of Danish society that one Danish author has described and named Jante Law (Axel Sandemose, *A Refugee Crosses His Tracks*, 1933). It's a bit like 'tall poppy syndrome' but is much more developed in its intricacies and considerably more widespread and accepted (albeit subconsciously) among the Danish population.

Jante Law clearly articulates the social and moral standards:

1. You shall not think that you are special.

2. You shall not think that you are of the same standing as us.

3. You shall not think that you are smarter than us.

4. Don't imagine yourself as being better than us.

5. You shall not think that you know more than us.

6. You shall not think that you are more important than us.

7. You shall not think that you are good at anything.

8. You shall not laugh at us.

9. You shall not think that anyone cares about you.

10. You shall not think that you can teach us anything.

Unfortunately, I was totally unaware of The Jante Law when I attended my first parents' meeting at my daughters' preschool. I guess, from the Danish parents' perspective, it looked like I came there with both barrels blazing. I had the gall to think that I knew some better ways to do things and to suggest that some changes be made. My ideas did not seem too radical to me. For example, that the children wash their hands before eating. However, the reaction was so aggressive. It was as if I had asked them to change their religion.

I really don't think Danes would argue so vehemently against hand-washing under normal circumstances (I hope not, anyway). I think it was because I, an outsider, broke several Jante laws and had to be dealt with accordingly. I was told that if I didn't like the way things were then I should go someplace else. I have been shunned by half of the parents since. There were some parents there that I thought probably felt sorry for me but they didn't dare defend me because of the potential repercussions from their more conservative compatriots.

I was wandering around a bit dazed and confused after this experience so it was a great relief when my Danish language teacher explained the Jante Law in class. It helped put things in perspective a bit and gave me some guidelines to keep out of trouble in future. As it turned out, most of the people in my class had had a similar experience at some time. If only the Danes issued a copy of the Jante Law to new arrivals at the airport. It would save a lot trouble.

My language class is a valuable support group in my struggle to understand the mysteries of the Danish culture and language. Believe me, one needs a lot of support to learn a language with a written form that bears little resemblance to the spoken form. That's bad enough, but one also has to make noises that one would usually associate with an intellectually challenged person afflicted by a severe speech impediment.

It is often said that the Danish language is not actually a language, but a disease, and that it helps to have a potato in your mouth while you're speaking. Even if foreigners do manage to conquer the language, the natives often still do not understand them because of their accents. Most Danes are not used to hearing foreigners speak Danish and find it hard to tune their ears to it.

My ongoing struggle with spoken Danish continues to make life quite difficult and embarrassing. For example, a few months ago I was in a cafe in Copenhagen with a Danish friend and I wanted to ask the waitress for some teaspoons. I checked with my friend who confirmed that I should say: '*Har du nogle skeer?*' The little confidence I had quickly dissipated as I saw a look of mortification creep across the waitress's face. At this point, I resorted to asking in English. I told my Danish friend what had happened and repeated what I had said. She suggested that the waitress probably thought I had asked '*Har du nøgen skede?*' or, in English: "*Have you naked vagina?*" These two sentences sound almost the same in Danish.

Needless to say, I won't be going back to that cafe in a hurry. In fact, I rarely go to cafes and restaurants in Denmark at all. Not only because I frequently embarrass myself, or because it's so expensive but because of the poor air quality. The smoke is so thick in these places that I'm inclined to start combating the cigarette-wielding patrons with a fire extinguisher.

It's not only cafes and restaurants, however. It seems that smoking is acceptable everywhere in Denmark except medical buildings. It's like Australia 30 years ago. There has been a half-hearted attempt to stop smoking in some public buildings. I've seen 'no smoking' signs at the local university but the abundance of ashtrays, supplied by the university, tend to undermine the whole idea of a serious smoke-free policy. In other words, smoking is not allowed *unless* you really, really want to. The staff can even smoke in the preschool building. In fact, 40% of Danes smoke and there is no age restriction on those wishing to buy cigarettes.

The first December I was here I noticed a "no smoking" sign in the local supermarket. I was absolutely thrilled that progress was finally being made. In my hasty exuberance I wrote to the management and congratulated them on their new non-smoking policy. I had a prompt reply in which I was informed that the only reason there was a non-smoking sign was that they were selling fireworks. Smoking would be allowed again after New Year's Eve.

In a way, the Danes cannot be held totally responsible for their devotion to the odious weed. After all, they love their Queen and everything she does. And what she does most, is smoke. She is the only yellow-toothed monarch that I have seen and, oddly enough, she is patron of the Danish Cancer Society. Perhaps she considers it some sort of insurance policy.

While the obsession with smoking must put a terrible strain on the public health care system, the Danes are still Vikings when it comes to disease, pain and medical treatment. Well, I assume it is pure Viking bravery that has made the use of anaesthesia superfluous in Denmark. Few women in Denmark are allowed the luxury of an epidural during childbirth (the Royals are an exception of course). A Danish friend told me they gave her something called a 'bee sting', which is an injection that causes a stinging pain in the back. The theory is that the pain in the back takes your mind off the pain in your front. It is certainly an innovative idea. I can't imagine why the 'bee sting' hasn't caught on in other countries.

My Danish neighbour went to the extent of moving to England for the birth of her two children so that she may at least have the option of pain relief. She was too terrified to have her babies here. She's seen a lot, she's a nurse.

One of my husband's work colleagues recently had a hip replacement operation. They did give anaesthesia this time, but only a local. They kindly offered that he might bring some headphones if he wanted to drown out the sound of the power tools. There's not much you can do about the smell of burning flesh and bone though I guess.

Before I knew of this unusual aversion to pain-killers and sedation, I had the misfortune to need a routine procedure myself. I had undergone the same procedure in Australia some years ago but only under sedation. I won't go into much detail about it, just to say that it involved a part of the body one wouldn't normally present to a stranger, except, perhaps, from the window of a fast moving car.

You can imagine my surprise when I realised that things were proceeding without the sedation. I quickly pointed out to the doctor that

I was still conscious but he told me that sedation wasn't necessary. Not necessary for whom? *I* certainly find it necessary and I think they probably did as well, when they heard how loud I could yell.

I've heard many stories from many foreigners about the odd approach the Danes have to medicine. When questioned about their methods, the Danish doctors usually cite Danish studies that have shown that they do not need to do this test or treat this symptom or give that medicine. I think it likely that these studies are commissioned by the person responsible for saving money on public health care.

I would also like to point out that doing research based on a country with a tiny gene pool of culturally pure specimens is not necessarily conclusive and perhaps they should open their minds to the findings of researchers from the outside world. After all, I'm a foreigner and I'm missing the Viking gene. I need to be treated differently!

However, I really am trying to conform by observing and imitating Danish traditions. I'm not going to start smoking but there is another favourite Danish practice that looked pretty safe to me. Flag waving. It's one of the first things you will notice upon arrival in Denmark. Danes love to whip out their flags at every opportunity. Most Danes have their own flagpoles in their gardens. They have miniature flags to decorate their Christmas trees and for birthday decorations. They even eat them in the form of ice creams. However, the real significance of the flag was driven home to me when I made yet another affront to Danish sensibilities.

The previous owners of our house left us their flagpole and their flag. They also left a list of flag days and rules of flag usage. Unfortunately, our Danish was not up to the task of deciphering most of this. We did know that most Danes put the flag up on birthdays so we decided to do as the Danes do and we put the flag up for one of ours. Unfortunately, we forgot to take it down. A concerned neighbour came by the next day and told us that we had better take the flag down. He said while *he* didn't mind, the other neighbours were getting upset. Apparently, if you leave the flag up after sunset, you are saluting the devil. No wonder they were having a meeting about us. The neighbour that was voted spokesperson was probably terrified of us. It's amazing how patriotism can embolden one.

I haven't been game to put the flag up again for fear I will forget to bring it down before sunset. The neighbours might think I'm trying to provoke them. Every time I think about it I imagine I hear an angry crowd assembling in our front garden and I peer out nervously to see them carrying burning torches and pitchforks and chanting 'kill the devil worshippers!'.

I am, of course, being paranoid. It's just that sometimes I am overwhelmed by incomprehension. When it gets that way I try to remember what an experienced expatriate told me before I left Australia. She said that when I came across customs that seemed to defy logic I should try to remember that it all has its purpose in the overall functioning of the culture. I guess when I have a better overview of the culture things will start falling into place.

In the meantime, aspects of my life that I once took for granted have been thrown into question and have to be re-evaluated. I've gone from being a reasonably articulate, respected and useful member of society to an illiterate, mute, ignoramus who must daily battle though a sea of prejudice (theirs and mine). I wonder if that famous Australian expat Mary Donaldson is having more luck than I am in Denmark. Although, I guess you can call 'going out with a crown prince' pretty lucky.

Leah Quinn has been living in Denmark for two years with my German-born husband and two Australian-born daughters. I have a degree in English and Sociology and before coming to Denmark I was a website designer. Now I'm a 'trailing spouse' and stay at home with my children muttering to myself.

LA REVERIE

Today I don't want to be Me.
Today I don't want to be Nice.
Today I want to be Godzilla,
Gigantic, Gargantuan Gorilla.
Stomping, Shaking,
Bashing, Bruising and Breaking
Everything in my Way.

Get Out before I Destroy You,
And your Cold, Callous, Rhinestone-Cowboy antics.
You haven't cared what you have done.
Pretenders of Industry, Power Poker Players,
Cutting Deals with Ice-pick Spokes,
Sticking our lives like Cubes in the bottom of your whiskey glass,
To be Sucked in by your Spray Spittle and Spat out on a whim.

Out of My Way, before I Tramp on you,
Crushing your electronic smiles.
We trusted you. You were Big and Friendly,
(You gave us some shares to soften us up.)
Powerful, Impressive, Modern, Slick.
Slick Flick with your Telephonic Stick.
And Quick.
You Cut out Everything, Scissoring our Roots:
Global lifelines to friends,
Solid schools for the kids,
Settled home hearth for the family,
Proud Job for Dad.
Fingered
By your Phoney Faceless Foul-Ups.

All gone?
No prob. No matter.
You'll be right.
Life's like that sometimes.
You have to take the good with the bad.
Now don't be angry.
Just be nice. Tomorrow's another day.

But I don't want to be Nice.
I want to be a Gorilla,
And Rip Off Your Contemptible Corporate Head.

Some days being an expat can get you down a little and I guess the day I wrote this poem in August 1999 was one of those days. Writing it was good therapy. Being an expat means you have to be resourceful and on this particular day I needed every inner resource I could muster.

My husband and I had just been told that all our plans were going to change, that head office no longer wanted to open a Paris branch after all. Our reason for being out of Australia had just evaporated. They were changing strategic direction, not because there was any real lack of success, but because they needed to save money. In this instance saving money was more important than making it. It was definitely more important than the consequences to our family.

So began a story that is probably quite familiar to seasoned expats who are living and working overseas because 'The Company' has posted them there. It is the downside to all the glamour and pleasure of the off-shore experience, the little-mentioned time when you realise that your life is not your own, and instead you are a pawn on the chessboard of some executive's self-saving strategy. The kind of corporate player who floats a brilliant idea, brings it into half-baked existence then, when things look grim, moves on, leaving the remains for the next poor bloke to clean up, while you are left holding the proverbial baby, making apologies for the mess that has been made to the people who believed in you.

In our case this brilliant idea was to open a European branch of 'The Company' in Paris and we were to do it. With our Australian house still unpacked, and the removalists promising all would be well and that they would leave the house keys with the neighbours, we boarded our plane. Not to France—'The Company' hadn't been able to quite get that signed off, so while they pondered their position, we flew to Switzerland, to spend time with my husband's family. There we would wait until we could be told where our destination was to be. I remember sitting on the balcony of my in-laws' apartment looking at the snowy peaks of the Alps wondering if someone would tell the packers so our furniture would reach us. Two weeks later we were told no, it wouldn't be Paris, yet. For the moment it would be London.

Our arrival in Paris didn't take place for six months. In the intervening period we had to put our children into school, find a temporary home and wait for all the paperwork and bureaucratic hassling to be completed in order for an Australian family to legally live and commence a business in Paris. None of that had been started prior to our departure. As my husband is Swiss and not French (and therefore not possessing an EU passport) the juggling and manoeuvring became quite entertaining. We watched and waited as French bureaucrats got a handle on the notion that a Swiss-born Australian—working for some Australian telecommunications business with an office in London—wanted to start up a business in competition with France Telecom. *Oo-la-la!*

So six months was spent in London. Thinking, as one does, that a house with a garden would be just the shot for this Australian family, we soon learnt that living in an apartment with two kids can sometimes be a more suitable abode. In those six months we had eight days of sunshine and when the garden turned to a bog I quickly learnt why the British invented Wellington boots. It occurred to me on more than one occasion that England may be actually sinking under all the watering it receives, especially when the roof tiles and walls of houses grow succulent moss. When the news reports started discussing the collapse of some southern coastlines into the sea, taking the houses resting atop the cliffs with them, I knew my suspicions were well founded.

With the safe arrival of the furniture in London we all started the process of adjusting to the cultural gap. Our eight-year-old daughter quickly took it for granted that a few of her classmates were real princes and princesses from a place called Borneo. However, she became confused by the notion that they were attending school in London and not in Sydney, when she was shown the location of Borneo and its proximity to Australia. It was also here that she was introduced to the idea that children could have their own business cards when the heir to the Cadbury throne was handing his out at recess. She still has it, all beautifully decorated with a black London taxi, in case she ever needs a quick supply of non-Swiss chocolates for the future.

For our twelve-year-old son adaptation involved, among other things, getting used to travelling to and from school alone on the Northern Line of the London tube in all its suffocating peak-hour press, stoppages in blacked-out tunnels, and mazes of underground inner-city walkways.

As for me, well I learnt that one thing the English do well is history. My cultural apprenticeship commenced by watching *The Antique Roadshow* and other such enlightening programs while wondering how on earth I was going to adapt to not working any more. These shows made me feel I was actually residing in a living museum and while the English seem to suffer from a lack of many important things (sunshine, space, good beaches, just to name a few) they do not lack in history and they have created an enormous industry selling that history to themselves and everyone else.

Having so much history surrounding me, and being totally homesick and miserable under the slate grey rain, it was no wonder that I began to read Robert Hughes' *A Fatal Shore*. It was from his account that my unemployment dilemma was solved and I began the metamorphosis from teacher-librarian into author. To find something to get my research teeth into I immediately took myself off to the British Library, told them I was writing a book, gained a one month reader's card which later turned into a five year reader's card, and began researching and writing my first novel, *The Sarsaparilla Souvenir*. This is a memoire of First Fleet convict, Mary Broad. My love affair with the British Library continues today.

We were all just starting to accept our new life when one day in February, in the middle of the school year, we were told to start packing, we were on our way to Paris!

What excitement! The thrill of flying over for the weekend, selecting our nineteenth century apartment located twenty minutes walk from the Arc de Triomphe and our arrival on a crisp sunny day when the first daffodils and tulips were bobbing their colourful heads under a bright blue sky in the Parc de Monceau. We were fascinated watching for the first time, the stick-insect machine lift our belongings from street-level up to the apartment because the staircase was too narrow and the lift too small. We were taken by the romance of that first night listening to the sounds of the Parisian traffic and hearing the notes played by the local organ-grinder and the screeching of his monkey. We had fun throwing copper coins down to him, watching them land on the dog poo encrusted pavement as the sun set over the grey Parisian rooftops and hearing his reply, with robust Gallic emphasis, '*Merde*!'.

Ah, Paris! Has there ever been a more romantic city? From art galleries to cathedrals, from cobbled-stoned streets with names like *Rue de Rustic* to cafes such as *Le Cafe Vigny*, whose claim to fame is its continuing existence in neighbourly proximity to the site where the Statue of Liberty was constructed before being shipped out to New York. These days the *Vigny*—as we affectionately called it—is the drop-in-stop for morning coffee among expat mothers whose children attend the nearby Ecole de Bilangue. Over coffee we exchange tips on how to survive everything from the French lack of service in all commercial matters, to the French gynaecologists' lack of a sensitivity and joke about the Anglo dislike of full-body nakedness.

Of relevance to our position was how best to survive the annual medical examination required for the renewal of the obliquitous *Carte de Sejour* (Permission to Stay in France Card). Hours can be spent standing in line (who said it is only the English who like to queue?) publicly holding your little sample of urine! Seasoned expats, no doubt, have overcome such coyness but for the new expat, these matters take on great importance in conversations over coffee.

So there we were, totally relishing all the wonders and joys and *petites quelque chose* of Paris, expecting to be there for three years, when one day, six months into our sojourn, a phone call was received to say that someone in head office had changed his mind. The telephone company was ending our life in Paris with a phone call!

For the children it was tragic. They had only just started to settle into their French international schools, made new friends again, adapted to their new life in an inner city apartment, just got over the worst phase of learning a new language but without being given the time to move into the pleasurable phase of accomplishment and communication. Our departure would again, be in the middle of the school year. Their new school would be the third in a little over twelve months. All the re-birthing phase over again.

Our son was going to have to give up Saturday afternoons at the movies on the Champs-Elysees with all his school friends. Our daughter was going to miss out on more birthday parties at the beauty salon—the latest fashionable kids party venue at the time. For my husband, no more sunset wanderings down to the Louvre, strolls along La Seine or playing *petanque* at Les Tuilleries. For me, no more weekend trips into French country villages, tasting divine regional delicacies and wonderful local wines. No wonder I turned to poetry!

It really was sad for my husband. All the efforts trying to establish the business from scratch in a market where you were considered crazy to attempt such a feat but in which he was showing early signs of success due to his knowledge of the culture. Normally, no Aussie would have stood a chance without such inside understanding of the way the French do business but all his hard work went for nothing. To be told to choose between a job that no longer existed in Sydney, to sit at a desk and do nothing till 'something came up', or to go back to rainy England to sit at a desk and do nothing till 'something came up', was a disheartening choice. He was stuck between a rock and a hard place.

Yet there is probably one thing that the expat experience teaches you more than anything else. To be an expat you have to be flexible—you have to see the bright point when all else seems black. You must seek the funny side, especially when the joke seems to be on you. You must look to the 'other side', find the Garry Larson perspective, and above all, you must move on.

In that sense, the expat life becomes a metaphor for the journey of life that we are all on. So having changed before, we accepted the new challenge of changing again—not to go back but to go on. This time it was to Geneva.

My husband jumped commercial ship and moved to a Swiss telco, only to have the rug pulled out from under his feet again. From the time he signed on the dotted line to a couple of months when later started in his new post, the job had been changed—the boss had once again moved on. Not to be defeated, we moved into a new house, kids started new schools in the French system where all subjects were taught in French with only six hours of English a week and I started a new novel, *Whispering Shadows*. We all hunkered down to endure the adaptation process once again.

Geneva is a city that may only be about the size of Adelaide but its history has made its reputation and character truly international. It is the home of many international organisations including various arms of the UN and the International Committee of the Red Cross.

So here we landed. This time our setting was rural France. Even though we were only fifteen minutes out of one of the most cosmopolitan cities in the world we were in the French outback, on the frontier with Switzerland, and in a village where the Mayor has more horses than people under her jurisdiction. In our immediate vicinity there is a wilderness area that provides cross-country skiing in winter and hundreds of kilometres of walking trails in pine forests during summer. Nearby is an international casino, Lake Geneva and the yacht club that sent out the Swiss winner of the America's Cup and CERN (The European Centre for Nuclear Research). It was at CERN that Tim Berners-Lee invented what is now known as the World Wide Web.

Now we are once again masters of our own destiny. After a few months my husband changed jobs once more, this time employed in an international company based in Geneva. As Swiss citizens we are locals but as Australians we are still a long way from home.

The children still see themselves as Aussie yet when we go back for visits we know we hold another dimension now: the dimension of the international experience. It is at once our loss and our gain. The paradox of being both and neither. Our kids have now joined the group called 'Third Culture Kids' where the children are living outside of their origins mixing more easily with others like themselves, seeing themselves as 'international' rather than having loyalties to only one place.

And so what have we achieved? Our goals for our kids are to have them experience both their heritages: the Australian and the Swiss. Now that they are bilingual they can live and work in either region as adults. They have experienced life in more than two cultures, met children from all over the world, and understand that their futures are only limited by their own imaginations rather than by any geographical boundary.

For my husband, he has attained his dream of living and working on the international scene. Coming from Switzerland he has always been exposed to the idea of a multilingual and multicultural life. As a hang-gliding nutter he can now fly in the Alps when here, and over the ocean and the desert in Australia.

As for me, well I am still making the transition from being an Australian teacher-librarian to international author. I have yet to see my books published but haven't given up hope. Each story is a new journey and every place I visit provides potential for a future story. My expat journey has been as emotionally demanding as the children's, though they have done a far better job of the linguistic side of life. My outer journey is mirrored in my books, where my characters face the challenges of growing outside of their home environments : the first as a convict exile in Botany Bay, the second as an Australian adolescent facing adult consequences in a foreign world.

All my life seems a journey now: whether it be the inner life of my imagination or the outer life of the expat, mother and wife. They have all been demanding, rewarding, and expanding voyages. For all the heartache, the anger, the disappointment and disillusionment, there have been exquisite times of joy, renewal and success. I still yearn for home, but it is the home of the high place, the place from where I can look back to see how far I have come, as well as to see the misty path of the future. It is the Dreaming Place: *La Reverie.*

Jo Anne Rey currently has a dual career of wife and mother. The other occupations, I realise, sound like Soviet-era economic plans, 'expat for five years', 'ex-teacher-librarian for five years' and 'yet-to-be-published author for five years'. However, it is the continuing support from my loved ones that gives me the freedom to keep exploring all my dreams.

SOME SNAPSHOTS OF LIFE

The BBC television series 'Brits Abroad' showed real life Brits living in various locations around the world. I especially stayed home the night they featured Hong Kong. By this time I had already committed to a position in Hong Kong, and had a few weeks left in London before I relocated. In a half hour episode I was introduced to a couple of interesting characters depicted as typical Hong Kong expatriates. One was a middle-aged woman with a cultured English accent who lived with her millionaire husband on the Peak. She had a very nice, spacious apartment with fabulous views over the harbour—mmm, my decision to go to Hong Kong was looking good. An ex-history teacher, she lived the life of a typical *tai tai* (a woman who financially does not need to work). A member of the ladies' club in the midlevels, she was filmed playing a game of tennis with her *tai tai* friends then lunching with them. She had recently established her own business, and proudly introduced an S&M playroom complete with rubber suits, whips and cages! Her successful and enterprising new business, Fetish Fashion, was conveniently located on the Escalator that transports many wealthy expats to their homes each night.

Another Brit abroad in Hong Kong was a young East End guy who hadn't made it in the investment banking scene in London so thought he'd try his luck in Hong Kong. He proudly stated that he'd made a fortune and was living the good life. Out on a junk trip with his mates, he was getting very drunk on beer, and used his mobile phone to arrange for more beer to be delivered to the junk. It was too late to back out of my move to Hong Kong, but I was wondering whether Hong Kong was going to be all about cocky young guys earning too much money and wanting to entice me to a playroom in Fetish Fashion!

Arriving in Hong Kong, I was met at the airport by my new firm's driver and transported to the Furama Hotel, which was to be my home for the next month. Sitting in that car, I was stunned by the dehumanisation of Hong Kong. A mass of high-rise buildings, as far as I could see, reminded me of the ant farm I'd had when I was a child. The see-through walls of my plastic sand-filled ant farm had allowed me to see the ants going about their daily lives. This is what Hong Kong seemed to be—one big ant farm where I could lose myself and never be found again. In between the clusters of buildings I caught glimpses of stunning turquoise water and an active working harbour. I sat very silently in that car trying to reach some sort of acceptance that this city was to be my new home.

I went to bed very early, with the hotel room curtains open. *I must not panic, I must not panic.* The next morning I looked out of the window onto Chater Garden and saw hundreds of women gathered in small groups. It sounded like an aviary. This was overwhelming, how could I venture out into the crowds below? It was only later that I discovered this was a Sunday phenomenon, and the women were Filipino maids enjoying their day off.

I was on a mission. It was my first week in Hong Kong, and I only knew one person in a city of seven million. Ange, my friend, who qualified with me in Melbourne, was coincidentally, a lawyer in the firm I had joined. Although she had a broad Australian accent, her parents were from Hong Kong so she spoke Cantonese and was willing to help me find my feet. We hit Causeway Bay on the weekend. Or more appropriately, Causeway Bay hit us. Was this what shopping was like in Hong Kong? Crossing roads involved seemingly all of humanity pushing us forward with no appreciation of my Australian need for personal space. How could I do this every time I needed to go shopping? We spent hours pounding the pavements, looking at furniture shops. This wasn't going to be my only Causeway Bay experience, as Ange was organising my return to make more purchases once I had found a flat. I had already decided I was going to live near the Escalator. I had lived at eight different addresses in London over a six year period, and my priority was being able to walk to work. Surely that same priority would apply to my commute in Hong Kong. I contacted an agent who said she had the perfect building for me—Manhattan Heights in Kennedy Town. I walked into the brand new building right on the waterfront and was surprised that it looked like an up-market hotel foyer, complete with marble and a chandelier. The views were stunning, described by the agent as having the 'wow factor'. Who needs to be able to walk to work anyway? Gosh, that was easy, I had my new home. Now, time to get out and meet some new people.

The Wombat Hole. What sort of name is that for a bar? I decided to attend the monthly drinks put on by the Australian Association of Hong Kong. Turning up on my own, I paid my entrance fee and stuck on my name tag, decorated with a bright orange sticker to ensure everyone in the room knew that it was my first time to the drinks function. Immediately I found myself embraced by a group of women who were discussing the schools their children attended. I asked them what they did for work, to find that none of them worked, they spent their time on various hobbies and going to a place called Shenzhen for shopping—well, that was good news, so I didn't have to shop at Causeway Bay after all. Moving on, I found myself talking to a group of teachers. One of the teachers, Louise, took pity on me and empathised with me on how embarrassing it was to have the orange sticker on my name tag. I proceeded to get drunk, and made plans to join the teachers for a birthday dinner at a restaurant in Wan Chai the following week. Mission accomplished, I had made some new friends.

Meanwhile, back at work I was told that I needed a Chinese name for my business card. How cool, imagine having a Chinese name. Would I have to learn how to say it? Translators had come up with two alternatives for me. Did I want to be a beautiful intelligent woman, or a young ambitious girl? The roughly phonetic translation would provide me with Chinese characters with meaning!

A few weeks into my induction into Hong Kong I was asked out on a junk trip. Oh, I know all about junk trips from the coverage on 'Brits Abroad'. The email told me to be at Queen's Pier at 11 am to go on Retsam, the firm's junk. A stunning luxury boat drew into the pier and we climbed aboard. Beers were handed out, people dispersed to the front of the junk, the roof, and inside where the airconditioning was frigid and unwelcoming. We stopped near Red Hill to do some waterskiing. Fabulous, I hadn't been waterskiing since I was at university. Next stop was Lantau Island at Lower Cheung Sha beach. We were transported to the beach in the motorboat, and had lunch in the Stoep, a South African BBQ restaurant right on the sand. So, this is it, life in Hong Kong!

Did I want to be in the firm's dragon boat team? Of course! Imagine being able to tell people at home that I'd paddled in the races at Stanley. Imagine too not having to work on Saturday mornings because training sessions were scheduled. A mini bus transported us from Central to Stanley for the first training session. We trustingly left our bags and clean clothes on the beach, and waded through water full of old rubber gloves, shampoo bottles, plastic bags and other discarded rubbish to climb into the long wooden boat. Our coach was a Scottish partner in the firm, a short rugby player who took the training sessions very seriously. For two hours we tried to coordinate our strokes, but somehow still ended up accidentally saturating the person behind with a rogue stroke. I put so much body movement into my strokes that I rubbed a raw blister on my bottom that proceeded to stick to my underwear for the next week. Afterwards we showered and dragged ourselves off to the Smugglers Inn to re-hydrate on beer. Training continued for six weeks, a team spirit evolved and I made some new friends. One of these friends asked me to accompany her to Sunny Paradise.

What on earth is Sunny Paradise? Feeling brave and curious, I said yes and a HK$30 taxi ride later we stopped at 341 Lockhard Road in the heart of Wan Chai. Those in the know visit Sunny Paradise for a regular massage and a unique Hong Kong experience. We emerged from the lift to a room with rows of black leather lounge chairs and foot-stools. After changing into a bathrobe, unflattering disposable underwear and slipping on a pair of plastic scuffs, we took a seat, put our feet up, and started relaxing. Complimentary food was available, including fresh watermelon or orange juice, toasted ham and cheese sandwiches, fresh papaya, and the special noodle dish of the day.

My friend was a regular patron and asked for her favourite masseur, identified by an allocated number. I lay down in the massage room expecting a gentle Swedish style massage when strong hands dug deep into the pressure points in my back and manipulated my limbs into positions that I didn't think were possible. Bravely I gave my masseur permission to walk on my back while she held the hand rails attached to the ceiling. It felt distinctly odd to have her feet rubbing my neck, and I found myself holding my breath as she walked up and down my back, her weight feeling heavier than I'm sure it was. Burning hot towels were piled up on my back, and my last attempt to remain alert and engaged in the process failed. I floated back to the changing room with smudged eyes and messy hair.

How many people outside of Hong Kong know that 40 percent of Hong Kong is national park? Most of my friends have an image of Hong Kong as a shoppers' paradise, with a stunning harbour and many high-rise buildings. As did I. It was a pleasant surprise to discover that hiking is one of the great pleasures of Hong Kong. The views can be truly spectacular, and the walks rewarding, accommodating different standards and preferences. One of the most spectacular walks is around the Peak. The combination of natural harbour and man-made city is breathtaking. But it's not like hiking in the Australian bush, or on the public footpaths dotted throughout the English countryside. Hong Kong hiking is unique. Paths are often concreted, with handy steps for climbing or descending steep hills. Local Chinese hikers often carry around portable radios or cassette players, listening to Chinese opera or the races. Old men with rolled up white singlets expose Buddha style bellies. On humid days the atmosphere is like walking through a tropical jungle, in contrast to the winter months when warm clothes are a must. In the summer months large black spiders with orange backs emerge from the thick foliage and scare any hikers who have the endurance to be hiking in 36 degree heat and 90 percent humidity.

However, it was the day-to-day working life that was the most interesting, and different from my experiences in Europe and Australia. Lunchtime was sacred. It didn't matter if there was an immovable deadline, the office would become a canteen at lunchtime, with people slurping noodles and eating rice in small friendly groups crowded around desks. I sampled my first (and last) moon cake at work, when the HR manager brought one to my office during the moon cake festival. Members of my team would quite often bring in small gifts of chocolates or toiletries for the other team members. A mouthwatering cake from Cova or the Mandarin Cake Shop was a must for someone's birthday. We had a tea lady, what a luxury! I would get out my Cantonese phrasebook each morning and make her smile with my attempts at speaking simple Cantonese phrases. She couldn't speak any English, was severely humpbacked, but had a wonderful spirit and I enjoyed our childlike exchanges.

One of my team members watched her boyfriend die of cancer over an eight month period. Another team member had her first child (a son), and another would occasionally make me a meal to take home. I was in a supportive and wonderful environment and found the cultural experience both rewarding and at times frustrating. I learnt never to show my frustration or annoyance, as this would be regarded as a loss of face by my Chinese colleagues. Instead I learnt to be more patient and, most importantly, I learnt that although I was so very different from many of the people I worked with, I could also be their friend.

One aspect of expatriate life in Hong Kong, which I was initially shocked by but very quickly learned to appreciate, was the employment of maids. Typically Filipino, but also Sri Lankan, Indian and Thai, they work for an extremely low salary and keep home for the busy locals and expatriates. Noi, my Thai maid, works for me three to four hours a week. In that time she cleans my 699 square foot flat and prepares wonderful Thai meals. When I took some time off work Noi agreed to teach me how to cook my favourite Thai meals. She'd arrive at my flat with bags of exotic ingredients that I hadn't heard of or seen before. Noi would patiently show me what each ingredient looked like, and how to peel, cut and prepare each for the different dishes. During those cooking lessons I learnt a great deal about Noi's life and her family back in Thailand. She was supporting her parents, brothers and sisters through her work in Hong Kong and could still find some money to send back to the local school to help out the children of other families. One day Noi announced that she was to be married, and two weeks later I attended a civil wedding ceremony as a witness. A translator ensured that Noi understood the Chinese celebrant and within ten minutes it was over and Noi was a married woman!

Hong Kong is a surprising city. In the three years I have lived in Hong Kong my feelings towards the city and its population have varied considerably. Quite strong culture shock affected me during the first six months. I was drawn to reading books about the adjustment process that any expatriate would normally experience in relocating to a new country: the initial euphoria and fascination being replaced by depression and then a rejection of all those things that weren't like home.

I met the Australian consular at a networking drinks evening in my first few months and found myself telling him about the surprising emotions I was going through, and how as an avid traveller throughout Asia I hadn't expected to experience any sort of significant culture shock. He was newly arrived, and a few days later I was having dinner with the him and his wife, sharing our thoughts on being new arrivals in Hong Kong. I also discovered in my first year the sadness of having made friends and losing them so quickly when they moved away from Hong Kong to return home. But I made new friends, and very much appreciated how easy it was in Hong Kong to meet new people. Unlike my six years in London, most of the friends I made in Hong Kong were also away from home, and far more open to new friendships and experiences than if they were still at home. The mix of nationalities made every outing a cultural experience in itself. Local Hong Kong friends have been harder to make, and although expats will commonly dismiss this as a product of Hong Kong, I believe it's fairly typical of inhabitants in any city, particularly those who haven't travelled or lived elsewhere.

SARS. It used to stand for Special Administrative Region, the description given to Hong Kong after the British handover to China in 1997. Today it is more likely to be used as an acronym for Severe Acute Respiratory Syndrome. As if Hong Kong didn't have enough problems with an ongoing recession and record unemployment. SARS, a new form of pneumonia, hit the headlines around the world, and became the focal point for Hong Kong residents and visitors. It was all too easy to dismiss when the first few cases were elderly people with pre-existing illnesses. But when SARS started killing healthy people under 40 the world reacted, the WHO issued a travel advisory warning, and the population of Hong Kong donned masks and became obsessed with the daily statistics covering the number of new cases, the number of deaths, and the number of recoveries. TVB Pearl and World, providing the two English news slot available on local television, alternated between headlining the Gulf War, and headlining SARS. To wear a mask or not to wear a mask? Did wearing a mask really protect the wearer from catching SARS? Could you catch SARS from pushing a lift button if an infected person had pushed it before you? Was the treatment being provided by the Hong Kong hospitals making patients better or worse? It was overwhelming. Panic hit one day when a 13-year-old boy placed an announcement on a Chinese language website that Hong Kong was quarantined. I had popped to my nearest supermarket to find long queues of people, not a trolley in sight, and a buzzing atmosphere. My Thai maid had been rung up by her Chinese employers and asked to buy enough rice and cooking oil for three months! My friends and I debated the merits of wearing a face mask, carrying around disinfectant gel, and washing our hands at every available opportunity. Yes, I did wear a mask—twice—in the cinema. After all, the peer group pressure to conform was enormous. The *South China Morning Post*, Hong Kong's premier English language newspaper, ran a Haiku competition. A Haiku is a three lined poem—the first line has five syllables, the second line has seven syllables, and the third line five syllables. My Haiku was published:

Who SARS life's easy?

Hong Kong SARS it can't get worse.

I SARS life goes on.

Tracey Sawyer left Melbourne in 1993 to live and work in London for a legal publishing company. After three and a half years she joined an international law firm and while based in London she travelled to the company's 18 overseas offices to supervise a project she had initiated. In August 2000 Tracey left London to work in Hong Kong.

WHAT HAPPENS NEXT IS UP TO ME

On New Year's Eve 2002, I boarded a plane in Sydney as a child. I walked off that plane in Paris as an adult. I've spent the months afterwards trying to catch up. I grew up in Goulburn, NSW, about an hour's drive from Canberra. I was 17, 11 months and 16 days. By that stage, I had the job of being a Goulburn teenager down to a fine art. I had a well-worn daily routine of going to school, working at McDonald's and living at home. I felt comfortable in a life I knew so well. I knew everything. Happy as I was, I certainly was not content. No matter how busy I was, I still felt bored. Long grown out of school and small town life, I counted down the days until school was over, when life could truly begin. Without minding how I got there, 2003 was the year to spend in Europe. University was for 2004. I had to do something first.

Becoming an au pair appealed because the job involved children and included accommodation. So I started searching for families on the internet. Since I was very young, daydreaming often led to picturing myself sailing down the canals of Venice, viewing Paris from the Eiffel tower or dancing in Spain. Idealistic and travel show-inspired as these thoughts were, they simmered away inside me for years. Now I was at an age to act on them. I was bursting out of my skin.

After corresponding over the internet to families in my dream locations, I narrowed my search down to three—one near Milan, one in Paris and the other in the south of France. I didn't know what to do. Life in the south of France sounded like a dream... complete with four boys under the age of 10 in a job that wouldn't allow me to go to French lessons, a legal requirement for au pairs in France. There was Max and Lily, whose previous au pair had talked up life with them in Paris and sounded really sweet. But... Riccardo and Lorenzo looked gorgeous and I'd have my own car...

In the end, the family in Paris offered me a job which I gladly accepted. Clicking 'send' on the email saying 'Dear Géraldine, I would love to come and work for your family in Paris for a year' is the best move I've ever made. Not once have I wondered if life with another family would have been better.

It must have sounded crazy to people who asked what I would be doing after school. I'd reply I was going over the other side of the world to work and live with a family I'd found on the internet. This sounded especially crazy to my parents. But that's how things worked out, and thankfully so. Imagine how Mum and Dad must have felt: their first child leaving the nest having found some people to live with in France—for a year. The bills rolled in. Passport, visa, travel insurance, medical certificate, translating paperwork into French, plus a plane ticket. All for a daughter whose income was from an after-school job at McDonald's, who wanted a farewell party and spending money in one of the most expensive cities in the world. Mum and Dad have been fantastic. Mum woke the family up on the morning I left for overseas with John Denver's 'Leaving On A Jet Plane' blasting out of the stereo. My parents didn't make a huge scene at the airport. The three of us shed a few tears, while my younger brother and sister were reluctant to participate. I walked through the departure gate, they walked out of the airport, carrying with them the giant keg of Vegemite that had earlier tipped my hand luggage over the limit.

Finally, after nearly 18 years of being under the charge of my parents, I was responsible for myself. That shift occurred the day I became responsible for two children, Max and Lily. I now find it hard to imagine that for so long I knew nothing of their existence. Now they are the centre of my world. I could easily write volumes about their antics, my observations of them and the smallest of attributes that make up their personalities; already so well developed and defined. I love these kids to bits, I'd wrestle tigers for them.

Lily was the first member of the family I met. After a big Bonjour!, she grabbed my hand and pulled me upstairs into what was the first of many hours playing in her room. This action sums her up well: bubbly, enthusiastic, full on! Aged five, her smile is contagious, she keeps me in stitches and we have loads of fun together. In two words, Lily is pure sunshine. Of course, there are moments when I want to send her to her room and she wants to send me back to Australia. Occasionally, her defiant attitude spreads a look across her face which shouts: 'Don't even think about telling me what to do!' The Little Miss Too Big For My Boots attitude, which thankfully doesn't emerge too often. She knows when she has misbehaved, and it is not too hard to forgive her when she takes my hand, lips wobbling as she says 'Excuse me, me sorry'.

Max is better described as a little man rather than as a little boy. I have never met a child like him, he thinks on a deeper level and is more sensitive than most boys *my* age. He is seven years old, gorgeous, charming, well mannered and will have the girls flocking to him in the future. He loves winning and is very dedicated to succeeding. An intense hatred of failure and incapacity to accept he's lost a soccer game mar his positive attitude. He adores his parents, sticks up for his sister and likes cooking. We can have a serious conversation together in one moment, and wrestle and be silly in the next. I love spending time with Max.

I was talking with a few friends before I left, when one asked me my French family's surname. Expecting something exotically French, she thought I was joking when I replied 'Smith'. There are 13 pages of Smiths in the Sydney white pages, and one single Smith in the Paris phonebook. Steve's half-American. He and Géraldine are both journalists and both very successful. I admire the way they balance work and family life— Géraldine's always home in time for baths and meals. They have made settling in easy and have made me feel like part of the family. If a future au pair was to ask my advice, the first thing I'd tell them was to check out the family thoroughly. I love my French family, and I am very lucky.

People are different, and this difference increases when you throw in a city like Paris plus a new culture and language. Plus we all have our own little quirks, habits and oddities. The Smiths see the meat I cook as a total mistake, whose deserving place is in *la poubelle*. As far as I'm concerned, what they view as the perfectly cooked side of meat should still be out munching grass in a paddock. While this is one of many small cultural clashes, we fortunately haven't driven each other mad.

This au pair arrangement is an intimate way to get to know a stranger. Inviting someone into your home to look after your children involves a high level of mutual trust. I'm trusting them not to exploit national regulations for having an au pair: they are the only people I have to fall back on in the entire Northern Hemisphere if I get into trouble. On the other side, they are trusting an 18 year-old from a small Aussie town to look after their children. Not only does she not speak the language, she's clueless about their lifestyle. Trusting a stranger with your children and your house (and therefore everything that goes with it) is a big deal. So I appreciate how much trust and respect I have been shown by Géraldine and Steve.

What my life in Paris would be like sounded simple before I came. In many ways, it is. I walk two well-behaved children to school, spend two hours at French school, pick up the children at 4.30 pm and keep them entertained and under control until their mother comes home. I lend a hand with baths, dinner, and babysitting. Sounds rather two dimensional. Before I left the above details were all I had about my new life. So it was hard to imagine what the coming year would be like. A lot of people asked me before I came if I was scared. I had no idea what to be scared of. I'd never been out of Australia before. I had no idea what I was getting myself into!

Asking me what I expected to find in 2003 was like asking a blind person to describe the colour blue. I came here with no expectations, just enthusiasm and a massive suitcase. Now that I'm living the dream that occupied my thoughts for so long, that paper thin, two dimensional description has been inflated and come alive. Every day has taught me something new, dropping a new challenge at my feet and adding to my experience. On occasions Max and Lily have run to me because a bigger child was giving them a hard time in the park. What on earth could I say to a surly 10-year-old in French that wouldn't lead them to beat up both kids because their au pair talked like a toddler?

I studied French for the first three years of high school. In state exams, I was awarded distinction certificates. Fat lot of good they did for me. Sure, I could count, tell you what day it was or ask for an orange juice, '*si vous plaît*', but not outside of the classroom! Fortunately, many people speak English in Paris and so do Géraldine and Steve, otherwise I would have been silenced. Not speaking French was extremely isolating. My course didn't start until February, so the only people I could talk to were Géraldine and Steve. For the eight hours Max and Lily were at school, I didn't talk at all. It actually wasn't as hard as one would expect to cope with the kids when we didn't speak each other's language. The essential words were there, or soon were found in the dictionary that's permanently attached to me. Being young and intelligent, Max and Lily pick up English at a rate that makes me insanely jealous. If they hear a word but not it's meaning, they are able to use it themselves after hearing it a few times. I think the first two words they learnt from me were 'be careful'. I had no idea how to say that in French, but they picked up on its meaning thanks to my tone of voice and the number of times it was first said.

I was really looking forward to starting French lessons. Finally, I'd meet people. People like myself who'd know what it's like to be in a country where you don't know anyone or anything. Plus I'd be learning how to speak French. French is not something I find easy to learn. There are several elements vital to learning a language. Such as the vocabulary itself; the practice of learning a word, and remembering it, the way it is spelt and pronounced, and whether it is masculine or feminine. Accent is another factor—I can't roll my r's properly just like the French have difficulty saying English words with a 'th'. Grammar also takes time. I find the little words that construct a sentence are more difficult than bigger words. I can grasp a noun or adjective, even verbs after I've memorised them. But the two and three letter words, the conjunctions, the building blocks of a sentence, slip like soap in wet hands. Their meanings are as vague as the words themselves, yet they are essential to getting a message across. These words float around in my head in a cloud of uncertainty that flows through my hand to pen to paper, easy to be struck with a red cross by the teacher.

But the joy that comes from being able to tell a stranger to turn right when they ask for directions, having a decent conversation with Max and Lily and catching *Water Rats* dubbed in French is made even sweeter when I look back on how much I knew when I arrived. Not only will French be the most frustrating and infuriating challenge I've conquered in life so far, it will also be the most rewarding.

If someone speaks to me in public, in a shop for example, they will speak to me in English if they can. I know I don't look French, but is it really that obvious? I've told people I'm Australian, and they say 'But you don't look Australian!' Or when they hear my accent, they say 'You don't sound Australian!' then what do I look like? What do I sound like? The answers vary. I've been told that I look northern European and Russian. I've been told I sound English. Americans think I'm Irish because I don't sound like the Crocodile Hunter. But more often than not, the French think I'm American. Which was interesting when the war in Iraq began, especially around the area I live. The pro-Iraq sentiment reverberated throughout the 20th area. Graffiti scrawled on walls screamed against George Bush. One day I was locked in a McDonald's by three girls who thought I was American and therefore deserved it. This is a side of Paris I had never dreamt of encountering. But it is one that has taught me a lot, and while not always pleasant, it has opened my eyes.

So has this year been easy? A big fat NO answers that question. Amazing, enlightening and more than I could have asked for? Truly. But not easy. Indeed, there have been times when I've only just kept my head above water. Thanks to those moments when I'm sure the Smith family wants to pack me in a box and deport me, the good times feel like I'm flying. When talking about having a gap year between school and university last year, it was the common belief that it was valuable in our development and progression beyond school. So has this been the case? How have I changed, and how will this change affect the person I'll be when I go home? New situations lead to new ways of thinking, the mind is manipulated to the point were things you've believed in all your life don't seem so true anymore. Sometimes I miss the person I was at home. She's still in me, but a different environment will bring out different sides of a person. We wear t-shirts in summer and coats in winter, so of course everyone would be a bit different living in Paris after growing up in Goulburn. I can be more indecisive now. The decisions I'm making are a lot bigger than what I've dealt with in the past, and therefore have greater consequences. I now think things through more. Everything isn't black and white anymore, I think in shades of grey.

Patience is also something I lacked before I became an au pair. I couldn't stand waiting 30 seconds for the microwave. Looking after a five and seven year-old has revolutionised that. Every time we go somewhere, I think of how long it would take me if I was by myself, then I double it and add extra time for skinned knees and snails. I've learnt to enjoy every minute instead of counting down to the next. As I have mentioned, life in country NSW was far from complicated. It was like a well worn pair of slippers: lots of warmth and fuzziness, always to be found with ease in the same place, under the bed. So if life in Goulburn is a pair of slippers, Paris is a pair of Gucci pumps. Glamorous, daring and expensive ... can start to pinch ... need to be broken in.

I like knowing about everything that's going on at home, and it doesn't seem a huge effort to take the time to keep in touch with my family. My mum emails me every day, and I try to do the same. Even a short 'not much news ... still no rain' is great. Big deal if there isn't any news and the lawn's dead, my mum thinks to email every night, no matter how tired she is and how much ironing needs doing. Mum asked me on the phone once if I'll be ready to come home at the end of the year. I don't think she liked my answer: 'I don't know' I wasn't supposed to say that! I was meant to say something along the lines of 'Of course, I already know what time my plane leaves!'

Life would be a lot more simple if I had a crystal ball. But seeing what I have done in the past six months, with no foresight makes me realise I prefer the uncertainty of it all. I would do nothing differently. So what about the next few months? Few months—two words that both excite and sadden me. Will I be able to stick up for Max and Lily in the playground? Will I walk off a plane in Sydney at the start of 2004, bringing a gorgeous, decent Frenchman with me? I have no idea. I'm 18, and what happens next is up to me.

Rebecca Thistleton finished school at Trinity College in Goulbourn before leaving for a year in France. Unless she cannot bear to leave Paris, she plans to studying at Australian National University to become a journalist after which she intends to return to Europe. She will be going home to her parents, Franki and John; and her siblings Elyse and Luke.

DISLOCATIONS AND TRANSFORMATIONS

Maurice and Val Webb have been dislocated expats off and on for some 33 years, becoming expats by default rather than by design. In the 1970s, medical specialist practice in Australia still required the approval of Mother England. For Maurice, that meant a year or so at St Mary's Hospital, Portsmouth, England, while he sat the exams for membership of the Royal College of Obstetricians and Gynaecologists. We toted two toddlers half-way across the world and, after the usual Australian pastime of visiting as many European countries as possible in a short time, planned to head back to Australia. Towards the end of our time in England, however, Maurice was offered a nine month fellowship to study at the world famous Mayo Clinic in Rochester, Minnesota. Apart from its significant career advantage, what gypsy Australian couple would turn up a look at America before heading home? However, nine months soon expanded into ten years as Maurice went onto the staff at the Mayo Clinic as a consultant in gynaecologic oncology and surgery.

Despite this wonderful opportunity, Maurice was a displaced Australian at heart, never missing an opportunity to tell colleagues at length of Australia's advantages and splendours. When pressed, his dominant reason to return was to be able to sit on the front porch in his shorts and read the paper! While this may not be earth shattering to someone who has never left Brisbane, it seemed like paradise for a Queenslander in Minnesota where, for five months of the year, the weather is akin to a Siberian winter! In his sub-zero exile, Maurice had contained his fantasies by wearing shorts in the house with the heating running high; cultivated an indoor plant jungle; and persisted in dashing to the mailbox barefoot and in shorts, even through the snow, to the puzzlement of neighbours. He had perfected living concurrently in two countries: working at his computer while plugged in via earphones to the

Brisbane radio talk shows. Dietary supplements for this dual existence—Promite, Milo, custard powder, Pavlova eggs, Australian jam, mustard pickles and pickled onions—were lugged periodically across the Pacific.

After ten years of this, the front porch won and we returned to Brisbane. Maurice established a gynaecologic cancer centre for Queensland and also had a private practice in gynaecologic oncology. We bought a home in Moggill among the pineapple farms and settled back into Australian life, albeit clinging to a few peculiarities acquired in the US. Although the early years of return were sweet and fulfilling, the Mayo Clinic is hard to beat as a place to work. In 1988, seven years later, the family packed up again and made the trip back to Rochester where we have remained ever since.

What of the rest of the family? Val (Skerman) had grown up in St Lucia, trained in science at the University of Queensland, and was working on her Masters in Microbiology when we married in 1966. Two children, Helen (1967) and Paul (1969), appeared by the time we left for England and Karen (1972) was born in Rochester, Minnesota. Despite its international patient clientele, the Mayo Clinic hospital notes recording Karen's delivery read, 'Mrs Webb is from Australia but she speaks English quite well.' The Mayo Clinic's 1970s policy of employing only one of a couple led Val into another career. Her pen and ink drawings resulted in two hardcover books of sketches and the opening of *Val Webb Galleries*, an art gallery featuring American and international artists. When Maurice decided to return to the front porch in Brisbane in 1981, Val's career took another turn. She became Superintendent of Public Relations and Development for the Wesley Hospital and served at state and national levels in the Uniting Church of Australia. She also began religious studies at the University of Queensland as part of her own faith journey. With the return to America in 1988, Val continued her studies and earned a PhD in Theology in 1996. She now teaches Religion at Augsburg College in Minnesota, and each February at Whitley College in Melbourne. She has also published more books—*In Defense of Doubt: an Invitation to Adventure* (1995), *Why We're Equal: Introducing Feminist Theology* (1999), *John's Message: Good News for the New Millennium* (1999) and *Florence Nightingale: the Making of a Radical Theologian* (2002).

What happens to children when their earliest experiences of life suggest to them that the world is their oyster? Helen, Paul and Karen returned with the family to Australia in 1981 with varying degrees of enthusiasm. It is often hard to know, in the magnitude of parental decision-making, how such a move might affect the offspring—saying goodbye to friends, fear of the new, loss of the familiar. Some thrive on it; some harbour pain that does not necessarily surface at the time. A Minnesota-trained principal, and teachers at St. Peter's Lutheran College in Brisbane who understood such transitions, eased some of that pain for the older children. Our daughter Helen came home ecstatic the first week. The school chaplain came from a little town a few miles from Rochester and, when he found out where Helen was from, spent the next fifteen minutes of class comparing notes with her on the after-Christmas sale at Dayton's, Rochester largest department store! Our youngest had a more traumatic first day at elementary school in Brisbane. Shy at the best of times as a child, Karen went with her mother to meet the principal. He said, 'Good morning, Karen,' to which she whispered, 'Hi.' He frowned and said, 'No, Karen, you don't say 'hi.' You say good morning Mr ... ' What a champion start for a nine year old, born in the US, and trying a new school and country for size!

Interestingly, our son Paul was the first to trek back across the Pacific. On his way to his current height of 6 foot 10 inches, Paul played basketball in the Australian schoolboy teams through high school, and was the youngest player ever recruited into the Brisbane Bullets—during his final year of high school in 1986. That exposure led to several scholarship offers from American universities and he left for the University of Richmond, Virginia, on a full college scholarship. While we knew it was a great opportunity for him, this international family separation was hard for everyone. An article Val wrote at the time reflects the feelings so many expat families experience because they have chosen to embrace the whole world as their home and a lifetime of brave goodbyes to children, parents and friends, staying calm on the outside but breaking up inside:

> This immanent farewell will be like an explosion. I wish it could have happened in moderation, in stages, like when he learned to walk. I see sons that break slowly with the family—college in a nearby town, an apartment in the same suburb, a wife and family in a small house across town, a promotion within the state, not out of school,

home and country in one single stroke. We are moving along routinely day after day knowing he is going, but doing the normal and repeatable things. We pretend it will be like this for always, but I am watching him without him noticing. I am recording each movement, each expression, and each reaction, to recall on replay in the months ahead. I try to make each last routine an event. He is an inward and complete person who does not talk much about the conversations of his soul, but I know those conversations take place often. I will miss those moments when the door stood ajar and I was invited inside to share those dreams.

This parting proved to be short as the family returned to Rochester in 1988, the following year. Richmond, Virginia was a short flight away. We could enjoy Paul's basketball games with the Richmond Spiders, even seeing them reach the NCAA Sweet Sixteen. We were close by when he quit his basketball scholarship after three years in order to graduate, a wise decision that helped him go on and earn a PhD in marine biology from the University of Santa Crus, California, and become a Professor at Roger Williams University in Bristol, Rhode Island where he lives with his American wife Alexis and children Rhys and Kyle.

The return to the US was also positive for our eldest daughter Helen (now Helen Salmon). She had finished her degree in speech pathology at the University of Queensland as we left Australia, and a theatre career filled her horizons. She was accepted into a theatre degree program at St Olaf College, Northfield, Minnesota, an hour from Rochester. On completing this degree, Helen followed in the family footsteps and took off into the world—to London where the action was. Rather than wait to be discovered waiting tables in some restaurant somewhere, she found a fringe theatre she liked and offered to volunteer, beginning a decade dedicated to London theatre. She is now Director of Development at the Royal Court Theatre in Sloane Square and totally anglophiled, even to the extent of acquiring an English husband Steve and step-son Daniel— although her hybrid Australian-American-English accent keeps those Londoners who care about pigeon-holing by dialect guessing!

For our youngest, Karen, the move back to the States was difficult as she had to enter an American high school two years before graduation when friendships had already been made in the cliquey pattern of high schoolers. Karen missed her friends and her Australian activities, even though she worked hard and entered into the spirit of Mayo High School. When she went on to St Olaf College, Northfield two years later, she felt, for the first time, more settled, as others were also 'newcomers'. Armed with an anthropology degree at the end of four years, Karen went to San Francisco and then Los Angeles, working in various aspects of the travel industry, including selling adventure travel to Australia! Now, as our only American-born child, Karen has returned to *Australia* to live!

How did the cycle begin again? After years of encouraging others to discover the beauty of distant places, Karen and her partner, American-born Sean Wolfson, decided to flee their long commutes in Los Angeles traffic for more peaceful climes. In September 2002, they set off for Australia, equipped with determination, a camping tent and a good map, and spent two months driving from Brisbane almost to Adelaide to find the perfect place to live and the perfect bed and breakfast guesthouse to run! After looking at every beach and mountain view, together with about fifty guesthouses of all shapes and sizes, they settled on Mudgee, New South Wales—a beautiful little town with a flourishing wine industry. In December 2002, they took possession of the Mudgee Homestead Guesthouse, a spacious and elegant Federation style home with six en suite guestrooms wrapped around by a verandah overlooking an idyllic valley and its vineyards. Snuggled under Mount Buckaroo, their only close neighbours are the thirty or so kangaroos who have claimed possession of their spread. When they marry in December 2003 at Mudgee, they too, like Karen's siblings, will cement a life of living between two worlds with their non-Australian partners.

The cycle has started again for more than them. Maurice retires from the Mayo Clinic in October 2003 and we are also returning to Australia as home base, building a small cottage on the Mudgee Homestead Guesthouse's forty acres. Gypsies once again, we will spend the northern winter each year in Australia and the rest of the year visiting children in England and America; writing; and volunteering, particularly in developing countries, in our specialties of medicine and religion until our two minds or four knees give out. When friends express surprise at such dislocation and mobility at this stage of life, we try to explain that this has always been our life as people of two lands. Even during our years in Rochester, we have explored over one hundred countries and are still counting!

Such comments from people make us ponder what 'home' means. For some, it is a town or a country; for some, it is ethnicity; for others it is a particular childhood house that takes precedence forever in the mind over any other subsequent house or occupants. For us, it is relationships. Being together as a couple and as a family has enabled us to call anywhere 'home'. We are thankful to have the opportunity now to return physically to our Australian roots for part of each year, because there is something about ethnicity that is embedded too deep to ever discard. In fact, we have become more Australian the longer we have been away—and an Australian accent is a decided advantage in an America obsessed with Down-Under, even if Crocodile Dundee and that crazy new crocodile hunter is all they know about it. That does not, however, replace the joy of discovering what 'home' is for other people, wherever in the world that may be, accepting their generous invitations to linger awhile in their country and place and enjoy that wider relationship, larger family, broader globe. Do we have to belong to one culture or country, or does the shortening of distances, both physically by flight and mentally by attitudes and interconnectedness, make us simply members of one great human family, held together, but also distinguished, by whatever gives us our roots and centeredness?

Maurice and Val Webb are looking forward to the paddocks of Mudgee for the Australian summer and travelling and volunteering for the rest of the year.

Kopi susu

'See that man down there, waving the red handkerchief? Well, that's your dad!'

My Mum's words still ring clearly in my ears as I recall that day almost 50 years ago, in October 1953, when our passenger ship *The New Holland* berthed at Tanjung Priok Harbour in Jakarta, Indonesia, after a three week journey from Australia. My initial reaction at seeing this short, stout, smiling Asian man peering up at us as we peered back down curiously at him over the ship deck was that this person could not possibly be my father! Why, he was Chinese looking—nothing like the Western fathers all my friends had in Australia. He was also greeting us in broken English. Could Mum possibly be mistaken? Had she forgotten that we were Australians? Surely, somewhere out there, my sister and I must have a tall, fair skinned, Australian father, who could speak proper English!

That, however, was my introduction to both my Indonesian Dad and to Indonesia itself—a country where I was to spend, on and off, almost half of my life. A country where I was to experience the most memorable, and often challenging, times of my life; to witness history in the making; and to discover my own true identity as a bi-cultural citizen of the world.

Now, even at 55 years of age, I remember vividly my first few years living in Jakarta as an Aussie kid, a post-war baby, born to an Australian mother and an Indonesian father. In Indonesia I was classified as an *Indo* (Eurasian), one with fair, light brown skin (to Indonesians, the colour of white coffee). This is a label I have not been able to shake off for all these years. A label which instantly describes a mixed heritage, where one parent is Western and the other Indonesian, a mixture which seems to hold the utmost fascination to Indonesians. Recently, I met a senior Indonesian government official who, as it turned out, was more interested in my background than in the business I had come to discuss. He took one look at me, asked if I was *Indo*, then proceeded to spend almost the entire session comparing my looks with a famous *Indo* MTV presenter (about 30 years younger than me!), very popular at the time!

My older sister, Triena, was born on Christmas Day 1945, a year after Mum and Dad had met in Sydney. An Indonesian officer in the Dutch East Indies Navy, Dad was on R&R in Sydney, along with hundreds of other young Indonesians. Mum was a nurse at a local Sydney hospital. At the time, Dad and Mum were 20 and 17 years respectively. Despite this, they had the maturity of a much older couple, choosing to go against the mainstream, entering into a mixed marriage, totally unacceptable in those days. Mum would often tell us over the years how she and Dad would walk down the main roads of Sydney in those days, only to be jeered at and sometimes spat at, simply for daring to break with tradition and marry a person of a different race. Mum and Dad held their heads high, determined to get on with their lives.

Mum also recounted how she and Dad had become enthusiastically involved in the free Indonesia movement in Sydney. In the late 1940s, it was this group which was largely responsible for encouraging the Australian government to support the battle of the Indonesian people for independence against the Dutch. Little did Mum and Dad know that they would soon be confronted by their very own personal battle, a battle to save their own family from being split up by Australian government policies.

In 1947, Dad, along with thousands of other Indonesians, was deported from Australia back to Indonesia, under Australia's White Australia Policy. Triena was a one year old. Mum was four months pregnant with me. This controversial episode in Australian history was to separate Dad from his young family for the next six and a half years, and it was to change the course of my life forever. I was six years old before I met Dad, or begun to understand my Asian heritage.

From 1953 to 1959, I grew up in Indonesia. Triena had decided to return to school in Australia in 1956, staying with family friends. Fearing I would lose my command of English, Mum arranged for me to have Australian correspondence lessons, since the only school in Jakarta for English speakers was far too expensive. There was always great excitement when the large envelope containing school materials arrived from

Australia every few weeks—in those days we relied heavily on the postman. He was our main link back to Australia. Our other lifeline was Radio Australia, which we used to sit and listen to at midday every day.

One day in 1959, I overheard Mum telling Dad that I should return to Australia to continue my education. I was 12 at the time. The thought of going back to Australia, of which I had vague memories, did not go down well with me. It was six long years since I had left Australia. I was now used to a completely different lifestyle—I mixed mainly with Indonesian and Dutch children; spoke more Dutch and Indonesian than English; was used to a tropical lifestyle, sleeping under a large white mosquito net, and watching grey *cicak* (geckos) climb up and down the walls at night; I had become strongly attached to our maid who took care of my every need; I was always chaperoned everywhere; and was used to eating exotic food. Why would I want to return to Australia? How would I fit in to a new culture and environment? What would the schools be like? All these questions started to haunt me.

In 1960 I arrived back in Sydney, in winter. It was cold and strange. Yet I was soon to realise that this move back to the West was to be a good form of character building for me. At 13 years old, I quickly became independent—going places on my own; managing my own finances; learning to do housework; completing tasks by a deadline—in short, assuming greater responsibility and maturing rapidly into a confident young lady. At 16 years and 10 months I was driving myself around and could even change a car tyre and oil.

However, at first I found life in Australia lacking vitality and warmth. Australians, while friendly, basically minded their own business. In Indonesia, I was accustomed to everyone knowing and, indeed, feeling they had the right to know, almost everything about you. Often strangers in Indonesia will strike up a conversation by asking: '*Dari mana?*' (Where are you from? Or it could also mean: Where have you been?). To me, this was always a cue to give them my whole life story in five minutes flat. From then onwards, we would end up chatting like long lost friends!

In Australia, however, people might be curious about you but would not want to delve into your background, let alone private life. I soon learnt in Australia that if you were asked: 'How are you?', the expected, polite answer would always be: 'Good thank you', even though you may be feeling half dead or wanted to tell the other speaker all your ails and woes. That would just not be appropriate, especially at first meeting. For me, this was hard to adjust to. The Asian part in me has always had this intense desire to know as many details as possible about people I meet but I soon began to accept that in Australia, you just get on with your life and mind your own business, not everyone else's!

I commenced school at Sydney Girls High, where five years later I was elected School Captain. As a teenager raised in Asia, I was not as rowdy as the Australians, nor as outspoken. I was a good student, and always respectful to the teachers. Throughout my teens I was forever mindful of my parents' advice. My Indonesian Dad would say: 'Don't do anything to embarrass the family. Be careful, as you are a girl. Study hard.' My Australian Mum, on the other hand, would say: 'Enjoy your life and always do the best you can. If anything happens, I am always there for you.' From my Mum I also learnt to greatly appreciate my dual heritage and to explore both cultures freely. To this very day it has always amazed me that my passion for Indonesian language and culture has been inherited from my Western mother, not my Asian father.

Somehow, my being elected School Captain made it into the local Indonesian papers. I still keep the photo of myself, with the caption which reads: 'Indonesian girl becomes Captain of Australian school'.

By this stage in my life, I was becoming used to being referred to as *Indo, bule* (Western) or *kopi susu* (white coffee) when in Indonesia; and Asian or Indonesian when in Australia. So being referred to as Indonesian in that Indonesian article both amused and confused me at the time. What *was* I really? Where did I *really* belong? Somehow, it seemed that I would always be different, in both the Indonesian and Australian contexts. Being Eurasian had its challenges, I was soon to learn.

My daughter, Michelle, many years later, participating in an ABC radio talk program on multiculturalism, referred to herself, also the product of a mixed marriage, as being like a *chameleon*—a creature with the ability to change colour according to its surroundings. As I went back and forth between Indonesia and Australia over the years to come, I was getting good at changing colours: my accent, my mannerisms, my dress, my views, and the way I adapted to different cultural situations, according to who I was with, and what I thought was called for in the situation.

After completing an honours degree at Sydney University, I married a young Indonesian Colombo Plan student in Sydney. Being starry eyed and romantic, I believed that before the wedding, all I had to worry about was my wedding dress. But finding a church in Sydney which would agree to marry us was a major obstacle we had to overcome first. In the 1970s, Church of England-raised young women like me were not encouraged to marry Moslem men, and in a church at that ... Horror of horrors! When we finally found a minister to marry us in the University of Sydney chapel, we were relieved, but nevertheless left wondering what all the fuss had been about. I also recall how even the night before our wedding, Dad wanted me home by 9 pm, like all good girls.

Fourteen years later, my husband and I moved back to Indonesia with our two young children. Prior to that, I had been teaching Indonesian language and literature at the University of Sydney, and later at Griffith University in Brisbane.

Within six months of returning to Indonesia, I had decided to divorce my husband. In very practical Western terms, I read up widely on the subject of divorce, planned the actual date I would leave my husband, told the children and relatives of my plans, then set about to make the necessary arrangements. My husband, being groomed to take up a senior Indonesian government position, was totally opposed to the idea. In Indonesia, a good wife just does not leave her husband. I was summonsed by my husband's superior and his wife, who proceeded to advise me how the divorce would jeopardise my husband's career, not to mention his reputation among his peers. Would I change my mind, they asked. I sat quietly in the large plush office in central Jakarta, trying to act as meek and mild as I knew a good Asian wife should. Inside, however, I was intrigued at how such a personal decision as to whether we should or shouldn't divorce could be decided by my husband's boss. I smiled sweetly, promising the boss that I would re-consider. Once outside, I turned to my husband and told him that there was no turning back. My mind was made up to go ahead with the divorce.

Eight years later, at a state function in Jakarta in honour of the then US President, Bill Clinton, my husband's former boss and I met again. He leant over to me and said: 'I remember you... I see you didn't take my advice!' I was momentarily stunned, but in typical chameleon style, I just smiled sweetly. This boss went on to become the third President of Indonesia in 1998.

From 1984 onwards, I was a single mum, struggling to raise two children in Indonesia. On the day I left my husband, I had only AUD$50 to my name. Initially, I toyed with the idea of returning to the security and stability of life in Australia. Under Indonesian law, however, children belong to the father. Returning to Australia would have meant either leaving the children in Indonesia, to be raised by their father, or forging our exit documents. After much soul searching, I finally decided to remain in Indonesia. For months, I gave Indonesian lessons to the Australian community in Jakarta, for an hourly fee. Some close Australian friends actually sent me food parcels now and then, to help us get by. For the children's education, the Australian Correspondence School came to our rescue, just as it had done when I myself was a child in Indonesia. But, despite the hard times, we managed well. And to this very day I attribute surviving the highs and lows of my life to my practical Australian outlook, combined with the Indonesian attitude I had learnt to accept, namely that whatever life dishes out to you is your *nasib* (fate/destiny)— just ride the waves and you will eventually reach the shore.

In 1985 I found a well-paid job at the US Agency for International Development (USAID) at the American Embassy in Jakarta. Working for the Americans in Indonesia has been one of the highlights of my professional career. The Americans were confident people, knew their strengths and limitations, were keen to get ahead in life, and made the most out of a situation. At the embassy, I quickly earned a reputation for being completely bilingual, which led to some exciting interpreting experiences: in 1989, for the visiting then US Vice President, Dan Quayle and his wife; and in 1994, for Hillary Clinton, visiting with husband, the then US President, Bill Clinton. Former US President George Bush was also on the list of dignitaries I met Mohammad Ali had the pleasure of teaching Indonesian to Paul Wolfowitz, the current US Defense Secretary, during his term as US Ambassador to Indonesia.

In 1996, the project I was working on at USAID ended. By then, both of my children had left Indonesia, returning to Australia to complete their tertiary studies. Even my faithful dog of 13 years, Polly, died that year. These were all significant milestones in my personal life.

Since mid 1996 I have been Country Director for an Australian company in Indonesia. Keen to make a difference, I have managed my office of 30 local staff by introducing a blend of Eastern and Western practices in most aspects of our work. At staff meetings, for example, all staff, down to the cleaner, are afforded the chance to report on their work, to have their say—a totally alien situation in Indonesia but, nevertheless, much appreciated by staff. Best practice policies must be acceptable in both Western and Eastern contexts. Staff from lower socio-economic backgrounds are often extended a helping hand by the company. To break down the barriers, we celebrate Moslem, Christian and Chinese festive periods. In short, we pride ourselves on adopting the most democratic and harmonious means to achieve the company's goals. It is truly an example of unity in diversity. In our multistorey office building we stand out as a shining example of how a Western company can work very effectively, and successfully, without losing its Asian context. And with a female boss at that!

As I look back on my time in Indonesia, I realise how enriched and exciting my life has been. Each of my days is different, each experience contributes to the intricate and colourful fabric of my life. I continue to be enlightened by the diversity of this amazing country, without for one moment believing that I fully understand all of its complexities. I continue to feel a strong sense of contentment—a feeling which comes with the acceptance of myself for who I am, of situations which I cannot change but must learn to respect, and finally, of the fact that it's important to be able to 'ride the waves' on whatever journey life takes you.

Isla Winarto was born in Sydney in 1947, and has two children, Andre and Michelle, and one grandchild. She taught Indonesian language and literature at the University of Sydney and Griffith University in the 70s and 80s, then moved with her family to Indonesia. After working at USAID for 11 years, she became Country Director for Indonesia of IDP Education Australia. She has co-authored two text books for students of Indonesian. Her BA Honours thesis was titled 'Modern Indonesian Women Writers'.

CONTRIBUTORS TO THE BOOK PROJECT

A Joseph Adams
Kate Armstrong
   and Christopher Nelson
Kelly Atkinson
Antasia Azure
Vicki Baensch
Tereze Bartholomew
Anna Batsone
Simon Bell
Allison Bennett
Claudine Berrisford
Andrew Best
Peter Blackwell
Robert Boehm
Gabrielle Brabander
Kylie Brennan
Mary Brice
Peter Brice
Gillian Bridgewater
Caroline Brothers
Yanti Brown
Denise Burns
Theresa Byrnes
Nerella Campigotto
Vivian Carrington
Carol Chang
Chia Chien Cherry Chang
David Cherry

Kimerley Clarke
Lee Cooper
Samuel Coppin
JoAnn Corkill
Fleur Cornelius
Russell Cotter
Paul Cranch
Ian Creber
Sharon Croxford
Silvia Cuevas-Morales
Bryn Davies
Charlotte de Gohan
Natalie Delary-Simpson
Adrian Donati
Vicki Douglas
Kristina Dryza
Ted Dwyer
Felicity Edge
Lynette Edge
Sophie Edmonds
Sexy Enrique
Caroline Everett
Marion Fennessy
Stacey Flurscheim
Christian Flurscheim
Meredith Fogg
Lisa Foulis
Craig Francis

Eric Fraser
Stephanie Fuger
Nicholas Galloway
David Gard
Jenny Gates
Benjamin Gilmour
Susana Gonzalez
Jane Grinling
David Guilfoyle
Stephanie Hanbury-Brown
Michaela Hansen
Teresa Harvey
Colin Heathcote
Christopher Heidemanns
Karen Heins
Murray Henman
Steven Hessling
Vicki Heywood
Virginia Hood
Catherine Howse
Louise Hunter
Made Ikan
Edmund James
Selina Kayman Joseph
Ben Julien
Kate Juliff
Jenny Kendall
Alicia Kennedy
Tony Kennedy
Lionel Kerr
Rosemary Kneipp-Avril
Paul Kromwyk
Elizabeth Kugler
Lakock
Sean Lawson
Josephine Lee

Margaret Leehane
Cherie Lehman
Mac
Cindy Mac
Anne MacGregor
Sister Margaret Mary Martin
Nicole Mays
Trish McAvaney
Kathleen McCormack
Fiona McDougall
Julie McLean
Jessica Michaels
John Miller
Robert Miller
Philip C Minter
Minty
Rean Monfils
Bradley Morris
Stewart Mullin
Sharyn Negus
Martie Newcombe
Michelle Newton
Caroline Nicholls
Ciaron O'Reilly
Suzann Osborne
Jane Paech
Ian Parry
Emma Pearse
Sylivia Petter
Karl Anthony Phillips
Helen Pitt
John Poljak
Belinda Prinzen
Prospector
Stella Pulo
Leah Quinn

Jo Anne Rey

Geraldine Ricca

Aaron Roberts

Leanne Robins

Sally Robson

Susan Rooke

Kate Roth

Belinda Lee Russell

Laurence Salmon

David Sangira

Tracey Sawyer

Charlotte Schibiger

Tim Schildberger

Marge Seufert

Joan Short

Marie Smyth

Beth Spencer

Peter Stephenson

Catherine Stok

Alison Stuart

Mary Summers

John Sved

Adam Taylor

Rebecca Thistleton

Chris Trott

Sue Turnbull

Jeff Turner

Stuart Ward

Maurice and Val Web

Carole Westbrook

Amy Whereat-Terdjman

Erica Wikander

Alex Williams

Trevor Williams

Isla Winarto

Michelle Witton

Michael Young

Donna Young

Denise Young